Eating Disorders in the 21st Century

Eating Disorders in Males

Muscularity and Fragility: The Two-faced Ianus of Male Identity

Two-faced Ianus. Magnani Palace, Reggio Emilia, Italy.

EATING DISORDERS IN THE 21ST CENTURY

Additional books in this series can be found on Nova's website under the Series tab.

Additional E-books in this series can be found on Nova's website under the E-books tab.

EATING DISORDERS IN THE 21ST CENTURY

EATING DISORDERS IN MALES

MUSCULARITY AND FRAGILITY: THE TWO-FACED IANUS OF MALE IDENTITY

EMILIA MANZATO
TATIANA ZANETTI
MALVINA GUALANDI
AND
RENATA STRUMIA

EDITED BY
RENATA STRUMIA

Nova Science Publishers, Inc.
New York

For permission to use material from this book please contact us:
Telephone 631-231-7269; Fax 631-231-8175
Web Site: http://www.novapublishers.com

LIBRARY OF CONGRESS CATALOGING-IN-PUBLICATION DATA
Eating disorder in males / Renata Strumia ... [et al.].
p. cm.
Includes bibliographical references and index.
ISBN 978-1-61470-901-5 (softcover)
1. Eating disorders in men. I. Strumia, Renata.
RC552.E18E28343 2009
616.85'260081--dc22
2010012169

Published by Nova Science Publishers, Inc. † New York

CONTENTS

PREFACE

Eating disorders are less common in males than in females, occurring generally 10 times more frequently in women than in men. In spite of similar symptoms in men and women, men are less likely to be primarily diagnosed as suffering from an eating disorder and they are at risk of being under-diagnosed.

Eating disorders in males are a complex phenomenon. The emblematic figure of the two-faced Janus, who faces in two opposite directions, may reflect the swinging between two opposite aspects of male identity, one more linked to the inner *animus,* which is identified more with feminine fragility, and the other more linked to strength and muscularity, which are stereotypic masculine features, as they reflect both protection from the external world and the ability to fight and dominate. This could be a possible interpretation of the male dilemma of eating disorders.

Epidemiology, clinical features, risk factors, weight and shape concerns, body dissatisfaction and a particular male anxiety on muscle mass are widely discussed in this textbook. One chapter deals with the relationship between eating disorders and sexual orientation, being that homosexuality is a recognized risk factor for eating disorders in men.

Medical complications are widely reported. Step by step, it is explained how to proceed for a correct medical assessment and "staging" of the patients.

One chapter is dedicated to skin signs due to the malnutrition, self-starvation and purging practices which can be found in eating disorders. As skin conditions are perceptible and visible, well recognized dermatological problems may help in the identification and disclosure of an eating disorder among those patients who deny their illness.

Finally, some clinical cases of medical and psychiatric interest, which may address specific clinical aspects, are reported. The aim of these clinical vignettes are to help primary care physicians recognize eating disordered subjects early and diagnose them as early as possible while also taking into account the medical complications. In each clinical case the authors give an overview of psychiatric, medical and nutritional assessment and, at the end, summarize the points of greatest complexity (the delay of diagnosis is one of these points).

This textbook is particularly addressed to primary care physicians, psychiatrists, psychologists, dieticians, nurses, and to all the people who work with adolescents, in a social and sport context.

FOREWORD

If we think of the different psychiatric disorders as an expression of the malaise of the historical moment which they represent, no mental disorder better expresses the discomfort of our time than Eating Disorders (EDs).

From anorexia to bulimia and binge eating disorder in obesity, EDs represent an intriguing area both from a clinical and speculative point of view. Even more complex and interesting is the field of EDs in the masculine gender.

EDs in males are stimulating a growing clinical interest for the peculiarities of its expressions, which are different from the same phenomenon in women, as is the difficulty of approach and treatment.

For these reasons, EDs in males have represented a true challenge for clinicians since the very beginning of the first approach.

Through this book we aim to give an overview of the most relevant studies on EDs in males and at the same time to provide an easy reference tool with useful information for clinical practice.

This book is dedicated to all health care professionals and to those who may have an initial request for help or who first suspect an eating disorder in adolescents or men and if properly informed, may contribute to an early diagnosis and a proper treatment.

As this manual has been primarily addressed to Primary Care Physicians (PCPs), a wide section has been dedicated to the medical approach. It is not unusual in fact that the first approach to the male patient takes place in the ambulatory of a Primary Care Physician, whose fundamental role is to detect as early as possible ED related symptoms, even when the patient is in a position of denial or concealment.

A step by step approach is presented to provide PCPs a concrete tool for diagnostic framework.

The special focus of this book is on male anorexia and bulimia. We opted not to include topics about Binge Eating Disorder which would have required a specific focus and an in-depth examination on the complex field of obesity.

In addition to medical and psychiatric aspects, we focused on social and cultural characteristics that differentiate Eating Disorders in males from EDs in females which makes it difficult to approach these patients.

We have therefore divided the work into three parts: first, a theoretical part, a second clinical part and a third part where some clinical cases are described and discussed.

The manual comes from the desire to share both the studies and the ten-year clinical experience of the ED Italian team of Ferrara, and does not aim to be exhaustive, but to be a stimulus to maintain a lively curiosity and a scientific interest in the study of EDs.

LIST OF ABBREVIATIONS

AN	Anorexia Nervosa
ANbp	Anorexia Nervosa binge purging
ANr	Anorexia Nervosa restrictive
ASA	Acetil Salycilic Acid
BED	Binge Eating Disorder
BIA	Bioelectric Impedance Analysis
BMD	Bone Mineral Density
BMI	Body Mass Index
BN	Bulimia Nervosa
CD	Celiac Disease
DSM	Diagnostic and Statistical Manual of Mental Disorders
DXA	Dual-energy X-ray Absorptiometry
EDI	Eating Disorder Inventory
ED	Eating Disorder
ED-NOS	Eating Disorder Not Otherwise Specified
FAT	Fat Mass
FFM	Fat Free Mass
FSH	Follicle Stimulating Hormone
GID	Gender Identity Disorder
GMT	Gelatinous Bone Marrow Transformation
HR	Heart Rate
IBD	Inflammatory Bowel Disease
IBW	Ideal Body Weight
LH	Luteinizing Hormone
MD	Muscle Dysmorphia
MDI	Muscle Dysmorphic Inventory
MRI	Magnetic Resonance Imaging
OEGDS	Oesophago-Gastro-Duodenoscopy
PCP	Primary Care Physician
PPI	Proton Pump Inhibitor
RMR	Resting Metabolic Rate
TGA	Trans Glutaminase Antibodies

PART I. THEORETICAL ASPECTS

PREFACE PART ONE

Part One of this book addresses important theoretical aspects of eating disorders (EDs) in men.

In Chapter 1, some brief historical notes are presented to face EDs in their evolution throughout the ages, up to and including the modern DSM IV-TR criteria.

Chapter 2 deals with the epidemiology of Eds, taking into consideration what is reported in the scientific literature about distribution, clinical characteristics and risk factors for EDs in men.

Chapter 3 and 4 focus on clinical features of EDs in men. Weight and shape concerns, body dissatisfaction and a particular male anxiety on muscle mass are addressed in chapter 3 while chapter 4 deals with the relationship between EDs and sexual orientation, being that homosexuality is a recognized risk factor for EDs in men.

Chapter 5 provides specific data about the relation between some sporting activities and the risk of developing an ED in men.

Chapter 6 deals with adolescence, considered one of the strongest predisposing periods for the onset of EDs even in male subjects, while chapter 7 emphasizes the importance of family environment and its relational functioning, especially for those male ED patients who are younger and still live with their families.

Psychiatric comorbidity, treated in the last chapter of this first part, represents a complex and difficult issue in the field of EDs in general and specifically in EDs in men. Therefore, it is important that all professional figures who get in touch with a male affected by an ED and above all, general practitioners, be aware of the relationship that exists between psychiatric disturbances and clinical aspects- such as compliance, evolution and prognosis- of the eating disorder .

Chapter 1

BRIEF HISTORICAL NOTES

T. Zanetti

ABSTRACT

The relationship between human beings and food is complex and of great interest.

In this introductive chapter we will give just a few hints to frame the phenomenon of self starvation and disordered eating. Disordered eating has been found throughout the ages, and with many different meanings according to the time and according to the culture. In many periods, fasting was not considered a psychic or a psychiatric condition and it was not considered an illness. For instance, during the middle ages, when self starvation was used for ascetic reasons with the aim of reaching a spiritual closeness and union with God.

We have to wait until 1689 before we get the first description of a condition labelled "nervous consumption": starting from that description by Richard Morton we will come to describe the modern form of Eating Disorders as classified in the different versions of the Diagnostic and Statistical Manual of Mental Disorders.

Current diagnostic criteria for full syndrome Anorexia and Bulimia nervosa as well as Eating Disorders Not Otherwise Specified (ED-NOS) will be presented at the end of the present chapter.

INTRODUCTION

Disordered eating can be considered a transversal phenomenon throughout the ages. People have practiced self-starvation for religious, political, and cultural reasons in different contexts in different times.

Fasting habits can be found, for instance, among Catholics during Lent or in Muslims during Ramadan.

Egyptians engaged in purging rituals to remain healthy.

Again, Romans had a vomitorium where they could vomit food in order to eat again during their feasts.

Fasting was used by holy saints (for example Saint Catherine of Siena) so much so that "holy anorexia" became the term used to describe self-starvation aimed at reaching a higher level of spirituality and closeness to God. Fasting was also thought to be used by witches.

That is, on the one hand, fasting saints abstained from eating to purify themselves, not to be impure and so to reach God; on the other hand, under the Inquisition, women could be accused of witchcraft if they didn't reach a certain weight. It was thought that underweight women were those under demonic possession and were therefore considered "witches," and were burned.

We are still far from obtaining the true, current meaning of anorexia or bulimia.

These forms of eating behaviours were not viewed as an illness: in fact histories of men and women who fasted in the past have been interpreted as examples of anorexia by applying "a posteriori" modern diagnostic criteria.

For those who are interested in these forms of eating behaviours used in different historical ages some works are worth to reading, like "From fasting saints to anorexic girls: the history of self starvation" by Vandereycken and Van Deth [1], or "Holy anorexia" by Bell [2]. And for those who are familiar with the Italian language may also enjoy "Ascetismo, digiuni e anoressia" by Santonastaso and Favaretto [3], which is an interesting source of knowledge in this field.

Even in the past, fasting was reported more often in women than in men and self inflicted starvation for religious and ascetic reasons was enormously lower in men- as medieval hagiography can testify.

In 1689, Richard Morton, an English physician, gave the first description of a patient with anorexia nervosa, a 16 year old boy, son of a minister, and he referred to his illness as a "nervous consumption" [4].

He later described the case of Mr Duke's Daughter, who at 18 years old, stopped her monthly courses, lost appetite and began to lose weight. He described symptoms of consumption which couldn't be related to any recognized medical condition and were related to "cares and passions of her mind."

In the early 1870's, anorexia was described by two neurologists, separately. Sir William Gull, in England, thought that self-starvation for "nervous loss of appetite" was not linked to medical diseases like tuberculosis or diabetes but could be considered a separate nervous disease that he called for the first time: "anorexia," which means "lack of appetite" [5].

In the same period in France, Charles Lasegue, a student of Claude Bernard, described clinical cases marked by self-starvation and high levels of activity, which occurred mainly among young women who were pleased with their food restriction, didn't want to eat more and denied their thinness.

He referred to this condition as "hysterical anorexia" [6].

Both Gull and Lasegue considered "anorexia" a nervous disorder.

At the beginning of the 1900s, with the discovery of new assessment techniques for in-depth analysis of endocrine functions, there was a shift from nervous to endocrine explanations of this illness.

In 1914, Simmonds described a theory suggesting an endocrine origin of the disease [7]: starvation in anorexia, namely progressive pituitary cachexia, was thought to be due to the destruction of the pituitary gland.

This association between anorexia and Simmonds' disease was later denied.

In the 60's, Professor Arthur Hamilton Crisp introduced the term "fat phobia" in order to describe anorectic attitudes towards the body [8]. He described this concept to explain the anorectic need to loose weight in order to take the body under control and the intense fear of gaining weight even in severely underweight conditions.

This concept is still recognized to be a core feature of anorexia nervosa.

Professor Crisp has left us an explanatory model for anorexia nervosa, viewed as a "flight from growth" [9]. According to him anorexia nervosa, which has its onset mainly during adolescence, acts like a morbid reaction to puberty, like an involution linked to the difficulties in growing.

Eating less and starting to lose weight is interpreted as a way to escape from the high responsibilities of growth: by losing weight, in fact, one has a regression to prepubertal weights and conditions.

One put himself into an "avoidance position.." Restrained eating, thinness or emaciation and "secondary amenorrhea" (in women), are therefore egosyntonic symptoms, useful to stop from growing.

In the early 60's, Hilde Bruch saw in anorectic behaviours and attitudes the struggle for personal autonomy, a search for a sense of identity, of self-competence and effectiveness [10].

She masterly described common psychological features in anorectic patients, like body image disturbance, a sense of ineffectiveness, a lack of interoceptive awareness, dependence and autonomy difficulties, that is to say, personal and interpersonal areas which seem to be compromised and need to be repaired.

This author gave an important contribution for the understanding of body image disturbance regarded as the result of a constant interaction of biological, psychic and social forces. She introduced the term "interoceptive awareness" to describe a lack of self-awareness found in eating disordered patients based on the inaccuracy of recognizing and conceptualizing bodily needs. The accuracy in recognizing stimuli coming from inside and outside of the body is linked to one's own sense of control. By controlling food, shape and weight one gives themself the illusion of controlling theirself and their own life.

In 1979, the world famous British psychiatrist Gerald Russell published his work describing a new disorder as "an ominous variant of anorexia" characterized by episodes of binge eating, sense of shame and guilty and use of compensatory behaviours [11]. He named it "bulimia," which we can consider today "the younger and different sister of anorexia.." There were three key-points for the diagnosis: 1) presence of powerful intractable urges to over-eat, 2) seeking to avoid the fattening effects of food by introducing vomiting, or abusing purgatives or both, 3) a morbid fear of becoming fat.

The term bulimia is derived from the Greek word "ox-hunger" indicating a great hunger. It literally translates to: "so hungry that one could eat an ox or can eat as much as an ox."

In Xenophon's Anabasis, written in about 370 B.C, "ox-eating" was the term he used to describe a state of hunger and exhaustion when he saw his soldiers eat huge quantities of food after fighting in a war and after crossing snowy mountains in extreme physical and climatic conditions.

Only in 1980 did the classification system of mental disorders, which provided a reliable basis for defining mental disorders, include anorexia and bulimia as separate syndromes. We can find the first descriptive and diagnostic approach classification of anorexia and bulimia as mental disorders in the third edition of the Diagnostic and Statistical Manual of Mental Disorders (DSM) [12].

There has been much progress in classifying these diseases, starting from that moment when diagnostic criteria for EDs underwent different evolutions [13] up until the latest version of the present DSM IV Text Revised [14].

DSM IV criteria, as proposed by the American Psychiatric Association, are reported below.

Diagnostic Features of Anorexia Nervosa

The essential features of Anorexia Nervosa (AN) are that the individual refuses to maintain a minimally normal body weight, is intensely afraid of gaining weight, and exhibits a significant disturbance in the perception of the shape or size of his or her body. In addition, postmenarcheal females with this disorder are in amenorrohea (Table I).

The individual maintains a body weight that is below a minimally normal level for age and height (Criterion A). When AN develops in an individual during childhood or early adolescence, there may be failure to make expected weight gains (i.e., while growing in height) instead of weight loss.

Table I. Diagnostic Criteria for Anorexia Nervosa

a) Refusal to maintain body weight at or above a minimally normal weight for age and height (e.g., weight loss leading to maintenance of body weight less than 85% of that expected; or failure to make expected weight gain during period of growth, leading to body weight less than 85% of that expected).
b) Intense fear of gaining weight or becoming fat, even though underweight.
c) Disturbance in the way in which one's body weight or shape is experienced, undue influence of body weight or shape on self-evaluation, or denial of the seriousness of the current low body weight.
d) In postmenarcheal females, amenorrhea, i.e., the absence of at least three consecutive menstrual cycles. (A woman is considered to have amenorrhea if her periods occur only following hormone, e.g., estrogen, administration)

Criterion A provides a guideline for determining when the individual meets the threshold for being underweight. It suggests that the individual weigh less than 85% of the weight that is considered normal for that person's age and height. An alternative and somewhat stricter guideline (used in the ICD-10 Diagnostic Criteria for Research) requires that the individual have a body mass index (BMI) (calculated as weight in kilograms/height in meters) equal to or below 17.5 kg/m. These cutoffs are provided only as suggested guidelines for the clinician, since it is unreasonable to specify a single standard for minimally normal weight that applies to all individuals of a given age and height. In determining a minimally normal weight, the clinician should consider not only such guidelines but also the individual's body build and weight history.

Usually, weight loss is accomplished primarily through reduction in total food intake. Although individuals may begin, by excluding from their diet what they perceive to be highly caloric foods, eventually end up with a very restricted diet that is sometimes limited to only a few foods. Additional methods of weight loss include purging (i.e., self-induced vomiting or the misuse of laxatives or diuretics) and increased or excessive exercise.

Individuals with this disorder intensely fear gaining weight or becoming fat (Criterion B). This intense fear of becoming fat is usually not alleviated by the weight loss. In fact, concern about weight gain often increases even as actual weight continues to decrease.

The experience and significance of body weight and shape are distorted in these individuals (Criterion C). Some individuals feel globally overweight. Others realize that they are thin, but are still concerned that certain parts of their bodies, particularly the abdomen, buttocks, and thighs, are "too fat." They may employ a wide variety of techniques to estimate their body size or weight, including excessive weighing, obsessive measuring of body parts, and persistently using a mirror to check for perceived areas of "fat." The self-esteem of individuals with AN is highly dependent on their body shape and weight. Weight loss is viewed as an impressive achievement and a sign of extraordinary self-discipline, whereas weight gain is perceived as an unacceptable failure of self-control. Though some individuals with this disorder may acknowledge being thin, they typically deny the serious medical implications of their malnourished state.

In postmenarcheal females, amenorrhea (due to abnormally low levels of estrogen secretion that are due in turn to diminished pituitary secretion of follicle-stimulating hormone (FSH) and luteinizing hormone (LH) is an indicator of physiological dysfunction in Anorexia Nervosa (Criterion D). Amenorrhea is usually a consequence of the weight loss but, in a minority of individuals, may actually precede it. In prepubertal females, menarche may be delayed by the illness.

For men, criterion D, which is the lack of menstrual cycles for three months, cannot be used. The corresponding criteria for men addresses a change in testosterone levels or loss of sex drive.

The individual is often brought to professional attention by family members after marked weight loss (or failure to make expected weight gains) has occurred. If individuals seek help on their own, it is usually because of their subjective distress over the somatic and psychological sequelae of starvation. It is rare for an individual with AN to complain of weight loss per se. Individuals with Anorexia Nervosa frequently lack insight into, or have considerable denial of, the problem and may be unreliable historians. It is therefore often necessary to obtain information from parents or other outside sources to evaluate the degree of weight loss and other features of the illness.

Subtypes

The following subtypes can be used to specify the presence or absence of regular binge eating or purging during the current episode of AN:

Restricting Type

This subtype describes presentations in which weight loss is accomplished primarily through dieting, fasting, or excessive exercise. During the current episode, these individuals have not regularly engaged in binge eating or purging.

Binge-Eating/Purging Type

This subtype is used when the individual has regularly engaged in binge eating or purging (or both) during the current episode. Most individuals with AN who binge eat also purge through self-induced vomiting or the misuse of laxatives, diuretics, or enemas. Some individuals included in this subtype do not binge eat, but do regularly purge after the consumption of small amounts of food. It appears that most individuals with Binge-Eating/Purging Type engage in these behaviors at least weekly, but sufficient information is not available to justify the specification of a minimum frequency.

Diagnostic Features of Bulimia Nervosa

The essential features of Bulimia Nervosa (BN) are binge eating and inappropriate compensatory methods to prevent weight gain. In addition, the self-evaluation of individuals with BN is excessively influenced by body shape and weight. To qualify for the diagnosis, the binge eating and the inappropriate compensatory behaviors must occur, on average, at least twice a week for 3 months (Criterion C -Table II).

A *binge* is defined as eating in a discrete period of time an amount of food that is definitely larger than most individuals would eat under similar circumstances (Criterion A1). The clinician should consider the context in which the eating occurred--what would be regarded as excessive consumption at a typical meal might be considered normal during a celebration or holiday meal. A "discrete period of time" refers to a limited period, usually less than 2 hours. A single episode of binge eating need not be restricted to one setting. For example, an individual may begin a binge in a restaurant and then continue it on returning home. Continual snacking on small amounts of food throughout the day would not be considered a binge.

Although the type of food consumed during binges varies, it typically includes sweet, high-calorie foods such as ice cream or cake. However, binge eating appears to be characterized more by an abnormality in the amount of food consumed than by a craving for a specific nutrient, such as a carbohydrate. Although individuals with Bulimia Nervosa consume more calories during an episode of binge eating than persons without BN consume during a meal, the fractions of calories derived from protein, fat, and carbohydrate are similar.

Individuals with Bulimia Nervosa are typically ashamed of their eating problems and attempt to conceal their symptoms. Binge eating usually occurs in secrecy, or as inconspicuously as possible. An episode may or may not be planned in advance and is usually (but not always) characterized by rapid consumption. The binge eating often continues until the individual is uncomfortably, or even painfully, full. Binge eating is typically triggered by dysphoric mood states, interpersonal stressors, intense hunger following dietary restraint, or feelings related to body weight, body shape, and food. Binge eating may transiently reduce dysphoria, but disparaging self-criticism and depressed mood often follow.

An episode of binge eating is also accompanied by a sense of lack of control (Criterion A2). An individual may be in a frenzied state while binge eating, especially early in the course of the disorder. Some individuals describe a dissociative quality during, or following, the binge episodes. After BN has persisted for some time, individuals may report that their binge-eating episodes are no longer characterized by an acute feeling of loss of control, but rather by behavioral indicators of impaired control, such as difficulty resisting binge eating or difficulty stopping a binge once it has begun. The impairment in control associated with binge eating in Bulimia Nervosa is not absolute; for example, an individual may continue binge eating while the telephone is ringing, but will cease if a roommate or spouse unexpectedly enters the room.

Table II. Diagnostic Criteria for Bulimia Nervosa

A) recurrent episodes of binge eating. An episode of binge eating is characterized by both of the following:

1. eating, in a discrete period of time (e.g., within any 2-hour period), an amount of food that is definitely larger than most people would eat during a similar period of time and under similar circumstances
2. a sense of lack of control over eating during the episode (e.g., a feeling that one cannot stop eating or control what or how much one is eating)

B) Recurrent inappropriate compensatory behavior in order to prevent weight gain, such as self-induced vomiting; misuse of laxatives, diuretics, enemas, or other medications; fasting; or excessive exercise.

C) The binge eating and inappropriate compensatory behaviors both occur, on average, at least twice a week for 3 months.

D) Self-evaluation is unduly influenced by body shape and weight.

E) The disturbance does not occur exclusively during episodes of Anorexia Nervosa.

Another essential feature of BN is the recurrent use of inappropriate compensatory behaviors to prevent weight gain (Criterion B). Many individuals with BN employ several methods in their attempt to compensate for binge eating. The most common compensatory technique is the induction of vomiting after an episode of binge eating. This method of purging is employed by 80%-90% of individuals with BN who present for treatment at ED clinics. The immediate effects of vomiting include relief from physical discomfort and reduction of fear of gaining weight. In some cases, vomiting becomes a goal in itself, and the person will binge in order to vomit or will vomit after eating a small amount of food. Individuals with BN may use a variety of methods to induce vomiting, including the use of fingers or instruments to stimulate the gag reflex. Individuals generally become adept at inducing vomiting and are eventually able to vomit at will. Sometimes, individuals consume syrup of ipecac to induce vomiting. However this is more rare. Other purging behaviors include the misuse of laxatives and diuretics. Approximately one-third of those with BN misuse laxatives after binge eating. Sometimes individuals with the disorder will misuse enemas following episodes of binge eating, but this is seldom the sole compensatory method employed.

Individuals with BN may fast for a day or more or exercise excessively in an attempt to compensate for binge eating. Exercise may be considered to be excessive when it significantly interferes with important activities, when it occurs at inappropriate times or in inappropriate settings, or when the individual continues to exercise despite injury or other medical complications. Sometimes, though rarely, individuals with this disorder may take thyroid hormone in an attempt to avoid weight gain. Individuals with diabetes mellitus and BN may omit or reduce insulin doses in order to reduce the metabolism of food consumed during eating binges.

Individuals with Bulimia Nervosa place an excessive emphasis on body shape and weight in their self-evaluation, and these factors are typically the most important ones in determining self-esteem (Criterion D). Individuals with this disorder may closely resemble those with Anorexia Nervosa in their fear of gaining weight, in their desire to lose weight, and in the level of dissatisfaction with their bodies. However, a diagnosis of BN should not be given when the disturbance occurs only during episodes of AN (Criterion E).

Subtypes

The following subtypes can be used to specify the presence or absence of regular use of purging methods as a means to compensate for the binge eating:

Purging Type

This subtype describes presentations in which the person has regularly engaged in self-induced vomiting or the misuse of laxatives, diuretics, or enemas during the current episode.

Non-purging Type

This subtype describes presentations in which the persons used other inappropriate compensatory behaviors, such as fasting or excessive exercise, but has not regularly engaged in self-induced vomiting or the misuse of laxatives, diuretics, or enemas during the current episode.

Eating Disorder Not Otherwise Specified (Ed-Nos)

The Eating Disorder Not Otherwise Specified ED-NOS category is for disorders of eating that do not meet the criteria for any specific Eating Disorder.

Examples include:

For females, all of the criteria for AN are met except that the individual has regular menses.

All of the criteria for Anorexia Nervosa are met except that, despite significant weight loss, the individual's current weight is in the normal range.

All of the criteria for BN are met except that the binge Eating and inappropriate compensatory mechanisms occur at a frequency of less than twice a week or for a duration of less than 3 months.

The regular use of inappropriate compensatory behavior by an individual normal body weight after eating small amounts of food (e.g. self-induced vomiting after the consumption of two cookies).

Repeatedly chewing and spitting out, but not swallowing, large amounts of food.

Binge-eating disorder: recurrent episodes of binge eating in the absence of the regular use of inappropriate compensatory behaviors characteristic of BN.

From American Psychiatric Association. ED. In: *Diagnostic and Statistical Manual of Mental Disorders*, (DSM-IVTR), fourth edition, Washington, DC: American Psychiatric Association, 2000, p.583-97.

REFERENCES

[1] Vandereycken, W; Van Deth, R. From fasting saints to anorexic girls: the history of self starvation. Athlone Press. London 1990.

[2] Bell, R. Holy Anorexia. University of Chicago Press. Chicago and London.1985.

[3] Santonastaso, P; Favaretto, G. Ascetismo, digiuni anoressia. Esperienze del corpo e esercizi dello spirito. Masson; 1999.

[4] Morton, R. Phthisiologia seu exercitationes de phthisi tribus libris comprehensae. Totumque opus variis historiis illustratum. S.Smith, London 1689.

[5] Gull, WW. Anorexia hysterica (apepsia hysterica, anorexia hysterica). Transactions of the clinical society of London. 1874 7 22-28

[6] Lasègue, EC. De l'anorexie hystérique. Archives Générales de Medicine.1873 21 325-403.

[7] Simmonds, M. Über embolische Prozesse in der Hypophysis. In "Archives of Pathological Anatomy" 1914 266

[8] Crisp, A H. AN. 1967 Hospital Medicine 28 713-718.

[9] Crisp A H Anorexia nervosa. Let me be. Amazon UK 1982

[10] Bruch, H. ED, obesity, anorexia nervosa and the person within. Basic books, New York 1973

[11] Russell, G. BN: an ominous variant of anorexia nervosa. Psychol Med, 1979 9 (3) 429-48.

[12] American Psychiatric Association Diagnostic and Statistical Manual of Mental Disorders Third edition Washington DC 1980

[13] American Psychiatric Association DSM-IV Diagnostic and Statistical Manual of Mental Disorders, fourth edition, Washington, DC:, 1994

[14] American Psychiatric Association DSM-IV Text Revised, Diagnostic and Statistical Manual of Mental Disorders, Washington, DC:, 2000

Chapter 2

Epidemiological Data

T. Zanetti

Abstract

Eating disorders are less common in males than in females, occurring generally 10 times more frequently in women than in men. Males are generally reported to account for 5-10% of anorectics and 10-15% of bulimics, as identified in community samples. In spite of similar symptoms in men and women, men are less likely to be primarily diagnosed as suffering from an eating disorder and they risk being under-diagnosed. However, males are not immune to eating disorders. It is therefore important to study differences between male and female patients as well as differences between men with eating disorders and men without eating disorders for a better understanding of the etiology and presentation of anorexia and bulimia. In fact, it is not yet clear what may predispose some men to develop eating disorders and what may protect others from developing them. In this chapter, after a brief presentation of methodological aspects in epidemiological research, we will focus on what is reported in the scientific literature with regards to prevalence and incidence, clinical presentation, psychological characteristics, risk and protective factors, as well as the course and outcome of eating disorders in males.

Some Notes on Epidemiological Research in EDs

Epidemiological research deals with the study of the distribution of the disorders with the purpose of determining which risk factors are involved in the development of the disorder.

Incidence and prevalence are two measures of the frequency of the disorders. Incidence is defined as the number of new cases in a specified period of time, usually in a year, and it is expressed as the rate per 100,000 of a population per year while prevalence measures the actual number of cases detected in a certain population at a certain point of time.

EDs are not widespread in the same way in every group of people. They are in fact more frequent in certain samples than in others due to the fact that some individuals are more at risk for developing an eating disorder. People who are considered to be at a higher risk are females, young people, namely adolescents or young adults, people living in Western countries or in industrialized and urbanized areas, and people belonging to particular professional groups, like models, dancers or athletes.

Epidemiological studies on EDs mainly aim to evaluate how EDs are widespread and to understand which risk factors are implicated in their development. Research studies conducted so far on EDs are difficult to interpret and compare, because of the important differences existing among them in regards to the choice of diagnostic instruments, the sampling criteria and the procedures used.

The prevalence of EDs in the general population is quite low and people suffering from an eating disorder often deny their illness and are reluctant in seeking professional help, and this can be even more prominent in males; thus, the identification of these cases can be problematic. For this reason, the use of clinical interviewers combined with the involvement of the patients' general practitioner in a clinical epidemiological survey can be of great importance in detecting them.

Most of the epidemiological studies have been carried out among the population considered at increased risk, such as for example young females, university students, athletes or dancers. Of course, findings from these studies cannot be generalized to the general population. Some other studies, on the contrary, have been carried out in the whole population (they are called community studies); community samples may add information on the natural course and outcome of these disorders.

The majority of research into the incidence and prevalence of anorexia has been done in Western, developed, industrialized countries as it has been demonstrated that EDs are more widespread in western culture. So, these results are generally not applicable outside these areas. EDs are generally considered "culture-bound syndromes," but recent cross-cultural reviews indicate an increase also in non-Western countries. Therefore, epidemiological studies are now carried out also in non-Western countries.

Some studies use a two-stage screening approach, while others use just self-report measures or just face-to-face interviews. The two-stage screening surveys are the most accurate procedure in epidemiologic research: one starts with a first screening in a determined population using self-reported questionnaires; people who are identified to be more at risk undergo a clinical interview, together with a randomly selected group that serves as the control.

Some studies include control groups while other studies don't.

Again, most of the epidemiological studies on EDs evaluated the prevalence of full syndromes of AN and BN and only few studies evaluated partial or subclinical manifestations of these disorders.

This great variability among epidemiological studies makes it difficult to generalize the findings. Anyway, according to the studies that are considered more correct, in relation to methodology, the average lifetime prevalence rates for AN and BN are around 0.3 and 1%, respectively, in young females, with an estimated prevalence of binge ED (BED) of about 1%. Lifetime prevalence rates of 5–12% are found for atypical AN and 1–5% for atypical BN and these rates go up to 14.6% in adolescents (14–15 years).

As reported before, young females are the most frequently studied sample but, as men are not immune to developing EDs; a growing number of surveys are now including males.

From now on, we are going to focus on epidemiological findings regarding male samples, sometimes compared to their female counterparts.

PREVALENCE OF EDS AMONG MALE SAMPLES

It is assumed that EDs among men are impressively less common than among women. It has been claimed that EDs can be considered female-gender-bound syndromes. But, as already said, EDs do affect men as well. The estimate female-to-male gender ratio seem to be 10:1 (more or less, according to the studies). Some authors state that the male to female AN prevalence ratio ranges from one to four males per 1,000 females with AN and the ratio ranges from 20 to 35 per 1,000 females for BN. In treatment centers there is approximately one male with an eating disorder for every 10-20 females [1]

Males are generally reported to account for 5-10% of anorectics and 10-15% of bulimics identified in the general population [2-3].

In 1991, Carlat and Camargo published an important review of BN in males in the American Journal of Psychiatry. According to these two authors, who conducted a very extensive literature search, bulimia affects about 0.2% of adolescent boys and young men [4].

Some studies on non-clinical samples of men with full and partial syndromes have found that partial syndromes are more common than the full syndromes [5-6] while some other studies run in the clinical population have reported that the partial syndromes are less common than the full ones [3]. As already reported in Chapter One, subjects with a partial syndrome are those who met all but one of the DSM criteria [7].

In 2001 a Canadian study, published in the American Journal of Psychiatry, compared males with full and partial EDs, men without EDs and women with EDs in the community [8]. The overall prevalence rate of full and partial EDs for men was found to be 2.0%. In this study the female-male ratio was 4.2:1 for full syndrome AN and 1.5:1 for partial syndrome AN while the female-male ratio for full syndrome BN was 11.4:1 and 1.8:1 was the ratio for partial syndrome BN.

A great difference was evident in the female to male ratio of full bulimia while a less marked difference was noted in the prevalence of partial bulimia.

The rate for full syndrome EDs in men, combining anorexia and bulimia together, was 0.3% compared with 2.1% for women.

Further examination in both clinical and community samples is needed as it may help in getting a better understanding of the distribution of men with EDs.

ARE MALES AN UNDER-DIAGNOSED SAMPLE?

Men affected by an eating disorder risk not ever being identified. One of the reasons has to do with the fact that they can be reluctant to recognize that they suffer from a disorder thought to be a "women's disease."

Moreover anorexia and bulimia are disorders characterized generally by a sense of denial. The ED's symptoms are not always seen as problematic or as manifestations of an illness. For men, besides these denial or resistance aspects, there can be the awareness that EDs are more common among females. The question then arises of the difficulties for men to seek help for their EDs when facing the fact that the proportion of males found in the community is greater than the percentage of males identified in clinical settings. They seem to be less likely than females to seek treatment. They may have some resistances in admitting to the disease and in seeking professional help because of feelings of shame.

It is therefore possible that only the most severe male cases of EDs arrive to clinical attention. They also risk going unrecognized because doctors can fail to identify male EDs.

In addition, men are screened with tests which have been constructed and validated for female populations. It is consequently more difficult to detect risk subjects among males by using scales or cut-off points used for females [9]. Again, some items, useful for exploring eating and body psychopathology in females, should be slightly different for males: for instance when asking for body image distress. In the next chapter we will focus on body image and the drive for muscularity in men so that differences of these concerns between genders will become clearer.

Age at Onset and Age at Presentation

In regards to women, it is well known that AN has a bimodal distribution with a peak at 14 years old and a second peak at 18 years old.

For bulimia a slightly higher age of onset is reported.

An older age of onset has been associated with greater weight loss, more purging behaviour during the acute phase of illness and a poorer outcome. This has been said for women. And what about men?

The small sample size of men in the studies don't always allow firm conclusions to be drawn.

Even though Crisp et al. reported similar age of onset of AN in the comparison between males and females [10] other studies suggested that the onset of the ED occurs generally later in men than in women.

In a review by Carlat and Camargo, for instance, men suffering from BN report a higher age of onset in respect with their female counterpart [4].

The older mean age of onset could be linked to the fact that puberty, the highest risk period for the onset of AN, for instance, begins and ends later in boys than in girls and it is known that puberty with all related physiological and psychological changes is considered one of the main stressors for the development of EDs.

Also Sharp et al., for example, reported that the mean age of onset in their male sample was later than the age of onset in their female counterpart: which is a mean age of 18.6 years in males versus 17.5 years in females [11].

The article written by Carlat, Camargo and Herzog published in 1997 in the American Journal of Psychiatry has to be considered an important source of data to better understand the etiology and clinical characteristics of EDs. It was based on a wide sample of 135 male patients.

As regards to the onset of the illness, it has been found that the age of onset is late adolescence to early adulthood, with a mean age onset of 19.3 years. They also found no differences among the different diagnostic groups. Differences were found, on the contrary, with regards to age at first treatment, where bulimic patients had an older age at first presentation for the delay between the onset and seeking help for treatment.

Males with AN restricting type waited 1.2 year before seeking treatment, AN patients of the bulimic subtype waited longer, about 4.3 years, while bulimic patients waited 8.4 years.

Chronological trends for men have not been yet established.

Braun et al compared males and females with a diagnosis of an ED who presented for their first admission at the New York Hospital [12]. The authors wanted to document a suspected increase in the number of males seeking treatment over time. They found that between 1984 and 1997 the percentage of males seeking treatment at their ED unit has increased.

An important study published on Eating and Weight Disorders in 2008 tried to determine the distribution of age of onset of EDs in men and to study the relationships between age of onset and demographic and clinical features [13].

The authors focused on the decade 1992-2002 and considered 70 men admitted to an inpatient Eating Disorder Unit in Iowa. The age of onset of the eating disorder, self-reported by each patient, ranged from 8 to 39 years old with a single peak around 14 years with a great part of men beginning their illness before they reached 18 years of age.

Consistent with previous reports by Carlat et al., this study also reported that the age of onset did not significantly differ by admission diagnoses: the AN purging subgroup reported an older age of onset, that is 20.7 years, while a mean age of 16.4 was found for AN restricting male patients, 16.7 for BN male patients and 16.9 for men with an EDNOS diagnosis.

In this study men with a younger age of onset were more likely to report hyperactivity than those with an older age of onset. Men with a younger age of onset were less likely to have used laxatives. No association was found between age of onset and vomiting and this finding replayed what was previously reported by Halmi et al. [14].

Age of onset and duration of illness were associated.

Is it True that EDs are Increasing in Males?

It is hard to give a definite answer to this question because findings on this issue are not great in number and are also not so consistent (12, 15-16]. The majority of studies are inclined to report a stability rather than an increasing trend for EDs in males.

Recent data suggests an increase in hospitalization rates for males with an ED and it seems that more men are now seeking treatment in the outpatients unit for EDs [12].

It has been claimed that there has been an increased referral rate of EDs to specialised clinics in recent years. What we do not know is whether this reflects growing awareness of these problems in the population and thus increased availability of treatment facilities or whether there is a real increase in incidence of EDs in men. A further question arises as to whether this increase is associated mainly with BN cases or with an increase in atypical cases of eating disorder rather than with any change in the rate of AN.

With the aim of examining any change over time in presentation rates of male patients, Button, Aldridge and Palmer recently analysed a cohort of 2554 patients assessed at Leicester Adult ED Service during the 21-year period between 1987 and 2007 [17].

Of this total sample 5%, corresponding to 128 patients, were males. The authors analysed the percentage of males presenting per year and they didn't find a clear trend of increasing over time confirming previous findings. The authors stated that these findings refer to patients presenting to a specialized ED service and cannot be representative of the community male sample, for whom further studies are needed.

Clinical Characteristics

For a better understanding of clinical features in men with EDs we can start by taking a look into some studies published in the recent past.

Vandereycken and Van den Broucke have gathered systematic information on clinical pictures of males with AN, referring to all case reports published in the years between 1970 and 1980 [18].

In general, it was found that male patients with AN resemble, in a striking way, their female counterparts in regards to clinical pictures confirming previous studies [19].

Through this comparative study of more than one hundred cases, they arrived at the following conclusions: the onset of anorexia in males occurs in pre-puberty, adolescence or in early adult life; at assessment male patients are significantly younger and present a greater weight loss; time of presentation, assessment, diagnosis and treatment is about 2 to 3 years after the onset; one third of cases include premorbid overweight; patients present typical anorectic behaviour and anorectic fears like female patients, in half of the cases bulimic episodes are present.

As regards to the 80's, some studies reported cases of bulimic males trying to understand symptomatology and demographic characteristics among males [20-21].

Features of male patients were compared to those of female patients by Margo [22] concluding that, as in the female sample, there was an increase in the referral of male anorectics from the mid-1970s. Anorexia in males began prevalently during adolescence even if some cases had an onset of over 25 years. Hyperactivity was more prevalent among males, confirming that for males a way of losing weight can be easily found in excessive exercise rather than in dieting. As in females, stressful life events were common antecedents of the disorder. Difficulties in relationships within the family were found, as well as a history of psychiatric illness in the family.

During the 90's, there was an increasing interest in male presentation of EDs and numerous studies in scientific literature gave their contribution to the understanding of EDs in men.

In Carlat and Camargo's review it has been found that the characteristics of bulimic men are similar to those of bulimic females although men are less troubled by their binge eating and are less concerned with strict control than females; males are less dissatisfied with their bodies, and they report less guilt, lower rates of depression and self-deprecation after bingeing and, in regard to weight control, the mean desired body weight is higher. Men rely less on laxatives, diuretics and diet pills to lose weight though they may have greater weight fluctuations during the course of their illness. Men don't differ from women in regards to the frequency of binge eating or purging, or on medical complications. It seems that bulimic males report high levels of psychiatric comorbidity, having substantial rates of concurrent mood and anxiety disorders as well as personality disorders.

An important finding reported in the various studies is the higher prevalence of premorbid obesity found in eating disorder male cases. A history of obesity is more prevalent among males than among females.

Another recurrent feature found in males is the different reaction towards body weight. Boys are more likely to be disappointed when they are underweight while girls report a higher drive for thinness, more body satisfaction if they are underweight, and higher prevalence of dieting. This can reflect the different cultural and gender approach to body image. So girls are more prone to desire to lose weight while boys are split: some wish to lose and some wish to gain weight.

Males with EDs may be overrepresented in certain potentially high risk working categories, that is in appearance-based jobs such as modeling or acting, food related jobs. These jobs are usually held by women.

As regards to sexual orientation, marked differences emerge in eating disordered men by diagnostic groups as emerged from the report on 135 eating disordered patients by Carlat, Camargo and Herzog.

A large part of bulimic men report homosexual or bisexual orientation while the great part of anorectic patients are recognised as asexual where asexuality is defined as the lack of all sexual interest for one year prior to assessment (as we can see in the diagnostic criteria the lack of sexual desire is one of the central features in male anorexia). The relationship between homosexuality and bisexuality and EDs in males will be the main issue in one of the following chapters.

The relationship between drug and alcohol abuse and bulimia among male has been studied but findings are not always consistent; sometimes they are contradictory. There seems to be a stronger association between drug and alcohol abuse and bulimic behaviours in men rather than in females though in some studies the reverse is reported. Again, future research can provide further data for better understanding this relationship.

Psychiatric comorbidity is common in men with EDs as most patients with an eating disorder also report a history of major depression disorder, substance abuse and personality disorders but we will go deeper into this argument in Chapter Eight.

As the course of AN among men in the general population is still unknown, a recent study conducted by Finnish researchers aimed to describe patterns, comorbidity and outcomes in men with AN in the general population [23]. Five cases and their co-twins were described in detail. Overweight commonly predated AN in all these cases while none of the co-twins were overweight during adolescence or in early adulthood. Premorbid overweight can lead to dieting and dieting is recognized as one of the main risk factors for AN. Affective and anxiety disorders were common among both the cases with AN and their concordant co-twins. Co-twins without AN reported affective (major depression) and anxiety disorders and symptoms of muscle dysmorphia. Symptoms of muscle dysmorphia like dissatisfaction for muscle bulk, frequent gym training and the use of substances to put on muscle were reported by the men who have suffered from anorexia and their co-twins: these symptoms represent an alternative phenotype of AN in men and it is known that anorexia and muscle dysmorphia share some characteristics such as body image disturbance, for instance.

In this case series the course of anorexia was transient even if, after recovery, some residual symptoms remained present.

The authors underline the anorectic men's difficulties to speak about their illness as they found that the majority of them never have spoken with anybody about their anorexia. They conclude underlining that "feelings of shame, isolation, and alienation related to their disorder were ubiquitous among them and appear to result from the double stigma of having not only a mental illness, but also a "women's illness."

Regarding the outcome of AN in males, it is worth underlining that we cannot rely on consistent findings. Significant differences between females and males on ED outcomes haven't been reported.

In the well-known study by Burns and Crisp on male patients with AN the outcome of the series compared very closely with a similar group of female anorectics [24].

They found that in a 2-20 year follow up, 44% had a good outcome, with stable weight restoration and normal sexual functioning. A good outcome was associated with good psychological and social functioning. 26% had an intermediate outcome and 30% a poor outcome. A poor outcome was instead associated with a longer duration of illness, previous treatment, and greater weight loss. Disturbances in family relationships during childhood and sexual anxieties were predictive of a less favourable prognosis.

For a detailed overview on clinical characteristics of eating disordered men the well designed and exhaustive book written by Arnold Andersen is really worth the read [25].

Risk Factors

Among predisposing factors the following are frequently reported by several authors: a family history of AN, obesity, eating concerns, weight and shape concerns, affective disorders, substance abuse, obsessive compulsive disorder, the exposure to stressful life events, the presence of certain personality traits like perfectionism, low self-esteem, excessive compliance and dependence on others' opinion.

A recent study conducted by Jacobi and collaborators [26] aimed at applying a risk factor approach to putative factors for EDs to deduce general taxonomy.

Risk factors were classified according to risk factor type and to risk factor outcome (into anorexia, or bulimia, into full or partial syndromes). Many factors are general and non-specific risk factors; few predated the onset of the illness and few differentiated among the ED syndromes.

Common risk factors were:

- Gender.
- Ethnicity
- Early childhood eating problems
- Childhood gastrointestinal problems
- Weight and shape concerns
- Low self-esteem and general negative self-evaluation
- Sexual abuse
- Other adverse experiences
- General psychiatric morbidity

Authors examined and found preliminary evidence that dieting, body image dissatisfaction and weight related teasing may have relevance for the development of the spectrum of weight related disorders.

Some risk factors for males are generally not different than the ones for females, but some are different.

Summing up the existing literature risk factors for men would include the following:

- Fatness or overweight during childhood
- Dieting(one of the main risk factors for both males and females)
- Participation in sports demanding thinness, such as runners etc.
- Doing a job that demands thinness (male models, actors, etc.)
- Living in a culture obsessed with dieting and physical appearance
- Homosexuality or bisexuality
- Victimization of sexual abuse

Precipitant factors reported in men generally overlap those reported for women and they include: being teased for being overweight, trying to control body weight and shape for athletic pursuits, feeling anxiety about sexuality, experiencing interpersonal difficulties, and managing separations like, for example, breaking up with a girlfriend. The presence of these factors can act like as an impetus for disordered eating in people who are biologically or psychologically predisposed to.

Positive self-esteem, emotional well-being, school achievement and family connectedness are, on the contrary, considered protective factors for both males and females.

Risk and protective factors for EDs seem similar across genders.

Further knowledge of risk and protective factors serve to guide health professionals in their intervention and prevention efforts.

The Importance of Studying Male Samples

As EDs and body image problems in men represent a peculiar phenomenon which need to be better known by clinicians and other health care providers, it is crucial to study characteristics of men with EDs, both in clinical settings (and here we probably find men with more severe symptoms and comorbidity) and in community samples.

It can be useful (for better understanding etiology and presentation of Eds) to study similarities and differences between men and women with an eating disorder, as well as similarity and differences between men with and without an eating disorder. It seems, in fact, that in men who develop EDs there is something different, as for example the higher likelihood to have homosexual tendencies. Moreover, the attention of the researchers has to be addressed to full syndromes and to partial ones, as these last ones are more widespread in the general male population.

REFERENCES

[1] McDermott, B. ED in boys and men. Ch 14 pg 59-61. In "ABC of ED." Edited by J Morris Blackwell Publishing 2008.

[2] Fairburn, CG; Beglin, SJ. Studies of the epidemiology of BN. *Am J Psychiatry*, 1990 147, 401-408.

[3] Carlat, DJ; Camargo, CA Jr; Herzog, DB. ED in males: a report on 135 patients. *Am J Psychiatry*, 1997 154, 1127-1132.

[4] Carlat, DJ; Camargo, CA Jr. Review of BN in males. *Am J Psychiatry*, 1991 148, 831-843.

[5] Taraldsen, KW; Eriksen, L; Gotestam, KG. Prevalence of ED among Norwegian women and men in a psychiatric outpatient unit. *Int J Eat Disord*, 1996 20, 185-190.

[6] Striegel-Moore, RH; Garvin, V; Dohm, FA; Rosenheck, RA. Psychiatric comorbidity of ED in men: a national study of hospitalized veterans. *Int J Eat Disord*, 1999 25, 399-404.

[7] American Psychiatric Association DSM-IV Text Revised, *Diagnostic and Statistical Manual of Mental Disorders*, Washington, DC, 2000.

[8] Woodside, DB; Garfinkel, PE; Lin, E; Goering, P; Kaplan, SA; Goldbloom, DS; Kennedy SH.Comparison of men with full or partial ED, men without ED, and women with ED in the community. *Am J Psychiatry*, 2001 158, 570-574.

[9] Woodside, DB; Garner, DM; Rockert, W; Garfinkel, PE. *ED in males: insights from a clinical and psychometric comparison with female patients*, in "Males with ED." Edited by Andersen AE. New York, Brunner/Mazel, 1990, pp. 100-115.

[10] Crisp, AH; Burns, T; Bhat, AV. Primary AN in the male and female, a comparison of clinical features and prognosis. *Br J Med Psychol*, 1986 59, 123-132.

[11] Sharp, CW; Clark, SA; Dunan, JR; Blackwood, DHR; Shapiro, CM. Clinical presentation of AN in males: 24 new cases. *Int J Eat Disord*, 1994 15, 125-134.

[12] Braun, DL; Sunday, SR; Huang, A; Halmi, KA. More males seek treatment for ED. *Int J Eat Disord*, 1999 25, 415-424.

[13] Forman-Hoffman, VL; Watson, TL; Andersen, AE. ED age of onset in males: distribution and associated characteristics. *Eat Weight Disord*, 2008 13, 28-31.

[14] Halmi, KA; Casper, RC; Eckert, ED; Goldberg, SC; Davis, JM. Unique features associated with age of onset of AN. *Psychiatric Research*, 1979 1, 209-215.

[15] Currin, L; Schmidt, U; Treasure, J; Jick, H. Time trends in eating disorder incidence. *Br J Psychiatry*, 2005 186, 131-135.

[16] Van Son, GE; Van Hoecken, D; Baltelds, AI; Van Furth, EF; Hoek, HW. Time trends in the incidence of ED: a primary care study in the Netherlands. *Int J Eat Disord*, 2006 39(7), 565-569.

[17] Button, E; Aldridge, S; Palmer, R. Males assessed by a specialized adult ED service: patterns over time and comparisons with females. *Int J Eat Disord*, 2008 41 (8), 758-761.

[18] Vandereycken, W; Van den Broucke, S. AN in males. A comparative study of 107 cases reported in the literature *(1970 to 1980). Acta Psychiatr Scand*, 1984 70, 447-454.

[19] Crisp, AH; Burns, T. The clinical presentation of AN in males. *Intl J Eat Disord*, 1983 2(4), 135-144.

[20] Robinson, PH; Holden, NL. BN in the male: a report of nine cases. *Psychol Med*, 1986 16, 795-803.

[21] Turnbull, J; Freeman, CPL; Barry, F; Annandale, A. Physical and psychological characteristics of five male bulimics. *Br J Psychiatry*, 1987 150, 25-29.

[22] Margo, JL. AN in males. A comparison with female patients. *Br J of Med Psychol*, 1987 151, 80-83.

[23] Raevuori, A; Keski-Rahkonen, A; Hoek, HW; Sihvola, E; Rissanen, A; Kaprio, J.Lifetime AN in young men in the community: five cases and their co-twins. *Int J Eat Disord*, 2008 41, 458-463.

[24] Crisp, AM. Outcome in AN in males. *Br J Psychiatry*. 1984 145, 319-325.

[25] Andersen, AE. "Males with ED." Edited by New York, Brunner/Mazel, 1990.

[26] Jacobi, C; Hayward, C; de Zwaan, M; Kraemer, HC; Agras, WS. Coming to Terms With Risk Factors for ED: Application of Risk Terminology and Suggestions for a General Taxonomy. *Psychological Bulletin*, 2004 130 (1), 19-65.

Chapter 3

MEN'S BODY IDEALS AND MUSCLE DYSMORPHIA

T. Zanetti

ABSTRACT

Weight and shape concerns are not only female issues. Men, particularly young men, are concerned with their appearance too.

A significant part of them are dissatisfied with some aspects of their body shape and weight and wish to put on muscle.

Cultural pressure for men to look a certain way, for instance with a V-shape figure, with a slim, toned-up and muscular body, can create body dissatisfaction as a discrepancy exists between the way they look and the way they ideally want to be.

In the present chapter, we will focus on the concepts of body image and body dissatisfaction in men. Afterwards we will give a look at a peculiar form of over-concern with the degree of muscularity: we will deal with muscle dysmorphia and its related symptom's characteristics.

BODY IMAGE

Body image has been defined as "the picture we have in our minds of the size, shape and form of our bodies and the feelings we have about these characteristics and parts that make them up" [1]

Body image is a complex, subjective construction that depends on several variables: some are external, like culture or a specific historical period, other are internal and are strictly related with the way a person perceives, thinks and feels about himself [2]. Key events in the life of a person and meaningful relationships can influence this construction, so that the mental representation of one's body is not a static concept but a changeable one.

As Schilder pointed out, "body image is continually changing and determines a physical, social and psychological *gestalt*" [3].

Although some researchers contended that body image disturbances should not be a required for the diagnosis of anorexia and BN [4], most clinicians consider it as a prominent symptom for both anorexia and bulimia to the point that body image distortion has been recognized as the core psychopathology of eating disorders. Weight and shape concerns are central in the minds of anorectics and bulimic patients.

As we saw in chapter one, which was about DSM IV criteria, "an intense fear of gaining weight or becoming fat even though underweight" is crucial and diagnostic for AN as well as the "disturbance in the way in which one's body weight and shape is experienced" and the "undue influence of body weight and shape on self evaluation, or denial of the seriousness of the current low body weight."

For subjects suffering from bulimia DSM-IV claims: "self evaluation is unduly influenced by body weight and shape" [5].

Kearney-Cooke and Striegel-Moore [6] described two possible pathways to the development of body image disturbance among eating disordered subjects.

Through a mental process, key relationships (with parents, peers, partners, etc.) and key events (events about body changes, like puberty or sexual experiences) leave some traces in the mind of a person. Relationships and events are "internalized" so that the relation between the external world and the person is kept in mind in "inner representations."

As the body reflects and "participates" in all human experiences, it can be seen as the mirror of the most important preoccupations, "the screen on which one projects one's most intense concerns" [7].

Projection is considered a key process in the development of body image disturbance and in the moment in which difficult internal states are put onto the body instead of trying to overcome these difficulties, one makes the effort to change the body.

A central theme in eating disordered subjects is the effort to keep the body under control when many other areas are felt to be out of control. People with an eating disorder generally feel negative about their body because they feel negative about themselves.

Body Dissatisfaction

Body dissatisfaction, that is to say the dislike of one's appearance, is quite common in the general population, especially among those people for whom the discrepancy between the way they are and the way they want to be is greater. This can be linked to high standards one can have, that means the expectations put on oneself (and this has to do with internal processes), or the suggestions and the models coming from outside stimuli.

Gender is considered an important factor in body image development: women in fact seem to be consistently more discontent with their body appearance, and this is often related with the idea that they are overweight and too fat [8].

Problems in parent-child communication, and later in parent-adolescent communication can have a role in filtering weight dissatisfaction.

In particular, fathers are likely to be involved with sons and this relationship, if positive and warm, can be of great importance in protecting children and helping them to cope with body dissatisfaction.

With regard to this issue an important cross-sectional study has been conducted in 24 countries and regions in Europe, Canada and the USA with the collaboration of the World Health Organization.

Authors aimed at understanding the association between body weight dissatisfaction among school-aged children and communication with parents [9].

A not surprising collection of data in this survey showed that girls were more dissatisfied than their male counterparts, body dissatisfaction was more common among overweight than non–overweight adolescents, and older adolescents showed greater dissatisfaction than younger ones. Difficulties in talking to the father were associated with weight dissatisfaction among both boys and girls in all countries while difficulties of talking with the mother, generally less common, was found to be rarely associated with body weight dissatisfaction among boys while this association was found to be common among girls. Among boys, body weight dissatisfaction was positively associated with difficulty in talking to father in 14 out of 24 countries.

Family environment and family relations and dynamics will be widely explained in Chapter 7.

Differences between Males and Females about Body Image

A great part of scientific literature on eating disorders explain the fact that eating disorders are more widespread among women than among men with the most significant differences between the two sexes being about cultural "norms and expectations" on thinness [10].

If body image traditionally refers to leanness and thinness for women, body shape in terms of muscularity is an important key for body image development in males [11-12].

If we define body dissatisfaction as the existing discrepancy between current body shape and ideal body shape, it is important to stress that in the last decades male models have become more and more lean and muscular at the same time.

Consequently body image and shape concerns are no longer just female problems: the available scientific literature and popular perception as well have evidenced that men may also suffer from body image problems and preoccupations [13].

Similar to what has been found for women, normative standards influence the degree of self-dissatisfaction and consequently this can have an impact on eating disorders psychopathology.

Therefore, when we consider eating disorders in men we have to take into account the new trends in society which lead to the achievement of an ideal body.

Strong messages are conveyed to girls and women about thinness, as well as strong messages being conveyed to boys and men about muscularity.

Drewnowski and Yee wrote about the stigma of thinness in men, and especially in homosexual men [14]. During the '80s men could easily associate the image of extreme emaciation to the starving body of HIV positive men. In gay communities images of wasted bodies, of underweight and ill bodies, could be linked to the devastating effects of AIDS. Harvey and Thompsom made the consideration that "the stigma of HIV/AIDS may have pushed gay, as well as heterosexual men, to obsess over their body image and to obtain a muscular physique. Men may strive for a muscular body to avoid being thought of as ill due to thinness" [15].

Over the last 30 years there has been a shift in how men view, think and feel about their body.

The media seems to play a central role in creating "ideal bodies."

In the case of boys and men, current socio-cultural standards suggest (or impose) the so called "V-shaped muscle structure," where ideally, the waist must be narrow while chest, arms and shoulders must be well-developed with very evident muscle mass.

Pope has published much on this issue, giving fundamental scientific contributions to the knowledge of body image in men. With the aim of analysing whether or not men in modern Western societies desire to have a much leaner and more muscular body than the body they actually had or perceived themselves to have, Pope and colleagues studied three groups of college men in three different countries: Austria, France and the USA. The subjects were asked to choose, through a computerised test, images corresponding to their own body, to the ideal body, to the body of the average man their age and the body they believed was preferred by women. In all three countries men showed a discrepancy between actual muscularity and their body ideals. In fact, men chose the figure of ideal body that was more muscular than their actual body and they believed that women would prefer a male body more muscular than themselves [16].

An important survey by Pope and colleagues focused on the value of male body in advertising and the use of male image for commercial aims.

In this original study, Pope and colleagues examined the proportion of exposed male and female bodies portrayed in advertisements in two American women's magazines, finding that between 1958 and 1998 in both magazines the proportion of undressed men has strongly increased, especially since the early 1980's. According to the authors, these trends in commercial advertising lead to hypotheses that the "male body is increasing in importance as a mark of masculinity- at least as judged from the actions of advertisers seeking to influence women's attitudes." [17]

With regards to females, it has been claimed that Barbie doll has become a role model for a lot of girls. Barbie doll's appearance, with her unrealistic proportions (extremely tall and extremely thin) has been a matter of controversial debates due to the fact that her shapes could induce anorectic attitudes.

The male counterpart of Barbie doll is called "Big Jim" in Italy, and is characterized by very large muscle mass, a narrow waist and huge chest and biceps.

Some authors hypothesized that the physiques of male action toys would provide some indexes of evolving American cultural ideals of male body image.

Pope et al. [18] measured examples of the most popular boys' action toys manufactured in the last couple of decades. They measured waist, chest, biceps circumferences and noticed that boys' action figures, including for instance Batman or G.I Joe, have reflected the growing muscle ideals as they have increased in size over time. Pope and colleagues, focusing on evolving ideals of male body image as seen through action toys, reported that from 1973 to 1998 the chest and the biceps of G.I. Joe significantly expanded (the biceps expanded from 12.2 to 26.8 inches!) while the abdominal muscles became more defined, like as in a body builder. Some contemporary figures exceeded even the largest human bodybuilder's proportions!

As for women, there have been theorized reasons why exposure to the thin-ideal body image may contribute to the development of eating disorders [19], for boys it has been hypothesized that the current media's portrayal of male images may lead to disordered thinking and behaviours because of the muscle-bound images that are presented.

When men see these images they may experience a sense of dissatisfaction with their own body and may have the desire to change it.

In comparison with women, men tend to exercise rather than diet in order to try and change their body.

Exercising can reach compulsive frequency, becoming more and more intense and prolonged and thus creating vicious cycles in men: the more they train, the more muscular they want to be.

Some choose to take anabolic steroids to speed up the process of "making muscle," despite well known side effects.

Of course ordinary training or weight lifting must be distinguished from muscle dysmorphia as in normal training appearance is not linked to overconcerns and body image distortions and it is not associated with unhealthy eating and weight control practices.

Differences can be found among different cultures: in fact body image disorders appear to be more prevalent in Western than in non-Western men.

Taiwanese men, for example, exhibit less dissatisfaction with their bodies than western men, as well as the fact that Taiwanese advertising places less value on the male body than Western media. Actually, American magazine advertisements portray undressed Western men frequently, while Taiwanese magazines portray undressed Asian men rarely, with a very different impact to the creation of an "ideal" body image. This difference may reflect the greater decline in traditional male roles in the West, leading to greater emphasis on the body as a measure of masculinity [20].

Halliwell et al. suggest that the effects of exposure to muscular male models among men seem to be moderated by gym use and exercise motivation [21].

Cohane and Pope recently reviewed the findings emerging from the literature on the "neglected issue of body image in boys" [22]. This study has been done using computer and manual search techniques on 17 studies that assessed body image attitudes in boys under age 18.

The results of this review were fairly consistent: it has been established that although boys generally display less overall body concerns than girls, body image problems in boys are common and often associated with impaired self-concept and self-esteem; body image problems in boys frequently focus on "bigness" and muscularity rather than thinness.

What about Muscle Dismorphia?

According to DSM-IV Body Dysmorphic Disorder (BDD) is a preoccupation with a mental, imagined defect in appearance leading to impairment in social or occupational functioning [5].

Men with a BDD can think and fear they are not lean enough, that they are too small or insufficiently muscular when in reality they look normal. This body distortion in men is labelled muscle dysmorphia or "reverse anorexia" and can lead to anything from profound distress to great difficulties in social relationships. In the comparison with others men with BDD feel inferior.

While many authors suggested muscle dysmorphia be classified as a subcategory of Body Dysmorphic Disorder, Chung, examining the historical aspects and proposed criteria for muscle dysmorphia and contrasting them with those of anorexia (being that anorexia focused on thinness and muscle dysmorphia focused on muscularity), suggests that both the historical and the clinical aspects of this syndrome are more consistent with a classification as an obsessive-compulsive disorder [23].

Anyway, this disorder has been associated in fact with impaired self-esteem, with symptoms of mood, anxiety and eating disorders, and with a high prevalence of anabolic steroid abuse. [24-26]

Men with MD can exercise compulsively in order to increase their muscle mass and the image they see in the mirror is never satisfying. Lifting weights, doing resistance training, and using steroids can reach obsessive compulsive levels: a vicious cycle can take place: the more they exercise (sometimes spending many hours in the daily gym) the more they complain to not bemuscular enough.

Muscle Dysmorphia has been described to be frequent among weightlifters and bodybuilders [27- 29].

As said before, the discrepancy between the ideal image and the actual one increases men's body dissatisfaction.

Men can feel ashamed of their body, and may also feel anxious and depressed. The exercise dependence may so strongly interfere with their occupational functioning that some men give up their well-paying job to submit to their daily training in gymnasiums constantly!

Knowledge on etiological factors for MD is still lacking. In this particular field further studies need to be run to better understand why some men develop such a distorted image about themselves while other men don't.

Reasons for the development of muscle dysmorphia can be found in patients' stories, in their family environment, in their experiences with peers, or in cultural exposure.

Literature about body dysmorphic disorder suggests that those people affected by muscle dysmorphia are more likely to have an experience of abuse in childhood [30].

It can be found that boys who later develop MD may have been small and weaker than other boys, and for that reason more frequently victims of bullism. Becoming stronger by strenuous exercise can represent a mean to react.

In one of the adolescents' bestsellers in Italy *"Tre metri sopra il cielo"*, one of the most read books by Italian teenagers [31], an important character named "Schello" is bullied and criticised by his peers. He is beaten and can't react because of his weak structure. Then he decides to react to bullying experiences and starts exercising to the point of exercise addiction and his body gradually changes in strength and structur. In many parts of this book "Schello" is seen doing long series of press-ups for the biceps. The ideal image to reach is that of "Conan," the famous film character.

An interesting study has been recently conducted by Wolke and Sapouna who examined whether childhood bullying victimization and MD have adverse effects on global psychopathology and self-esteem, and they tried then to understand if MD can play a role in moderating the effect of bullying victimization on general psychopathology and self-esteem [32].

This study was conducted among 100 bodybuilders who trained regularly in gymnasiums in South England and South Wales.

21% of them reported to have been victims of bullying during childhood. Those who recalled regular bullying victimization, in particular to have been beaten by their peers, also scored higher on the Muscle Dysmorphic Inventory (MDI), an instrument designed to assess discomfort and distress associated with the fear of being small and / or not muscular enough.

Those bodybuilders with higher scores on the MDI also reported lower self-esteem and higher levels of general psychopathology: early victimization experiences increase muscle dysmorphia tendencies and have a negative impact on psychopathology.

Some authors suggest studying the association between MD and personality disorders and psychiatric illness. Cafri, Olivardia and Thompson, for example, have analysed symptom characteristics and psychiatric comorbidity in males affected from muscle dysmorphia [33].

They found that, relative to controls, men with a history of muscle dysmorphia presented higher rates of mood and anxiety disorders. Again, muscle dysmorphic men were more dissatisfied with their appearance and with their muscularity, and reported more appearance checking and more bodybuilding dependence.

In conclusion, when facing the issue of body image and body image disorders in men one has to use different perspectives, thought by some to have overlapping areas with their female counterparts, but also must take into consideration some peculiar aspects of male body image.

Teasing in childhood and adolescence for being too thin or too fat or too weak, cultural pressure to be muscular and strong, a great emphasis on appearance, and advertising campaigns featuring idealized male body images can contribute to the construction of male negative body image.

Consequently, a negative body image can encourage unhealthful behaviours in men like dieting, disordered eating, exercise dependence and steroid abuse.

As body image has this enormous impact on the mind and life of subjects, it should be taken into account in the diagnostic process and in the treatment of eating disordered males.

REFERENCES

[1] Slade, P; Brodie, D. Body image distortion and eating disorders. A reconceptualization based on the recent literature. *Eur Eat Disord Rev*,1994 2, 32-46.

[2] Cash, TF; Pruzinski, T. *Body Images: development deviance and change*. New York:.The Guilford Press; 1990.

[3] Schilder, P. *Image and appearance of the human body*. New York: International University Press; 1950.

[4] Hsu, L; Sobkiewicz, T. Body image disturbance: time to abandon the concept for eating disorders. *Int J Eat Disord,* 1991 10, 15-30.

[5] American Psychiatric Association DSM-IV Text Revised, *Diagnostic and Statistical Manual of Mental Disorders*, Washington: DC; 2000.

[6] Kearney-Cooke, A; Striegel-Moore R. The etiology and treatment of body image disturbance. Chapter 15, 295-306. In Garner, DM; Garfinkel, PE. Handbook of treatment of eating disorders Second Edition., New York London, The Guilford Press 1997.

[7] Fisher, S. *Development and structure of the body image*. Hillsdale, New York: Lawrence Erlbaum; 1986.

[8] Rodin, J. *Body traps*. New York.: William Morrow; 1992.

[9] Al Sabbah, H; Vereecken, CA; Elgar, FJ; Nansel, T; Aasvee, K; Abdeen, Z; Ojala, K; Ahluwalia, N; Maes, L. Body weight dissatisfaction and communication wuth parents among adolescents in 24 countries: international cross-sectional survey. *BMC Public Health,* 2009 6, 9-52.

[10] Feingold, A; Mazzella, R. Gender differences in body image are increasing. *Psychological Science*, 1998 9, 190-195.

[11] Muth, JL; Cash, TF. Body image attitudes. What differences does gender make? *J App Soc Psychol*, 1997 27, 16 1438-1452.

[12] Toro, J; Gila, A; Castro, J; Pombo, C; Guete, O. Body image, risk factors for eating disorders and sociocultural influences in Spanish adolescents. *Eat Weight Disord,* 2005 10 (2), 91-97.

[13] Benninghoven, D; Tadic, V; Kunzendorf, S; Jantschek, G. Body images of male patients with eating disorders. *Psychother and Psychosom Med Psychology,* 2007 57 (3-4), 120-127.

[14] Drenowski, A; Yee, DK. Men and body image: are males satisfied with their body weight? *Psychosom Med*, 1987 49, 626-634.

[15] Harvey, JA; Robinson, JD. Eating disorders in men: current considerations. *Journal of Clinical Psychology in Medical Setting*, 2003 10 (4), 297-306.

[16] Pope, HG Jr; Gruber, AJ; Mangweth, B; Bureau, B; deCol, C; Jouvent, R; Hudson, JI. Body image perception among men in three countries. *Am J Psychiatry,* 2000 157 (8), 1297-1301.

[17] Pope, HG Jr; Olivardia, R; Borowiecki, JJ; Cohane, GH. The growing commercial value of the male body: a longitudinal survey women's magazine. *Psychother Psychosom,* 2001 70 (4), 189-192.

[18] Pope, HG Jr; Olivardia, R; Gruber, A; Borowiecki, JJ. Evolving ideals of male body image as seen through action toys. *Int J Eat Disord,* 1999 26 (1), 65-72.

[19] Stice, E; Shaw, HE. Role of body dissatisfaction in the onset and maintenance of eating pathology: a synthesis of research findings. *J Psychosom Res*, 2002 53 (5), 961-93.

[20] Yang, CF; Gray, P; Pope, HG Jr. Male body image in Taiwan versus the West: Yanggang Zhiqi meets the Adonis complex. *Am J Psychiatry,* 2005 162 (2), 263-269.

[21] Halliwell, E; Dittmar, H; Orsborn, A. The effects of exposure to muscular male models among men: exploring the moderating role of gym use and exercise motivation. *Body Image,* 2007 4 (3), 278-287.

[22] 22 Cohane, GH; Pope, HG Jr. Body image in boys: A review of the literature. *Int J Eat Disord,* 2001 29, 373-379.

[23] Chung, B. Muscle dysmorphia: a critical review of the proposed criteria. *Perspect Biol Med,* 2001 44 (4), 565-574.

[24] Pope, HG Jr; Gruber, AJ; Choi, P; Olivardia, R; Philips, KA. Muscle dysmorphia. An underrecognized form of body dysmorphic disorder. *Psychosom,* 1997 38 (6), 548-557.

[25] Olivardia, R. Mirror, mirror on the wall, who's the largest of them all? The feature of muscle dysmorphia. *Harv Rev Psychiatry*, 2001 9 (5), 254-259.

[26] Pope, CG; Pope, HG; Menard, W; Fay, C; Olivardia, R; Philips, KA. Clinical features of muscle dysmorphia among males with body dysmorphia. *Body Image,* 2005 2 (4), 395-400.

[27] Olivardia, R; Pope, HG Jr; Hudson, JI. Muscle dysmorphia in male weightlifters: a case-control study. *Am J Psychiatry,* 2000 157 (8), 1291-1296.

[28] Choi, PY; Pope, HG jr; Olivardia, R. Muscle dysmorphia: a new syndrome in weightlifters. *Br J Sports Med,* 2002 36 (5), 375-376.

[29] Mangweth, B; Pope, HG Jr; Kemmler, G; Ebenbichler, C; Hausmann, A; De Col, C; Kreutner, J; Biebl, W. Body image and psychopathology in male bodybuilders. *Psychother Psychosom,* 2001 70 (1), 38-43.

[30] Didie, ER; Tortoloni, CC; Pope, CG; Menare, W; Fay, C; Phillips, KA. Childhood abuse and neglect in body dismorphic disorder. *Child Abuse Negl*, 2006 30 (10), 1105-1115.

[31] Moccia, F. *Tre metri sopra il cielo*. Second Edition. Milano: Feltrinelli Editore; 2007.

[32] Wolke, D; Sapouna, M. Big men feeling small: childhood bullying experience, muscle dysmorphia and other mental health problems in bodybuilders. *Psychology of Sports and Exercise*, 2008 9, 595-604.

[33] Cafri, G; Olivardia, R; Thompson, JK. Symptom characteristics and psychiatric comorbidity among males with muscle dysmorphia. *Compr Psychiatry,* 2008 49 (4), 374-379.

Chapter 4

SPORTS AND EATING DISORDERS IN MALES

T. Zanetti

ABSTRACT

Among men weight and shape concerns associated to a deep body dissatisfaction may put them at risk of compulsive training and unhealthy eating and weight control practices. This can increase the likelihood of developing an eating disorder. Participating in special types of exercise and sports may result in a higher risk for controlling body and body weight using unhealthy methods. In this chapter, we address the relation between some particular sporting activities and the risk of developing an eating disorder in men.

We will focus on some studies published in the scientific literature about disordered eating in wrestlers, rowers, cyclists and jockeys.

HYPERACTIVITY, A SYMPTOM OF EDS

Patients with ED often use excessive physical activity to keep body weight low. Excessive exercise has an important clinical significance [1]. It plays a role in the aetiology, and in the development and maintenance of an eating pathology.

Compulsive exercise is, together with restrictive dieting, a way of exerting control over the body and body weight, and a way to achieve the goal of thinness and emaciation in anorexia nervosa.

In bulimia nervosa excessive exercise can be used after binge eating episodes to limit the consequences of great food intake: consuming calories by way of intense physical activity is a way of reducing the sense of guilt and distress. It represents a compensatory method in the diagnostic criteria of the non-purging type of bulimia nervosa. So, it can be considered a transdiagnostic phenomenon.

In patients with eating disorders, excessive exercise can take various forms: one can walk many kilometres every day, or can go swimming and swim an infinite number of lengths, or can go to the gym and exercise in an extreme way by doing impressive numbers of repetitions.

People with EDs feel compelled to exercise as a means of controlling their weight and shape. Physical activity is not intended for healthy or sporting goals, for fitness or for having fun. Physical activity is just a way of burning off calories.

The great amount of time spent exercising may strongly interfere with daily functioning. A person can come to the point of feeling distressed, nervous, anxious and angry when unable to exercise for any reasons (i.e. for climatic reasons or for physical injuries).

The most common ways to refer to this peculiar attitude are hyperactivity, compulsive exercise, obligatory exercise, exercise dependence or driven activity.

An update on the definition "excessive exercise" in eating disorders research suggests considering the exercise as excessive when its postponement is accompanied by intense guilt or when it is undertaken solely with the aim of influencing weight and shape [2].

Despite some significant advances in the understanding of this central topic in ED, much remains to be done in terms of future research about presentation, features, risk factors and the consequences of excessive exercise [3].

Eating and exercise disorders have been found in undergraduate men [4] and young college men [5]: professionals need to be aware of the dangers related to these distressing attitudes.

Athletes and Eating Disorders

EDs appear with relative frequency in sports, in particular in sports such as gymnastics, figure skating, or resistance sports, in which weight control is important.

Incidence and prevalence of eating disorders among athletes are higher in women than in men [6], reflecting the situation of the general population. Nevertheless some authors state that EDs do occur in male athletes as well: they are less prominent than in females and this can be a risk for missing them [7].

In 1992 the American college of sports Medicine coined the term "the female athlete triad": this is a serious syndrome comprising three interrelated components: disordered eating, amenorrhoea and osteoporosis [8].

The triad is caused by an imbalance between energy intake and energy expenditure and can be associated with medical morbidity [9]. Early recognition and intervention are essential. Amenorrhoea must be considered an indicator of this important problem. Of course, among men this peculiar indicator is nonexistent, therefore in men pathological conditions due to strenuous exercise is at risk of going undetected.

The relation between behaviours and attitudes that could promote eating disorders, like, for example, restrained eating or body dissatisfaction, and the presence of EDs in athletes is rather complex.

Common psychological features emerging among eating disordered athletes are low self-esteem, a distorted body image, inefficiency, perfectionism, sense of loss of control, compensatory attempts exerted through food manipulation and use of inadequate methods of controlling weight.

WHICH CAME FIRST, THE CHICKEN, OR THE EGG?

Is it a person prone to eating disorders who will start to participate in excessive sport activities or is it the participation in sport activities that may increase the risk for developing EDs ? This is still a hotly debated question.

SOME SPORTS ARE MORE AT RISK

Some sports require weight classes and athletes are classified according to their body weight, therefore some athletes have to control their weight constantly. Several studies report a higher level of dieting in athletes of light-weight classes and it has been hypothesized that dieting is a risk factor for the development of eating disorders. It is also true that restrained eating does not necessarily lead to EDs since a great number of persons who diet do not develop eating disorders.

Rowing, wrestling, and horse-racing are light weight sports in which performance is strictly related to the athlete's body weight.

Again, while for some athletes increasing the body size can be an advantage such as in basketball, in rugby or in sumo wrestling, for some other athletes body dimensions are not relevant but it can be essential to maintain low the fat body mass and relatively high levels of fat-free body mass to optimize their performance (like in football, in swimming or skiing). For some other athletes, their body weight is imposed by a specific weight category in which they have to fit in, in order to compete in that specific sporting activity.

In other sports body weight is controlled in order to get a better performance or for aesthetic reasons: for disciplines like diving or figure skating the aesthetic component has a great emphasis on the performance itself.

In some sports body weight is determinant for the admission of the athlete into a competition.

But whatever the sport is, if body weight has its own importance, the nutritional aspects consequently play an essential role.

With this held in regard, a Norwegian study about prevalence of EDs among elite athletes found that the prevalence of eating disorders is higher in athletes than in controls, in fact more athletes than controls had subclinical or clinical EDs [10]. The prevalence of anorexia, bulimia and eating disorders not otherwise specified was higher in female athletes than in male athletes and more common among leanness dependent sports and weight dependent sports than in other forms.

The prevalence of EDs among males was greater in antigravitation sports (22%) than in ball games (5%) and endurance sports (9%).

In a Finnish study about weight and diet, concerning female and male athletes, the prevalence of weight reduction attempts resulted higher in female weight-classes athletes than in endurance and ballgame athletes and controls. In males, the frequency of weight reduction attempts was also highest in weight-class athletes, confirming that the risk for disordered eating is dependent on the type of sport [11].

THE USE OF WEIGHT-MAKING PRACTICES AMONG WRESTLERS

Which is the worse adversaries for a fighter? Perhaps the balance and the need to keep his weight into a definite range.

Wrestlers are known for their extreme weight cutting strategies including fasting, food and fluid restriction and dehydration.

In a study conducted several years ago by Oppliger et al. in Iowa, 713 school wrestlers were investigated about weight loss practices, nutritional knowledge and bulimic behaviours [12].

Results showed a rate of people with bulimic symptoms higher than expected for adolescent males: the average wrestler lost 3.2 kg to compete, cycled 1.8 kg weekly and fasted 20 hours prior to weight-in. More extreme bulimic behaviours were found in 45% of the sample: 19% frequently fasted, 34% used rubber suits, 25% restricted fluids and 8% vomited.

ROWERS

In regards to rowing, light-weight categories exist, in which a rower must not overcome certain weight limits. According to the International Rowing Federation (FISA) the average limit weight for male rowers in the lightweight category is 70 kilos, 72.5 as maximum limit for the single rower (corresponding to about 160 lb). For female rowers, the average limit weight is instead 57 kilos, 59 for the single female rower.

A group of researchers at Yale University evaluated eating attitudes, dieting patterns, weight fluctuations and methods of weight loss in a sample of male and female rowers [13]. The results of this study indicate that rowing can be considered a sport in which eating and weight disturbances may be present and male athletes may be more vulnerable to these problems than previously recognized. In fact, females displayed more disturbed eating patterns and weight control methods than did their male counterparts, but male rowers were more affected by weight restriction than were female rowers. Lightweight male rowers reported greater weight fluctuations during the season and gained more weight during the offseason than did female lightweight rowers or heavyweight rowers.

Karlson and colleagues [14] hypothesized that rowers could show an increased prevalence of restraint in their eating behaviours but not an increased prevalence of eating disorder cases, because they are required to make their target weight but they are discouraged from further weight loss.

In their retrospective survey, where lightweight women rowers were compared to distance runners, they found that the use of pathologic weight-making behaviours is of significant clinical concern in rowers as rowing is associated with increased restrained and diuretic misuse.

But they didn't find increased prevalence in eating disorders.

RUNNING AND COMPULSIVE RUNNING

In a study aimed at exploring the similarity between patients with anorexia and a subgroup of male athletes designated as obligatory runners it has been found that obligatory runners resemble anorectics in terms of personality characteristics such as inhibition of anger, high self-expectations, high tolerance of physical discomfort, denial of potential serious debility and tendency towards depression [15].

Great preoccupation with food and an unusual emphasis on lean body mass were common features in the two subgroups and authors speculate that obligatory running and anorexia could represent an attempt to establish an identity.

Psychological and physiological features were also investigated in male runners, female runners and anorexia nervosa patients in a study by Powers, Schocken and Boyd [16].

They found that anorexia nervosa patients had significantly more evidence of psychopathology on all the psychological measures than either groups of runners. At physical examination fat content was low in anorexia nervosa patients but in the normal range for both groups of runners.

Some suggestive similarities were found between female runners and anorexics on body image tests, but not for the male runners. So the authors have concluded that despite hypothetical similarities anorexia nervosa patients and habitual runners share few psychological and physiological features.

AMONG JOCKEYS?

In horse racing there are two racers: the horse and the jockey; obviously the supplementary efforts a horse exerts during the race is related to the jockey's body weight. The lower the weight of the jockey the faster the horse runs.

Jockeys are usually low in height and follow rigid dieting to keep their weight under control. Current weight restrictions imposed on jockeys by the horseracing industry, however, can have an impact on nutritional status and consequently on their sporting performance and on their health.

Jockeys are in fact required to maintain very low their body weight and are also required to maintain precise weight control during competition. In preparation for racing many athletes reduce their weight by restricting their food intake, especially during the day before competition.

High percentages of jockeys routinely skip meals. Sauna-induced sweating and diuretics are methods employed for rapid weight loss [17].

In a study conducted by King and Mezey about eating behaviour in male racing jockeys the majority of the interviewed subjects reported food avoidance, use of saunas, abuse of laxatives, diuretics and appetite suppressants [18].

Recent studies focus on the impact of weight management and weight loss strategies used by professional jockeys on their physical and psychological health.

In a study conducted in New Zealand on jockeys' dietary habits and their potential impact on health Leydon and Wall [19] found that energy and carbohydrate intakes were below the recommendations for athletes. A high percentage of jockeys used a variety of methods to "make weight" including dangerous methods like diuretics, saunas, hot baths, restriction of food and fluids. 20% of the jockeys had symptoms of disordered eating and half of the sample was classified as osteopenic for the reduction of calcium intake.

EDs Among Male Cyclists

Disordered eating habits and nutritional deficits can position male cyclists in a risk category.

A study was conducted by Rielb and colleagues in Colorado [20] to identify subclinical disordered eating and dietary features among male cyclists. 61 male cyclists and 63 male noncyclists participated to this investigation: they completed questionnaires about nutritional patterns and about eating attitudes.

Cyclists scored higher on the Eating Attitudes Test compared to noncyclists, the nutritional test revealed that male cyclists may not consume adequate nutrients for their metabolic needs (see case report on a male cyclist in Part 3).

Five cyclists reported to suffer from an eating disorder. Half the cyclists believed eating disorders were common in the sport.

The National Collegiate Athletic Association Study

The prevalence of symptomatic eating behaviour and attitudes among female and male student athletes was investigated in Kansas in an important collaborative study with the National Collegiate Athletic Association (NCAA), published in the International Journal of ED in 1999 [21].

In this study 1445 students athletes from 11 divisions schools from 11 different sports were surveyed. The different sports were football, basketball, track, swimming, gymnastics, wrestling, cross-country, crew, tennis, Nordic skiing and volleyball.

More than one fourth of male and female athletes had episodes of consuming large quantities of food, males were more likely to have had a binging episodes of overeating on a daily basis than females. Females were more likely to feel out of control during an episode of bingeing than males. In regards to the frequency of vomiting, more females than males had vomited to lose weight at some time in their life (about 24% versus about 6%) and similarly more females than males had used laxatives and diet pills. There were no differences between the two sexes for the use of diuretics. Males were more likely to use saunas or steam baths to lose weight.

In summary, with different frequency, eating-disturbed behaviours also affected men.

More than 10% of females and 13% of males reported binge eating on a weekly basis, 5% of females and 2% of males reported purging behaviours like vomiting, laxatives and diuretics on a weekly basis.

With regards to body mass index, most subjects were in the normal weight range but 173 females and 44 males had a BMI between 15 and 20 and two subjects had a BMI lower than 15!

Desired fat content was reported by 341 females and 554 males. Both females and males want to be at a fat content below ideal; males were at a low normal fat content and females were at an abnormally low fat content, below that required for normal menses.

This study relied on self report questionnaires and didn't use a two stage methodology using both self-report and clinical interviews; some findings about prevalence of the disorders were deducted from athletes' responses: results indicated that 1.1% of the females met DSM-IV criteria for bulimia nervosa versus 0% for males. None of the students met DSM-IV criteria for anorexia nervosa. 9.2% of the females and .01% of the males were identified as having clinical problems of bulimia.

The athletes were asked if they believed they had an eating disorder and 11 females and 1 male said they had anorexia nervosa, while 21 females and 2 males reported they had bulimia nervosa.

The results of this study suggest that female athletes are at significant risk for developing eating disordered thoughts and behaviours, but also male athletes, even if at a lower level, can be at risk.

Preventive Efforts Are Needed

Eating disorders among athletes may be prevented.

Coaches, athletic department directors, trainers, students athletes, regulatory boarding members and parents of athletes need to be aware that emphasizing pursuit of low body weight and low percentage of body fat can have serious consequences on physical and psychological health.

Coaches and trainers need to be educated on the dangers and on the signs of what to look for in an athlete that may be suffering from an eating disorder. They should be able to recognize when healthy training turns into obsessive and compulsive activity with the unique aim of controlling weight and becoming thinner and thinner.

Both primary and secondary prevention intervention efforts are recommended.

A collaboration among coaches, athletic trainers, parents, physicians and athletes is required and necessary for recognizing, preventing and treating ED in the athletes.

The identification of cases among risk groups is an essential goal.

Psychoeducation of athletes, their family and coaches can be an important step in this direction.

"Mens Sana in Corpore Sano" (Iuvenalis, 100 A.C.)

Sport has always been a great mean of wellbeing, both from a psychological and a physical point of view. There are many documented reasons for being physically active. Physical training produces important physiological effects (on the cardiovascular system for instance).

Important psychological effects result in the improvement of life quality, in higher self-esteem, in lower levels of depression and anxiety, and in a better sense of control of one's own body, just to give some examples.

Just the practice of a sport activity cannot be considered a risk factor in developing disordered eating.

Therefore, it becomes essential to distinguish between behaviour aimed at maintaining a particular weight for sporting reasons and behaviours driven by the characteristics of patients with eating disorders.

Among men weight and shape concerns, associated with a deep body dissatisfaction, may lead athletes to compulsive training, as well as unhealthy eating and weight control practices. This can increase the likelihood of developing an ED as many authors previously underlined [22-23].

Fairburn and Beglin [24] suggested that a possible key to consider is the extent to which the individual's behaviour remains under his control. "*If subjects report that they are no longer able to control their eating habits or attempts to lose weight, this suggest that they have developed a clinical eating disorder.*"

REFERENCES

[1] Shroff, H; Reba, L; Thornton, LM; Tozzi, F; Klump, KL; Berrettini, WH. Features associated with excessive exercise in women with eating disorders. *Int. J. Eat Disord.*, 2006, 39, 454-461.

[2] Mond, JM; Hay, PJ; Rodgers, B; Owen, C. An update on the definition of "excessive exercise" in eating disorders research. *Int. J. Eat Disord.*, 2006, 39, 147-153.

[3] Meyer C; Taranis L; Touyz S. Excessive exercise in the eating disorders: a need for less activity from patients and more from researchers..." *Eur. Eat Disord. Rev.*, 2008 16, 81-83.

[4] Ousley L; Cordero ED; White S. Eating disorders and body image of undergraduate men. *J Am. Coll Health*, 2008 56 (6), 617-621.

[5] O'Dea JA; Abraham S. Eating and exercise disorders in young college men. *J. Am. Coll. Health*, 2002 50 (6), 273- 278.

[6] Augestad LB. Prevalence and gender differences in eating attitudes and physical activity among Norwegians. *Eat Weight Disord.*, 2000 5 (2), 62-72.

[7] Baum, A. Eating disorders in the male athlete. *Sports Med.*, 2006 36(1), 1-6.

[8] Golden, NH. A review of female athlete triad (amenorrhea, osteoporosis and disordered eating). *Int. J. Adolesc. Med. Health*, 2002 14 (1), 9-17.

[9] West, RV. The female athlete. The triad of disordered eating, amenorrhoea and osteoporosis. *Sports Med*,. 1998 26 (2), 63-71.

[10] Sundgot- Borgen, J; Torstveit, MK. Prevalence of eating disorders in elite athletes is higher than in the general population. *Clin. J. Sport Med.*, 2004 14 (1), 25-32.

[11] Fogelholm, M; Hiilloskorpi, H. Weight and diet concerns in Finnish female and male athletes.*Med. Sci. Sports Exerc.*, 1999 31(2), 229-235.

[12] Oppliger, RA; Laudry, GL; Foster,SW; Lambrecht, AC. Bulimic behaviours among interscholastic wrestlers: a statewide survey. *Pediatrics*, 1993 91, 826-831.

[13] Sykora, C; Grilo, CM; Wilfley, DE; Brownell, KD. Eating, weight and dieting disturbances in male and female lightweight and heavyweight rowers. *Int. J. Eat. Disord.*, 1993 14 (2), 203-211.

[14] Karlson, KA; Becker, CB; Merkur, A. Prevalence of eating disordered behavior in collegiate lightweight women rowers and distance runners. *Clin. J. Sport. Med.,* 2001 11 (1) 32-37.

[15] Yates, A; Leehey, K; Shisslak, CM. Running: An analogue of anorexia? *N. Eng. J. Med.*, 1983 308 (5), 251-255.

[16] Powers, PS; Schocken, DD; Boyd, FR. Comparison of habitual runners and anorexia nervosa patients. *Int. J. Eat Disord.,* 1998 23 (2), 133-143.

[17] Moore, JM; Timperio, AF; Crawford, DA; Burns, CM; Cameron-Smith, D. Weight management and weight loss strategies of professional jockeys. *Int. J. Sport Nutr. Exerc. Metab*, 2002 12 (1), 1-13.

[18] King, MB; Mezey, G. Eating behavior of male racing jockeys. *Psychol Med*, 1987 17 (1), 249-253.

[19] Leydon, MA; Wall, C. New Zealand jockeys' dietary habits and their potential impact on health. *Int. J. Sport. Nutr. Exerc. Metab.*, 2002 12 (2), 220-237.

[20] Riebl SK; Subudhi AW; Broker JP; Schenck K; Berning JR. The prevalence of subclinical eating disorders among male cyclists. *J. Am. Diet. Assoc.*, 2007 107 (7), 1214-1217.

[21] Johnson C; Powers PS; Dick R. Athletes and eating disorders: the national collegiate athletic associations study. *Int. J. Eat. Disord.,* 1999 26, 179-188.

[22] Davis C; Kennedy SH; Ravelski E; Dionne M. The role of physical activity on the development and maintenance of eating disorders. *Psychol. Med.*, 1994 24 (4), 957-967.

[23] Davis C; Katzman DK; Kaptein S; Kirsh C; Brewer H; Kalmbach K; Olmsted MP; Woodside DB; Kaplan AS. The prevalence of high-level exercise in the eating disorders: etiological implications. *Compr. Psychiatry*, 1997 38 (6), 321-326.

[24] Fairburn, CG; Beglin SJ. Studies of the epidemiology of bulimia nervosa. *Am. J. Psychiatry*, 1990 147, 401-408.

Chapter 5

Homosexuality, Gender Identity Disturbance and Eating Disorders in Men

T. Zanetti

Abstract

Anorexia and Bulimia occur primarily in females so that to be a female is a factor that increases the likelihood of developing an eating disorder.

Eating disorders occur, as we could see in the previous chapters, also in men, even if at a lower frequency. It has been estimated in fact that 5-10 % of all cases occur in males.

But what happens in homosexual or in bisexual men, or in the subgroup of subjects with a gender identity disorder?

Studies on the relationship between eating disorders and sexual orientation can be approached from two directions: 1) assessing sexual orientation and the presence of homosexuality and bisexuality among eating disordered male patients, 2) assessing the prevalence of disordered eating attitudes and behaviours in samples of homosexual and bisexual men.

Compared to their female counterparts, men with eating disorders appear to have higher prevalence of homosexuality and asexuality.

Homosexuality seems to act as a specific risk factor for eating disorders in males.

In this chapter, we will deal with the association between homosexuality and weight and shape and eating concerns as well as the association between gender identity disorders and eating disorders in men.

Anorexia and bulimia nervosa are predominantly considered diseases of girls and young women as it is assumed that the ratio of gender distribution relating to eating disorders is about 1:10 and therefore less common among men [1-2].

Some men cannot recognize or are reluctant to recognize the symptoms of an eating disorder because they may think that it is a "women's disease."

In addition EDs have an important impact on psychosexual development. In anorexia, for example, females stop their periods and amenorrhea is an important indicator of physiological dysfunction. The absence of three consecutive menstrual cycles is a diagnostic criterion.

It is also an important sexual indicator as girls and women with AN are alike pre-pubertal individuals from the sexual point of view.

The absence of three consecutive menstrual cycles cannot be, of course, a diagnostic criterion for men. For men, the corresponding indicator is low testosterone levels, causing decrease in sexual drive and performance.

"A widespread endocrine disorder involving the hypothalamic-pituitary-gonadal axis is manifested in men as a loss of sexual interest and potency." This is one of the diagnostic criteria of AN in men.

Sexual Orientation

The issue of the relationship between sexual orientation and eating disorders can be approached from two different perspectives: analysing eating disorder male samples to assess the prevalence of homosexuality or bisexuality or analysing homosexual and bisexual samples to assess the prevalence of EDs..

Men's sexual orientation may affect the risk for having an eating disorder.

Studies have found that, compared to heterosexual men, gay and bisexual men are more likely to have symptoms indicating disordered eating as well as have a partial or a full DSM-IV diagnosis of eating disorders [3-7].

Among eating disordered men an impressive number of them are in fact gay or bisexual [8-9].

In the male population in the USA about 3% have gay or bisexual tendencies [10] whereas in the male eating disordered population this percentage can reach 40%. Rates among different studies range from 14 to 42% [8,9,11,12].

Some authors explained this high prevalence with the so called "socio-cultural perspective."

Socio-cultural factors are in fact central to the development of eating disturbances as ideal body images portrayed in the media represent an unrealistic goal: difficult or even impossible to achieve. The discrepancy that lies between the ideal body and the real one contributes to the development of body dissatisfaction, of decreased self-esteem and disturbed eating attitudes.

Among women, for instance, the thin ideal, unreachable for the majority of them produces negative mood states and the conviction that only by becoming thinner one can get consideration, self-appraisal and self-worth.

The exposure to the thin-ideal media image, typical of our culture, can have a negative impact on women. If we take a look into the scientific literature about body image we can easily find that women who had been exposed to thin ideal media images by reading magazines, like for example Cosmopolitan, Vogue or Glamour, report increased body dissatisfaction compared to women who were not exposed to thin images [13]. It could be hypothesized, a causal link between exposure to thin images and increased body dissatisfaction in women.

Some authors suggested a similar pathway for gay and bisexual men who are subject to pressures and demands similar to those of heterosexual women [14].

For gay men a heightened focus on physical appearance and on physical attractiveness can be related to the need to attract other men.

According to this hypothesis homosexual men can be more likely to develop EDs because of possible excessive concerns with slim bodies and other attitudes traditionally associated with women.

Starting from the study by Arthur Crisp, who described in 1972 thirteen cases of anorexia nervosa in males [15], most of whom reported sexual difficulties, several studies in the following years described high rates of homosexual conflict in anorexic male patients [16-17].

In a study about symptomatology, psychosexual development and gender identity in 42 anorexic males published in the late 80's, male patients with primary AN presented signs of disturbed psychosexual and gender identity development [18]. Also, this data supports the hypothesis that males with atypical gender role behaviour are more at risk to develop anorexia or bulimia in adolescence.

In 1997, a fundamental study published in the American Journal of Psychiatry was undertaken to better characterize eating disorders in males.

In this study a large sample of male patients were assessed and the authors asserted that "without question, the most striking finding concerns sexual orientation."

In fact, of 122 male patients, 41% were heterosexuals, 27% were homosexual or bisexual, and 32% were asexual. Homosexuality and bisexuality were more common among bulimic men while asexuality was more frequent among AN patients and among patients with an eating disorder not otherwise specified. Asexuality was rare among bulimic male patients. Many subjects of this large sample reported that "their sexuality played an important role in the development of their eating disorder, and five homosexual men explicitly stated that their eating disorder began in response to pressures toward thinness in the gay subculture"[9].

In a study on homosexual men, Yager and colleagues found that 2.1% of them had a lifetime history of an eating disorder compared to the 0.33% of heterosexual men [19].

In another study it was investigated whether homosexuality predisposes males to have EDs. In the late 80's, Yager and colleagues studied a sample of homosexual male college students at the University of California at Los Angeles founding that the homosexual men had higher prevalence of binge eating problems, of feeling fat in spite of others' perception and of feeling terrified of being too fat, and of having used laxatives and diuretics to take weight and shape under control.

Moreover, several studies evidence that gay man scored significantly higher on the different scales evaluating eating psychopathology showing difficulties in the relation with food, weight and shape.

The lifetime prevalence of binge eating episodes in men is reported higher among homosexuals rather than among heterosexual men [22].

Homosexuality: A Specific Factor for EDs or a General One?

One can wonder if homosexuality can be considered a specific risk factor for eating disorders in men.

That is: should we consider homosexuality a specific risk factor for EDs or for the general psychopathology?

The cultural stigmatization of homosexuality might represent a source of psychological distress, and this could be linked to a higher risk of low self-esteem, depressive mood, anxiety and disordered eating. So, homosexuality can be considered a risk factor for general psychopathology.

To examine whether homosexuality is a specific risk factor for eating disorders Russell and Keel [23] studied heterosexual and homosexual men and found that homosexuals had greater body dissatisfaction, more bulimic and anorexic symptoms together with higher levels of depression, lower self esteem and less comfort with their sexual orientation. Sexual orientation was related to these psychopathological variables but even after accounting for depression, self-esteem and discomfort for sexual orientation, sexual orientation continued to account for a significant portion of variance for body dissatisfaction and eating disordered symptoms.

So, according to findings of this study, it seems that homosexuality can act as a specific risk factor for disordered eating.

Now, can homosexuality be considered a specific risk factor for EDs even in women? What happens among lesbians?

It has been suggested that lesbians and bisexual women are less prone to eating disorders [24-26] because they do not share with heterosexual women the standards of feminine beauty based on the idea of thinness. But while some studies indicate lower levels of body dissatisfaction and fewer symptoms of EDs in lesbians than in heterosexual women, some other studies found no differences between the two groups [27-29], claiming that lesbians are not immune to developing eating disordered symptoms [30]. On the contrary, one author studying sexual orientation as a risk factor for bulimic symptoms found higher levels of eating disorder psychopathology among lesbians (31).

So this is still an open question.

The Role of Abuse Victimization

Thinking about risk factors for the development of EDs in men, it has been supposed that abuse, both physical and sexual, can play an important role.

In Chapter 7 we will go deeper in this important and delicate issue.

Researchers put in evidence that gays and bisexual are more likely to have been victims of physical or sexual abuses during childhood [32-37]. Some studies reported rates around 15-43% for physical abuse and rates around 14-37% for sexual abuse in gays and bisexuals. This enormously high percentage of childhood abuse led some authors to examine whether there is an association between eating disorders and a history of childhood abuses in homosexuals and bisexual men.

Feldman and Meyer [38] found that in their sample of white, black and latino gay and bisexual men, 33% had a history of physical abuse and 34% a history of sexual abuse. An association exists between abuses and EDs: these researchers make the hypothesis that eating disordered symptoms may represent an attempt to manage the vulnerability and overwhelming emotional states associated with the abuse in the absence of more adaptive coping strategies as also happens for abused women [39].

Gender Identity Disorders and Eating Disorders

While homosexual men are considered to be at high risk for EDs as homosexuality is recognised to be one of the stronger risk factors, few studies exist about gender identity disorders and eating disorders.

A preamble has to be done: both gender identity disorders and EDs in men are not so widespread and common, so that the coincidence of the coexisting disturbances in the same person is of relevance.

Some authors in fact highlight a parallel between transsexualism and eating disorders, above all AN.

There are common features between the two disorders: the body image disturbance and high body dissatisfaction. In both disorders the theme of body image is crucial.

Transsexualism is a condition in which individuals identify with a physical sex different from the one with which they are born.

A person with apparently normal somatic sexual differentiation is convinced to belong to the opposite sex.

The DSM-IV [40] uses the term "Gender Identity Disorder" (GID) where two components must be present to make the diagnosis: the first is the evidence of a strong and persistent cross-gender identification and the second is a deep and persistent distress.

Transsexualism is defined in the ICD 10 [41] as a "desire to live and to be accepted as a member of the opposite sex, usually accompanied by a sense of discomfort with, or inappropriateness of, one's anatomic sex, and a wish to have surgery and hormonal treatment to make one's body as congruent as possible with one's preferred sex."

Transsexuals experience discomfort as a result of the desire to be a member of the opposite sex, that is "I'm a man but I don't feel like a man, I want to be a woman." The gender identity, that is the own sense or conviction of "maleness" or "femaleness" doesn't coincide with biological sex and genitals.

The term used by the researchers and the clinicians to define the distress resulting from conflicting gender identity and sex of assignment is "gender dysphoria."

In an article published in the International Journal of ED in 2002 [42] Hepp and Milos described three cases of transsexual patients who were suffering from an eating disorder: two male-to-female transsexuals, one 35 years old biological male with anorexia nervosa and the other 22 years old with BN and a history of psychiatric problems, and a female-to-male with AN complicated by psychiatric instability and alcohol dependence.

In all these three cases a very deep body dissatisfaction was present.

All these patients referred to a psychiatric outpatient service for Gender Identity Disorders not for Eating Disorders. The authors of this interesting report made the hypothesis that "for male-to-female transsexuals, underweight is a way to suppress their libido, and at the same time their way to correspond to a female ideal of attractiveness. For female-to-male transsexuals underweight is a possibility to suppress the secondary sexual characteristics and the menstruation."

The same authors and another colleague presented the case of AN in male monozygotic twins [43]. In this case both twins showed an atypical gender behaviour in childhood such as playing with girls' games and toys. Both started cross-dressing, one of them during childhood and the other one during adolescence. In adolescence their sexual orientation was revealed to be homosexual. One of the twins later developed a transsexual gender identity and ask for sex reassignment, the other developed a male identity but with effeminate behaviour and attitudes in appearance and clothing.

Both developed AN, one anorexia nervosa bingeing-purging subtype, the other AN restricting type and they both reached severe body mass indexes.

Also, Winston et al. reported two cases of AN in biological males with gender identity disorder [44].

The first refers to a 46 year old man characterized by educational difficulties, significant emotional deprivation and disturbed early relationships and a strong desire of thinness linked to the wish to achieve a more feminine aspect. He had "a history of a long-standing eating disorder. His symptoms included a desire to be thin, disordered body image, fear of fatness, self-induced vomiting and laxative abuse. The onset of his eating disorder was associated with the development of depressive symptoms, which he attributed to the fact that he could not be a woman. As a child he regularly took the female role in plays and began cross-dressing at the age of 6 or 7 years. During adolescence and early adulthood, he attempted to prove his masculinity by drinking heavily and becoming involved in football-related violence. However he never felt comfortable with a male identity." This man was treated successfully with inpatient treatment followed by an outpatient program. After a psychotherapeutic work-up and a weight stabilization program he has been referred to a gender identity clinic.

The second case, a 41 years old man, was referred to an ED Unit for a long history of eating problems starting when he was 28. He reported a strong desire to achieve a more feminine shape and it seems that this body dissatisfaction could cause a drive for thinness and consequently weight loss. He reported problems with his gender identity. He responded positively to gender reassignment surgery in a gender identity clinic improving both body satisfaction and self esteem.

Recently some other data has been presented about the eating and body image disturbances, and the self-esteem and depression issues in persons with GID [45]. Male to female transsexuals reported higher scores on restrained eating, eating concerns, weight and shape concerns, drive for thinness, bulimic attitudes, body dissatisfaction and body checking than did controls. Restrained eating, weight and shape concerns, body dissatisfaction and body checking reached high levels in female to male transsexual as well. Moreover, persons with GID reported higher levels of depression than controls. Even if in this study all these variables were not higher in GID subjects than in ED subjects, the reported results lead to enhanced knowledge, treatment opportunities and prevention programs for transsexuals.

The present chapter doesn't aim at being exhaustive about the relation between gender role and eating disorders in men.

It just wants to be a suggestion for thinking at this complex and delicate issue which surely needs further interest and research.

To sum up the findings on eating disturbances and male homosexuality, most of the authors (but not all) agree to consider gays and bisexual men at a greater risk to develop ED.

Scientific literature about the relation between gender identity disorders and eating disorders, on the contrary, cannot come to definitive conclusions, as it is substantially based on single case studies.

Therefore it is recommended to examine the gender identity problematic in the assessment of male patients with ED as it is also recommended to assess body dissatisfaction and eating disturbed attitudes in the assessment of transgender patients.

REFERENCES

[1] Garfinkel, PE; Lin, E; Goering, P; Spegg, C; Goldbloom, DS; Kennedy, SH; et al. Bulimia nervosa in a Canadian community sample: prevalence and comparison of subgroups. *Am J Psychiatry*, 1995 152, 1052-1058.

[2] Hoek, HW; van Hoeken, D. Review of the prevalence and incidence of eating disorders. *Int J Eat Disord*, 2003 34, 383-396.

[3] Carlat, DJ; Carmago, CA. Review of bulimia nervosa in males. *Am J Psychiatry*, 1991 148, 831-843.

[4] Woodside, DB; Garfinkel, PE; Lin, E; Goering, P; Kaplan, AS; Goldbloom, DS; Kennedy, SH. Comparisons of men with full or partial eating disorders, men without eating disorders, and women with eating disorders in the community. *Am J Psychiatry*, 2001 158, 570-574.

[5] Feldman, MB; Meyer, IH. Eating disorders in diverse lesbian, gay and bisexual populations. *Int J Eat Disord*, 2007 40, 218-226.

[6] Austin, SB; Ziyadeh, N; Kahn, JA; Camargo, CA; Colditz, GA; Field, AE. Sexual orientation, weight concerns and eating-disordered behaviours in adolescent girls and boys. *J Am Acad Child Adolesc Psychiatry*, 2004 43, 1115-1123.

[7] Strong, SM; Williamson, DA; Netemeyer, RG; Geer, JH. Eating disorders and concerns about body differ as a function of gender and sexual orientation. *J Soc Clin Psychol*, 2000 19, 240-255.

[8] Herzog, DB; Norman, DK; Gordon, C; Pepose, M. Sexual conflict and eating disorders in 27 males. *Am J Psychiatry*, 1984 141, 989-990.

[9] Carlat, DJ; Carmago, CA; Herzog, DB. Eating disorders in males: A report in 135 patients. *Am J Psychiatry*, 1997 152, 1279-1132.

[10] Laumann, EO; Gagnon, JH; Michael, RT; Michaels, S. *The social Organization for sexuality: sexual practices in the United States.* Chicago: University of Chicago Press; 1994

[11] Mangweth, B; Pope, HG; Hudson, JI; Olivardia, R; Kinzl, J; Biebl, W. Eating disorders in Austrian men: an intracultural and crosscultural comparison study. *Psychother Psychosom*, 1997 66, 214-221.

[12] Olivardia, R; Pope, HG; Mangweth, B; Hudson, J. Eating disorders in college males. *Am J Psychiatry*, 1995 152, 1279-1285.

[13] Hawkins, N; Richards, PS; Mac Granley, H; Stein, MD. The impact of exposure to the thin ideal media image on women. *Eat Disord*, 2004 12(1), 35-50.

[14] Morrison, MA; Morrison, TG; Sager, CL. Does body satisfaction differ between gay men and lesbian women and heterosexual men and women. A meta-analitic review. *Body Image,* 2004 1(2), 127-138.

[15] Crisp, AH; Toms, DA. Primary AN on weight phobia in the male: Report on 13 cases. *BMJ,* 1972 1, 334- 338.

[16] Pope, HG; Hudson, JI; Jonas, JM. Bulimia in men: a series of fifteen cases. *J Nerv Ment Dis,* 1984 174, 117-119.

[17] Scott, DW. Anorexia nervosa in the male: a review of clinical, epidemiological and biological findings. *Int J Eat Disord*, 1986 5, 799-819.

[18] Fichter, MM; Daser, C. Symptomatology, psychosexual development and gender identity in 42 anorexic males. *Psychol Med*, 1987 17, 409-418.

[19] Yager, J; Kurtzman, F; Landsuerk, J; Wiesmeier, E. Behaviors and attitudes related to eating disorders in homosexual male college students. *Am J Psychiatry,* 1988 145, 495-497.

[20] Siever, MD. Sexual orientation and gender as factors in socioculturally acquired vulnerability to body dissatisfaction and eating disorders. *J Consult Clin Psychol* 1994 62, 252-260.

[21] Williamson, I; Hartley, P. British research into the increased vulnerability of young gay men to eating disturbance and body dissatisfaction. *Eur Eat Disord Rev,* 1998 6, 160-170.

[22] French, SA; Story, M; Remafedi, G; Resnik, MD. Sexual orientation and prevalence of body dissatisfaction and eating disordered behaviours: a population-based study of adolescents. *Int J Eat Disord*, 1996 19, 119-126.

[23] Russel, CJ; Keel, PK. Homosexuality as a specific risk factor for eating disorders in men. *Int J Eat Disord*, 2002 31, 300-306.

[24] Schneider, JA; O'Leary, A; Jenkins SR. Gender, sexual orientation and disordered eating. *Psychol Health*, 1995 10, 113-128.

[25] Gettelman, TE; Thompson, JK. Actual differences and stereotypical perceptions in body image and eating disturbance: a comparison of male and female heterosexual and homosexual samples. *Sex Roles,* 1993 29, 545-562.

[26] Lakkis, J; Ricciarelli, LA; Williams, RJ. Role of sexual orientation and gender-related traits in disordered eating. *Sex Roles,* 1999 41, 1-16

[27] Beren, SE; Hayden, HA; Wilfey, DE; Cirilo, CM. The influence of sexual orientation on body dissatisfaction in adult men and women. *Int J Eat Disord*, 1996 11, 253-259.

[28] Brand, P; Rothblum, E; Solomon, L. A comparison of lesbians, gay men and heterosexuals on weight and restricting eating. *Int J Eat Disord*, 1992 11, 253-259.

[29] Heffernan, K. Eating disorders and weight concern among lesbians. *Int J Eat Disord*, 1996 19, 127-138.

[30] Share, TL; Mintz, LB. Differences between lesbians and heterosexual women in disordered eating and related attitudes. *J Homesex*, 2002 42, 89-106.

[31] Wichstrom, L. Sexual orientation as a risk factor for bulimic symptoms. *Int J Eat Disord*, 2006 39, 448-453.

[32] Balsam, KF; Rothblum, ED; Beauchaine, TD. Victimization over the lifespan: A comparison of lesbian, gay, bisexual and heterosexual siblings. *J Consult Clin Psychol*, 2005 73, 477-487.

[33] Corliss, HL; Cochran, SD; May, VM. Reports of parental maltreatment during childhood in a United States population-based survey of homosexual, bisexual and heterosexual adults. *Child Abuse Negl*, 2002 26, 1165-1178.
[34] Garcia, J; Adams, J; Friedman, L; East, P. Links between past abuse, suicide ideation and sexual orientation among San Diego college students. *J Am College Health,* 2002 51, 9-14.
[35] Neumark-Sztainer, D; Story, M; Hannan, PJ; Beuhring, T; Resnik, MD. Disordered eating among adolescents: associations with sexual/physical abuse and other familial/psychological factors. *Int J Eat Disord*, 2000 28, 249-258.
[36] Mitchell, K; Mazzeo, S. Mediators of the association between abuse and disordered eating in undergraduate men. *Eat Behav*, 2005 6, 318-327.
[37] Kinzl, J; Mangweth, B; Traweger, C; Biebl, W. Eating-disordered behaviors in males: the impact of adverse childhood experiences. *Int J Eat Disord*, 1997 22, 131-138.
[38] Feldman, MB; Meyer, IH. Childhood abuse and eating disorders in gay and bisexual men. *Int J Eat Disord*, 2007 40, 418-423.
[39] Dansky, BS; Brewerton, TD; Kilpatrick, DG; O'Neil, PM. The National women's study: relationship of victimization and post-traumatic stress disorder to bulimia nervosa. *Int J Eat Disord*, 1997 21, 213-228.
[40] DSM-IV Text Revised, *Diagnostic and Statistical Manual of Mental Disorders*, American Psychiatric Association Washington, DC:, 2000
[41] International Classification of Diseases ICD-10. World Health Organization 1994
[42] Hepp, URS; Milos, G. Gender identity disorder and eating disorders. *Int J Eat Disord*, 2002 32, 473-478.
[43] Hepp, URS; Milos, G; Braun-Scharm, H. Gender identity disorder and anorexia nervosa in male monozygotic twins. *Int J Eat Disord,* 2000 35, 239-243.
[44] Winston, AP; Acharaya, S; Chauduri, S; Fellowes, L. Anorexia nervosa and gender identity disorder in biologic males: a report of two cases. *Int J Eat Disord*, 2004 36, 108-113.
[45] Vocks, S; Stanh, C; Loenser, K; Legenbauer, T. Eating and body image disturbances in male-to-female and female-to-male transexuals. *Arch Sex Behav*, 2009 38, 364-377.

Chapter 6

EATING DISORDERS IN ADOLESCENCE

E. Manzato

ABSTRACT

So far we have focused our attention on Eating Disorders in adulthood, but we think it is appropriate to devote a chapter to the characteristics of eating disorders in adolescence because the peak of onset of these disorders is in adolescence and early youth.

It seems useful to start reporting two of the most well-known diagnostic classifications of eating disorders in adolescence and to give some reference points to Primary Care Physicians (PCP) or non-psychiatric specialists.

We'll devote the first part of the chapter to the description of typical adolescent problems and to stress the importance of the family in order to better understand the area in which one develops an Eating Disorder.

Then we will describe the possible role of some risk factors for the development of eating disorders in adolescence, such as low self-esteem, body dissatisfaction and the presence of stressful life events.

Finally, we focus on the risk of suicide associated with the presence of an Eating Disorder in adolescence.

First of all it is very important and also difficult to understand the very meaning of ED symptoms in adolescence. These disorders could be expressions of a momentary discomfort in the growth that is achieved through an aesthetic need for weight and shape control. On the other hand they could derive from deeper and more "archaic" difficulties to access adult psychological and relational functioning and they could represent a block in the normal process of evolution.

In order to get a clear diagnosis it is necessary to assess the evolution of symptoms over time.

During adolescence the different forms of disturbed eating behaviours may have in most cases a spontaneous remission. In adolescents who do engage, over a period of several months, in potentially unhealthy weight control practices, one should always suspect the possible onset of a partial or a full ED.

These observations are consistent with the fact that EDs are considered the third most prevalent chronic illness after obesity and asthma among adolescents [1].

In males, EDs may be associated both with difficulties in reaching a clear gender identity and with a suicidal risk determined by the frequent presence of depression.

From the diagnostic point of view, the majority of adolescents suffers from a partial syndrome (ED-NOS), still largely unrecognized in many health care settings (see chapter on epidemiology) [2].

The development of partial forms in adolescence follows different paths: most adolescents with a partial ED recover spontaneously, but some others develop a full ED.

The characteristics of this last part, developing a full syndrome, are not yet entirely clear: probably the adolescents who have more severe symptoms or more risk factors are consequently more likely to have a worse evolution.

The ED-NOS share common risk factors with full ED syndrome: one can think of a continuum in which the diet alone is not sufficient for developing an ED-NOS or a full ED but it requires the presence of other cofactors related to the psychopathology, relations and environment of the subject.

Among the risk factors we must also remember the genetic risk. Most studies have reported greater frequency of full or partial ED among relatives of patients [3].

Given the special characteristics of EDs in adolescence, amendments to the DSM classification used for adults were proposed. These changes are also influenced by the new guidelines on the diagnosis of EDs: in fact EDs might be interpreted either as discrete categories that are qualitatively different from dieting, or as a continuum ranging from normal eating to full ED syndrome.

In order to give an orientation to PCP about diagnostic symptoms in children and adolescents, we report here two classifications.

The first one is the classification of EDs inside the "Diagnostic and Statistical Manual for Primary Care, Child and Adolescent Version" [4].

DSM-PC Criteria for EDs

Dieting and body image behaviors:

- Dieting behavior or voluntary food limitation
- An obsessive pursuit of thinness
- Systematic fear of gaining weight that extends beyond normal dieting or body image
- Does not meet criteria for AN

Purging-binge-eating behaviors:

- Display binging and compensatory behaviours
- Does not meet criteria for BN

The second one is the English classification named " Great Ormond Street Criteria" that reports six eating disorder categories [5].

Great Ormond Streeet Criteria (GOS) for Typical and Atypical EDs

1) Anorexia Nervosa

- Determined weight loss
- Abnormal cognitions regarding weight and/or shape
- Morbid preoccupation with weight and/or shape

2) Bulimia Nervosa

- Recurrent binges and purges
- Sense of lack of control
- Morbid preoccupation with weight and shape

3) Food Avoidance Emotional Disorder

- Food Avoidance not accounted by primary affective disorders
- Weight loss
- Mood disturbances not meeting criteria for primary affective disorders
- No abnormal cognitions regarding weight and shape
- No morbid preoccupation regarding weight and shape
- No organic brain disease or psychosis

4) Pervasive refusal syndrome

- Profound refusal to eat, drink, walk, talk, or self-care
- Determined resistance to efforts to help

5) Selective eating

- Limited selection of food for at least two years
- Refusal to eat new kind of food
- No abnormal cognition regarding weight and/or shape
- No fear of swallowing and vomiting
- Low, normal or even overweight

6) Functional dysphagia

- Marked food avoidance
- Fear of swallowing and vomiting
- No abnormal cognitions regarding weight and/or shape

- No morbid preoccupation regarding weight and shape
- No organic disease or psychosis

Regarding bulimia nervosa we report now the proposal for a distinction in subtypes which are different from those currently in use in the DSM (purging or not purging) and based mainly on the presence of negative affect.

The distinction proposed by some studies on adults in "dietary" subtype and "dietary depressive" BN subtype [6] can also be applied in adolescents and can give more information for adequate treatment.

Dietary restraint models are based on evidence that binge eating is a response to dieting; it is accompanied by great concern for the physical form and there are no great negative affects.

The dietary depressive subtype, on the other hand, reported significantly more severe affective disorders, anxiety, poor impulse control and personality disorders.

The prognosis in this second subtype is worse.

This model was also studied in samples of adolescents [7] and demonstrated its validity, especially for therapeutic indications.

In regards to the depressive subtype, there is the need for a more intensive treatment to target depressed mood in addition to the eating disorder.

To better understand the characteristics of EDs it is important to mention the physical and psychological changes that adolescence induces and the subsequent problems related to a changing body [8,9,10,11].

Both males and females during adolescence undergo radical body transformations that lead them to seek new adaptations, which involve a real revolution in self-perception and self-knowledge.

The path of adolescence leads the individual from a child state to a recognition of an adult state: it is a hard work that requires one to move from a well-known situation to a new and unknown state.

It is a phase of discomfort as the psychological transformations and the inner representation of the body evolve more slowly than the somatic changes. It is as if the adolescent needed to take confidence with his own new body.

In order to restore harmony the adolescent makes different attempts to adapt his physical appearance to the external models (proposed by peers or the media). Males generally tend to lean towards the acquisition of an athletic and muscular body while females generally are prone to beauty treatments to achieve a more slim appearance.

The transition from puberty to adulthood is a natural step which is common to all humans but it occurs in different ways in different cultures and historical periods.

For example, in the western world puberty is a phenomenon that occurs at an increasingly early age and, on the other hand, the moment of separation from his own family is increasingly dilated owing to economic and social reasons.

In relation to their children, parents play a protective function: up to puberty they act as a protective screen. With the arrival of adolescence the physical and mental changes require them to take a different distance. A separation is needed to help their children to move away from them.

What happens in adolescence is what is defined by the psychoanalytic school as a "second process of separation-individualization" in which trauma and conflicts of the early childhood years are reactivated. The first separation-individualization stage happened in the first years of life.

Adolescence is therefore a stage that brings the boy to the identification of himself as a person, to test a separation and a different distance from their parents; for example the physical intimacy between the teenager and his parents changes. Affectionate physical contact exchanges typical of childhood are now lost.

The boy, in the attempt to assert his personality, may even have a total refusal of the family.

On the contrary, if the adolescent finds in his parents a good level of understanding and acceptance for his evolutionary changes, he may accept his changes without difficulty.

Even external environment's substitute parental figures may be helpful if they perform support and mediation activities. These important aids help the adolescent to maintain a cohesion and to reinforce his sense of identity and continuity despite physical and psychological changes.

When the physiological stage of separation-identification is not adequately supported, the adolescence loses the consolidation of the sense of identity and autonomy, with a feeling of relational emptiness that risks being filled by psychopathological symptoms. The answer that the family provides to the adolescent change is of essential importance: reassurance, calmness, and the ability to receive not derision or depreciation, are essential for maintaining the adolescent transition in the normal range.

If the adolescent experienced a mother who is sufficiently capable of care and adaptation to his (e.g. when she was pregnant) and others' physical changes (e.g. in the different stages of the child growth) they will be later able to take care of his own body.

If, on the contrary, the first care experiences were problematic, the adolescent will be deprived of resources and his difficulties in relation to the body will probably result in difficulties with food.

AN can be a way to express difficulties in relation to the world and the emotions by using the concrete language of food refusal.

As in childhood hunger and food, allowed to carry pleasant and unpleasant sensations in the relationship with the mother, so in adolescence AN uses this language to communicate the difficulties of getting in touch with the external world which can be perceived as dangerous and threatening.

The internal world too is perceived as threatening: by denying themselves food and causing hunger, the anorexic patient denies the emotional world that frightens him. So he can have the feeling of being able to manage it.

The refusal to eat is also a refusal to grow, to assume an adult and sexually determined identity.

For a male, to reach a male adult identity may mean to go away from the primitive relationship with his mother and to identify with the father figure.

It is a difficult process in which the mother must be willing to allow this step (the strength of a couple-type relationship and esteem for the partner plays a fundamental role) and the father must support the path of removal of his child from the mother, and to be able to bear his fantasies of rivalry.

Adolescence is a moment of transformation in the son but also in the mother, involving the fact of reorganization of her role and the need to elaborate a sort of mourning determined by the greater autonomy of her child.

There is a passage from the maternal care concerns to new anxieties related to the son autonomy and social entry. On one hand the mother can have the fear that the culture and the style followed by her son can lead him to dangerous and risky social conduct. On the other hand there can be also an anxiety that the son will not be accepted in his new social role by his peers.

Anyway the proper role of the mother is a “natural withdrawal:” to let her child be free to grow up.

The narcissistic withdrawal of the mother pushes her to invest again and in a different way in the relation with her partner (which sometimes can not be fully satisfactory).

The maternal ambivalence towards her son can lead her to exert control in respect to the controversial and aggressive son’s attitudes, which can be also addressed towards or against his body.

In adolescence, the body of the son no longer belongs to his mother but it is dressed and decorated according to the rules dictated by the culture shared with peers.

The adolescent body is a body which develop towards adult sexual functioning and this development leads him to look for new experiences outside the family.

The aid that a mother can give in this period to his son is to accept these physical and relational changes with joy and affection and to show him that nothing will be as before, but it will be better than before, and that the transformation will lead to new significant and worthwhile experiences.

In adolescence, the father too has the role of care giver, that of a supporting and empathic guide.

In the last few decades adult men who became fathers have suffered a crisis of their role driven by the need to find new models, other than those of their fathers, and to be more responsive to the needs of their sons.

Some fathers may adhere to a new model characterized by careful attention to the needs of their sons and by a greater presence in their sons’ life, namely, sharing maternal duties. Some other fathers may have attitudes which aren’t helpful to their children’s development.

The different attitudes can be summed up in three forms: the deserter father, the weak father and the jealous father [12].

The deserter father thinks of his son's adolescence as a time which should not care, the son "is great" and must look after himself. It is as if the son belonged only to the mother and the father lived in another dimension.

The weak father has a contradictory presence in relation to the adolescent son: even if he is seemingly concerned and interested, in reality he is a false father, who constantly seeks the approval of the children and instead of assuming a regulatory role, he puts himself in competition with the son.

The jealous father is a man unable to assume this role because he perceives it as a loss of his freedom and youth. He loses the opportunity to be helpful for his children’ process of growth and he isn’t able to estimate them.

In all the situations described above an essential aspect in helping the adolescent to grow is missing: that is, the respect for the child and for what he is experiencing and also for what he is lacking.

Feeling esteemed and loved is crucial for the adolescent who must rebuild his self-esteem in his process of separation. This self-esteem reconstruction helps him to live out all the difficult stages of the adolescent processing in a serene way.

The problem of self-esteem has been largely studied in the works about EDs in adolescence.

The term self-esteem refers to the value that an individual gives of himself, essential to feeling loved and accepted; it represents an important sign of psychological well-being.

The acquisition of self-esteem in the psychodynamic theories is related to the processes of evolution of the Self and of the first object relations: which means that the way in which the child had received affection and positive regards in the first years of his life will later influence his behaviour and his self-esteem as an adult.

Therefore, for the development of a good level of self-esteem in children, parents' attitudes are crucial.

Self-esteem is constantly tested by life experiences and by the changes that these experiences require.

Especially in adolescence, self-esteem can go down and this crisis can be related to physical changes or to the developmental tasks, to the difficult search for autonomy and to the development of sexual impulses.

Self-esteem is considered low when a person tends to judge himself inadequate or insufficient to meet the requirements of life.

In patients with EDs the levels of self-esteem are strongly influenced by weight and shape concerns.

A low self-esteem may be a risk factor in the development of EDs. It may be the result of the depression that often accompanies weight loss in AN, but it can also be a factor in the maintenance of eating disorders because it may be compensate by the ability to control hunger and weight.

Adolescence is a period of identity formation and when one's sense of identity is disturbed, the adolescent may prove great instability of feeling of the self, which can lead to low self-esteem [13].

The subjects with EDs are focusing on the physical body as a way of coping with the internal difficulties with the self.

Self-concept components that are characteristic of low self-esteem are insecurity or feelings of inadequacy with negative mood or depression, poor body image, poor adaptation skills and unrealistically high aspirations [14].

In adolescence in fact the personal appearance plays an important role in self-esteem [15] and a chronic low self-esteem is a vulnerability factor for the development of EDs [16].

A wide study on 200 adolescent males and females demonstrated that low self-esteem was significantly associated with depressive symptoms and problematic eating behaviours. The low self-esteem was a possible precursor to the onset of problematic eating behavior that could lead to EDs and the mediator was the presence of depression [17].

Depression in fact is one of most common mental health disorders seen in adolescence: studies have found the lifetime prevalence rate of major depression for adolescents varies from 10% to 28% with a higher prevalence among girls, while in childhood depression is more present in males [18].

Few studies, however, make comparisons between genders; one of these, done on a sample of high school students, points out that regarding the correlation between depression and ED, the genders share many more similarities than differences.

In fact there is a significant positive correlation between depression and EDs in both male and female samples. Regarding risk factors, poor body image satisfaction and little social support were correlated with disordered eating symptomatology in males, while, always in males, low self-esteem was more linked to depression [19].

We have seen as one of the components of low self-esteem is a poor body image in adolescence.

Body image is a complex mental construction that is related to psychological and relational aspects of the individual and it changes during the different phases of development and it is also affected by social patterns (Part 1 Chapter 3).

It is easy to see that a male adolescent may have a poor image of his body. In fact over the last twenty years, the standards of beauty have more and more emphasized the strong and muscular male body.

During adolescence the acquisition and internalization of the prevailing body shape models is of great importance and there is a close association between self-esteem and overvalued perceptions of body shape. The size of specific parts of the body may also be overestimated and this may support the development of an ED.

There is a difference however between adolescent girls and boys in terms of their receptivity to socio-cultural influences that favour thinness. Some studies found that in anorexic boys the influence of conversations, magazine articles and advertisements may be greater than in anorexic girls [20].

Adolescent male with AN, however, are generally less concerned about being fat than females and have contradictory concerns: they present desire for thinness on the one hand and the desire for building muscle mass on the other.

As males want to become more muscled, they increase physical activity, rather than using dietary restrictions [21].

This aspect is very important for secondary prevention: in males more than in females hyperactivity and exasperated exercise aimed at developing the muscles should always give rise to the suspicion of the debut of EDs.

In fact, the attitude of hyper-attention and care of body-builders could be a functional equivalent of the investment that characterizes the attitude of the anorexic female towards thinness.

At puberty, there is less redistribution of body fat in males compared to females and this is a possible explanation of the less intense fear of fat in males.

Among girls, the experience of menarche increases the worry about weight gain and this affects, consequently, the dietary restriction behaviour. Among males the body transformations seem to be elaborated more quickly, and perhaps in a less traumatic way [22].

The period of adolescence is itself a risk period for the development of EDs because it is a period of important changes. The vulnerability of adolescence towards EDs can be also determined by the presence of life events that may have a precipitating role.

By life events we mean any event or circumstance occurring in the life of an individual that may have the potential of altering an individual's present state of mental or physical health.

So it means not only negative events but also events with positive aspects.

For example, in an investigation of life events in the year prior to the onset of AN in adolescents it was found that adverse events such as separation, illness or death of parents, but also of positive events as achieving a scholarship place at an independent school were present.

In this study the adverse events were not associated with development of depression in adolescents suffering from AN [23] and therefore AN could be interpreted as a sort of equivalent of depression or maladaptive solution to parental adversity or conflict [24].

Sometimes it is the perception of events that is altered in adolescents with a predisposition to EDs: they perceive events as more stressful and have a low self-esteem, and they feel a sense of ineffectiveness or distorted impression of their social competence.

In general, however, it is not evident that there is a linear relation between life events and AN onset, the link may be mediated by the way of adolescents' reaction to the event itself.

We have to keep in mind that according to the cumulative stressors model for the development of disordered eating it is not the single event that should be considered as a risk factor, but it is the cumulative effect of multiple experiences that is more likely to lead to symptoms expression [25].

According to some studies, adolescents, and in particular boys, who use a coping style characterized by avoiding the problem and non-adaptively coping with the emotions are more at risk of developing an ED.

These adolescent males tend to feel overwhelmed by problems and blame themselves excessively [26].

When dealing with the theme of adolescence it is worth it to mention a very delicate issue, that is the risk of suicide in adolescent patients with EDs.

Even if the area of suicidality (intended as the set of suicidal thoughts, self-harming behaviours, suicide attempts and suicide) is very complex to be studied, especially in adolescence, the scientific data show a trending upward of suicide in adolescence.

A survey of U.S. teenagers between 13 and 15 years showed that 30% had thought about suicide at least once and 15% has seriously thought about it while 6% made a suicide attempt.

The presence of EDs during adolescence is a risk factor for suicide or attempted suicide and the suicidal risk is associated with EDs as a whole and as partial syndromes [27].

As above mentioned, the suicidal spectrum among people with EDs ranges from suicide to suicide attempts, until risk behaviours present for the life of the patient.

In fact, owing to the dissatisfaction with their bodies, many adolescents not only try to lose weight, but also engage in high risk behaviours such as drug and alcohol exposure, unprotected sex, risky driving etc. [28].

AN, especially in the binging purging subtype, has been identified as an illness associated with suicidality: rates of suicide in AN is more than 200 times greater than the suicide rate in the general population [29] and this data is also valid for adolescent patients with EDs.

A study that analyzed a large sample of patients with AN found that the presence of binge/purging behaviors is the most important factor that distinguishes the AN group with lifetime suicidal behavior from the group without AN suicidal behaviour [30].

The risk has been increased by higher body dissatisfaction, with low self-esteem levels and with a higher morbidity of mood disorders. Moreover, in the same study, it was noted how the development of binge/purging behaviour accelerated the suicidal behaviour.

What can lead to suicidal behaviour is mainly body dissatisfaction, in fact in adolescents with EDs a linear relationship between body dissatisfaction and the risk of suicide has often been reported.

So, these are feature which need to be carefully investigated in adolescents.

In BN the presence of suicide is lower: in a review that analyzed 80 studies with follow-up the rate of suicide in BN was 0.1% [31].

An Italian study on a sample of women showed that BN patients more at risk for suicide are those who, during adolescence have attempted suicide or had more frequent suicide ideas [32].

The picture is completely different if we look at the suicide attempts in ED samples.

The same study has investigated the lifetime prevalence of suicide attempts in eating disordered outpatients and found a significantly higher 18% in BN compared to AN, while other studies have found discordant data.

The variability of the literature data may be linked to the fact that in the analysed samples no distinction is made between the different subtypes of AN, restricting or binge/ purging: in the latter group in fact impulses' control is much weaker.

Also, in BN the purging behaviours are factors related to the presence of suicide attempts which are much more frequent in patients using purging methods such as vomiting or laxatives abuse compared to patients without purging methods [33].

This brief overview about the data on ED adolescents' suicidality highlights that particular attention must be paid during the interview to all the matters concerning suicidality and to all risk factors that can lead to suicide or attempted suicide.

References

[1] Fisher, M; Golden, NH; Katzman, DK. Eating disorders in adolescence: a background paper. *J. Adolescent. Health*, 1995 16, 6, 420-437.

[2] Chamay-Webe, C; Narring, F; Michaud, PA. Partial eating disorders among adolescents: a review. *J Adolescent Health*, 2005 37, 417- 427.

[3] Strober, M; Freeman, R; Lampert, C; Diamond, J; Kaye, W. Controlled family study of anorexia nervosa and bulimia nervosa: evidence of shared liability and transmission of partial syndromes. *Am. J. Psychiatry*, 2000 157, 3, 393-401.

[4] Wolraich, M; Felice, M; Drotar, D. The Classification of Child and Adolescent Mental Diagnoses in Primary Care (DSM-PC), child and adolescent version. Elk Grove Village IL, *American Academy of Pediatrics*, 1996.

[5] Bryant-Waugh, R; Lask, B. Eating disorders in children. *J. Child Psychol. Psychiatry*, 1995 36, 199-202.

[6] Stice, E; Agras, W; Telch, C; Halmi, K; Mitchell, JE; Wilson, T. Subtyping binge eating-disordered women along dieting and negative affect dimensions. *Int. J. Eat Disord*, 2001 30 (1), 11-27.

[7] Chen, EY; Le Grange, D. Subtyping adolescents with bulimia nervosa. *Behaviour Research and therapy*, 2007 45, 2813-2820.

[8] Montecchi, F. *Anoressia mentale dell'adolescenza*. Ed. Franco Angeli, Milano, 1998.

[9] Jeammet, P. *Psicopatologia dell'adolescenza*. Ed. Borla, Milano, 1999.

[10] Zappa, E. *Narciso a tavola*. Ed. Franco Angeli, Milano 2007.

[11] Cuzzolaro, M. *Anoressie e bulimie*. Ed. Il Mulino, Bologna, 2004.

[12] Pietropolli Charme, G . *I nuovi adolescenti*. Ed. Raffaello Cortina, Milano 2000.

[13] Fairburn, CG; Wilson, TG. *Binge eating: nature, assesment and treatment*. The Guiford Press, New York, 1993.

[14] Steinhausen, H; Voltrath, M; The self-image of adolescent patients with eating disorders. *Int. J. Eat Disorders*, 1993 13, 221-227.

[15] Tomori, M; Rus-Makovec, M. Eating behaviour, depression and self-esteem high school students. *Journal of Adolescent Health*, 2000 26, 361-367.

[16] Silverstone, PH. Is chronic low self-esteem the cause of eating disorders? *Medical Hypotheses,* 1992 39, 311-315.

[17] Courtney, EA; Gamboz, J; Johnson, JG. Problematic eating behaviours in adolescents with low self-esteem and elevated depressive symptoms. *Eating Behaviours*, 2008 9, 408-414.

[18] Gotlib, I; Hammen, C. *Handbook of depression*. Guilford press, New York, 2002.

[19] Santos, M; Richards, CS; Bleckley, MK. Comorbidity between depression and disordered eating in adolescents. *Eating Behaviors,* 2007 8, 440-449.

[20] Toro, J; Castro, J; Gila, A; Pombo, C. Assessment of sociocultural influences on the body shape model in adolescent males with anorexia nervosa. *Eur. Eat Disorders Rev.*, 2005 13, 351-359.

[21] Davis, C; Katzman, A. Chinese men and women in the United States and Hong Kong : body and self-esteem rating as a prelude to dieting and exercise. *Int. J. Eat Disord*, 1998 23, 99-102.

[22] Cotrufo, P; Cella, S; Cremato, F; Labella, G. Eating disorder attitude and abnormal eating behaviours in a sample of 11-13-yer-old school children: the role of pubertal body transformation. *Eating Weight Disord*, 2007 12, 154-160.

[23] Gowers, SG; North, CD; Byram, V. Life event precipitant of adolescent anorexia nervosa. *J .Child Psychol. Psychiat*, 1996 37, 4, 469- 477.

[24] Crisp, A H. *Anorexia nervosa: let me be*. Academic Press, London 1980.

[25] Levine, MP; Smolak, L. Toward a model of the developmental psychopathology of eating disorders: The example of early adolescence. In Crowther, J; Tennenbaum, D; Hobfoll, S; Stephens, M. *The etiology of bulimia nervosa. The individual and familial context*. Hemisphere. Washington 1992.

[26] Garcìa-Grau, E; Fusté, A; Mirò, A; Saldana, C; Bados, A. Coping Style and vulnerability to eating disorders in adolescent boys. *Eur Eat Disorders Rev*, 2004 12, 61-67.

[27] Lewisohn, PM; Striegel-Moore, RH; Seeley, JR. Epidemiology and natural course of eating disorders in young women from adolescence to young adulthood. *Journal of the American Academy of Child and Adolescent Psychiatry*, 2000 39, 1248- 1292.

[28] Pompili, M; Girardi, P; Tatarelli, G; Ruberto, A; Tatarelli, R. Suicide and attempted suicide in eating disorders, obesity and weight -image concern. *Eat Behavior,* 2006 7, 384-394.

[29] Sullivan, PF. Mortality in Anorexia nervosa. *Am. J. of Psychiatry* , 2005 152, 1073-1074.

[30] Foulon, C; Guelfi, JD; Kipman, A; Ades, J; Romo, L; Houdeyer, K; Marquez, S; Mouren, MC; Rouilon, F; Gorwood, P. Switching to the bingeing/purging subtype of anorexia nervosa is frequently associated with suicidal attempts. *European Psychiatry*, 2007 22, 513-519.

[31] Keel, PK; Mitchell, JE. Outcome in bulimia nervosa. *Am. J. Psychiatry*, 1997 154, 313-321.

[32] Favaro, A; Santonastaso, P. Suicidality in eating disorders: clinical and psychological correlates. *Acta psychiatrica Scandinavica*, 1997 95, 508- 514.

[33] Milos, G; Spindler, A; Hepp, U; Schnyder, U. Suicide attempts and suicidal ideation. Link with psychiatric comorbidity in eating disorder subjects. *General. Hospital Psychiatry*, 2004 26, 129-135.

Chapter 7

THE INFLUENCE OF FAMILY ON MEN WITH EATING DISORDERS

E. Manzato

ABSTRACT

This chapter will analyse the influence of the family environment on ED development. The family is in fact deeply involved, especially in the case of adolescent patients.

A brief overview of the different models of family functioning will be analysed. Then we will focus on the presence of psychiatric disorders in patients' relatives and on the presence of EDs in the mother which is considered one of the risk factors.

We will report back the results of major studies on children's traumatic experiences with a specific focus on the controversial aspects that sexual or physical abuses may have as predisposing factors for the development of an Eating Disorder.

The influence of family functioning on the development and maintenance of ED has always been emphasized.

A better understanding of the family history has many purposes:

- it helps to formulate etiopathogenetic hypothesis about EDs and allows the physician to identify at what stage of the patient's history difficulties arose that might have led to the development of the ED.
- it can give indication on ED prognosis: some studies correlate the severity and the course of EDs with the family functioning
- it allows a therapeutic intervention aimed at eliminating pathological dynamics within the family maintaining or exacerbating EDs.

Moreover, some authors explain the genesis and the perpetuation of EDs exclusively within the family relationships (systemic approach).

There are different interpersonal areas involved in every single family function. The rituals related to the pattern of consumption meals within the family are often an expression of relational familial dynamics and of the difficulties of growth in adolescent patients. The importance given by the family to aesthetic models proposed by the society is relevant as well: for example, parents who are strictly adherent to the models of leanness, shifting in rigid food and weight control practices, can affect in a decisive manner the aesthetic and food model of the son.

Therefore it is important to study not only the different types of relationship in the pathological families but also the features of the family functioning in general, with a particular attention to the mother-son relationship.

It is necessary to emphasize, however, that caring for a person with an ED is associated with psychological distress and poor quality of life for all the family.

Families may, in fact, have a malfunction due to the presence of an ED and the relationships become more problematic because of concerns related to physical and mental health of ED patients.

It is therefore important to thoroughly investigate the current family functioning and to trace the history of familial relations as well to understand their nature before the development of EDs.

The prevalent body of the literature about EDs refers to pooled samples, males and females or predominantly females, and does not point out the gender related differences. We will consider the more interesting data among these studies focusing on those concerning male patients with EDs.

Studies on families of patients with EDs tried to outline standards of family functioning and often turned their attention to patterns and functioning through several generations.

Hilde Bruch [1], one of the first authors who studied EDs, focused on the mother-child relation as one of the main causes of AN development.

Even Minuchin [2] in his book "Psychosomatic families" stressed certain pathological runs in families of patients with EDs, characterized by over-protectiveness and rigidity.

He defined the relations between family members as "over-involved," intrusive and hostile with a denial of the child's emotional needs. The same interpretation, that recognized in a single model of an altered family relation the cause of AN, was supported by the Italian Selvini Palazzoli [3].

The family relationships were also studied according to the diagnostic type of ED.

In anorectic patients various models of family configurations were proposed. They can be summarized into two types: families with "centripetal process" with excessive cohesion among family members, reduced emotional expressivity and poor contacts and exchanges, and a family dominated by the "centrifugal process," where there is lack of cohesion between family members and high presence of conflict [4].

Instead, in families of bulimic patients a degree of uniformity of familial functioning has been emphasized, characterized by chaotic communications, frequent conflicts among members, lack of harmony and "emotionally hot relationships."

Common characteristics in families of patients with ED are the excessive expectations on their children's performance and their adaptation to the successful social models, along with a relative social isolation of the family itself.

In a review on the role of family functioning and of sexual and physical abuse in ED, Treasure et al. [5] concluded that there is evidence of more family pathology in ED than in normal control families.

Patients with binge/purging AN seem to have a poorer family functioning, and a higher frequency of sexual and physical abuse than restrictors, while in patients with BN high levels of family disturbance seem to be associated with greater severity and chronicity of bulimic symptoms.

Psychiatric Problems in the Families

Among familial factors that influence EDs, an important factor is the presence of psychiatric disorders in patient's first or second degree relatives.

A recent review made on samples of female and male patients' families [6] showed that, despite the heterogeneity of methodologies and results, mood disorders (such as Major Depressive Episode) and anxiety disorders (such as Obsessive-compulsive disorder) among relatives of individuals with AN were over represented.

In general, mood disorders appear more frequently among female first degree relatives of individuals with restrictive type AN (10.4%) than in the control group (4%).

In particular, Major Depressive episodes were more frequent among relatives of patients with AN (with variations between 12% and 15%) compared with the relatives of healthy controls [7,8].

Still, in the area of AN there is a higher presence of mood disorders among relatives of ANbp forms (14% among first degree relatives) than in ANr forms (about 3%).

Among anxiety disorders the obsessive compulsive disorder is the most frequently found in families of ED patients and its prevalence is found around 10% in mothers of ED patients compared to 1.8% in control groups.

The presence of a mental disorder in the mother can represent a risk factor for the future development of an ED in the child. In fact a study on a large sample of adolescents taking into account patient gender differences [9] showed that risk factors like the loss of a loved one, high grade of parents demands, school results and family dysfunction were not different between genders. Differences were instead reported in regards to the presence of mental disorders in the mother, that was reported to be 17.5% in the boys' mothers *versus* 6.7% in the girls' mothers.

The presence of a psychiatric disorder in the family influences the severity of ED clinical picture, the compliance to treatment and therefore the prognosis.

The parental pathology can be related to stressful events for the child (as the separation from the mother or from a relative as in case of hospitalization), and in any case it can upset the quality of interaction during childhood.

Depending on the time in which the psychiatric disorders occur in ED patient relatives, one can have different effects: i.e. if a mother's depression occurs during patient childhood he can experiment an unsatisfactory mother-child relationship.

If the parental psychiatric problem occurs during patient's adolescence, the age most at risk for the ED onset, the parents may tend to deny the ED or may not perceive it, thus delaying treatment. Parental reactions and the consequent time lag in seeking help can influence the ED outcome [10].

Finally, the persistence of a psychiatric disorder in the family of a patient with an ED can prevent the teenager from any attempt towards independence, so keeping all family components in a situation of pathological stability.

If we look more specifically at the influence of a psychiatric disorder in the mother on child feeding, we can notice that several aspects of maternal mental health have been repeatedly associated with child feeding difficulties even if not leading to the development of an ED.

An interesting study by Blissett et al. [11] examined the contribution of maternal symptoms of anxiety and depression on difficult feeding interactions between mothers and children of different genders in a non-clinical sample. In boys, symptoms of maternal anxiety were significant predictors of mealtime negativity, and symptoms of maternal depression predicted food refusal behaviours. The study emphasized the need to investigate, without ignoring child gender, the maternal symptoms of anxiety or depression as factors that can affect the way a child obtains nutrition.

The anxiety linked to the parents' need to help their child to reach specific "gender-linked goals" may be associated with different feeding difficulties [12]. Depending on gender, parents themselves can be prone to accept and pursue slimness models for their girls and greater height and weight standards for their boys. This anxiety can strongly interfere with feeding patterns in the families and specifically on the development of a distorted body image in the children.

So, in general, the psychiatric disorders and distorted attitudes in parents may deleteriously influence the mealtime and may be predictors of feeding problems in children.

Disturbed Eating Attitudes in Mothers

Current or lifetime EDs in the mother may have an important role in the relationship with the children and conflict-related food and can contribute to the future development of an ED in children.

In the mother-child relationship, in fact, nutrition is one of the critical early tasks and it is one of the most important ways in which parents communicate with their infants.

Studies on the effects of mothers' eating disturbances on their children eating began in the '80s with descriptions of single clinical cases, sometimes dramatic.

Recent studies on pregnancy of eating disordered mothers highlight how the nutritional status of the woman represents the very first environment for the child.

Some authors reported that the offspring of ED mothers tends to be smaller in both weight and length than the offspring of control mothers, probably due to continuation of their ED throughout pregnancy [13].

In the late '90s Russell et al. studied nine children of ED mothers, of which 8 were males: the observations were made on mothers with AN whose children showed evidence of low weight for age and low height for age, that are the most sensitive indices of food deprivation [14].

The findings indicate that even for boys, there is a potential danger that anorectic mothers underfeed their children, leading to shortness of stature and physical frailty.

The reaction of children to food deprivation was studied as well: children tended to avoid asking their mothers for extra food and to refuse any temptation to eat food that their mothers could perceive as fearful, such as in the case of sweets.

Mothers with EDs, as well as all patients who suffer from these disorders, may find difficulties in distinguishing somatic sensations from emotional feelings; this can interfere with their ability to perceive the physical and emotional state of their son.

Another effect on nutrition of children whose mothers are affected by an ED is linked to the disturbed attitude towards body shape and weight that can indirectly affect the child's nutritional intake. In some cases this can lead to extreme behaviours such as limiting child's food intake or excessive controlling body weight [15].

In fact, because of their preoccupation with weight, shape and dieting, they may have difficulties in feeding their infants: the mothers with anorexia might underfeed their children while the mother with bulimia might ignore their children when they are engaged in overeating and vomiting or may even restrict the amount of food in the house in an attempt to limit their own food intake.

Some studies suggest that mothers with an ED and their offspring interact differently than mothers without any ED in the areas of feeding [16].

The mothers with an ED seem to be more intrusive during both eating and playing and seem to express more critical comments and fewer positive comments during eating than the mothers without any ED do [17].

More conflicts during mealtimes are reported between the mothers with ED and their children. Furthermore, mothers with an ED are prone to use food for non-nutritive purposes, for example to reward or to calm their child.

Mothers with an ED (more than mothers without any ED) may perceive their children to have greater negative affectivity: they may feel their children to be more hostile towards themselves and this can make their relationship more complicate.

Differences exist between male and female in their interactions with their eating disordered mothers: mothers may be mainly concerned about their daughters' physical form, from the other side daughters show greater avidity for feeding. In the case of sons this dynamic is less strong.

In conclusion, although there is no general agreement about the importance of EDs in mothers in the development of EDs in children due to the complexity of child feeding problems, there is the feeling that EDs in the mother can influence the food behaviour of the children, through the mediation of other risk factors that may contribute to the development of an ED.

For clinicians it is therefore important to search in the history of an eating disordered patient for the presence of a psychiatric disorder in first or second degree relatives, with a particular attention to the presence of an ED.

TRAUMATIC EXPERIENCES DURING CHILDHOOD

We will consider now another important issue: the role of experienced trauma in childhood as a risk factor for the development of EDs even if its causal role has not yet been completely clarified.

The experiences of physical and sexual abuse have been the most studied among traumatic events in childhood without any definitive conclusion [18].

It is difficult to determine whether the experience of abuse is a "specific" risk factor for an ED, because abuse is a risk factor for many forms of mental disease. It is even difficult to define it as a risk factor that predates the onset of the disorder and increases the likelihood of ED occurrence (no adequate longitudinal studies are reported).

Referring to the multidimensional theory by Garner on the etiology of EDs we might consider traumatic events as predisposing factors that may create a vulnerability basis for the development of an ED [19].

Traumatic experiences in children often occur in families where there is a high presence of psychiatric illnesses or a familial functioning characterized by high levels of aggressiveness. These factors may contribute to the failure of a secure attachment to caregivers and in this way they can be involved in the development of an ED.

Early studies on these aspects have been made on samples of eating disordered women around the '80s and the results showed a higher frequency of traumatic experiences in patients with BN.

The first large-scale research in patients with EDs [20] reported the presence of episodes of sexual abuse in 70% of the sample without any correlation with the type of ED.

The same authors extended their sample in a subsequent study [21] but they did not find any significant association between traumatic events and the ED diagnosis. This lack of relation was also shown in other studies comparing ED patients reporting a history of physical or sexual abuse with control groups.

The results of later studies showed how traumatic sexual experiences in childhood could be related to an increase of psychiatric disorders, not necessarily EDs [22], but the group of patients with EDs who had suffered sexual violence had more severe psychiatric disorders of obsessive-phobic nature.

In abused ED patients, personality traits characterized by low self-esteem, distorted attitude towards their own body and sexuality, aggressiveness, dissociation and multiple-personality disorders were also reported [23].

Vanderlinden and Vandereycken [24] reported that infancy trauma in patients with EDs might be associated with self-aggressiveness and dissociation disorders.

On the contrary, some authors found that the presence of self harm behaviour in ED patients might be one of the most important signs of a possible childhood sexual or physical abuse [25].

It was found, however, that purging, vomiting and body image disorders were more severe in ED patients who had suffered childhood physical or sexual abuse [26].

Few studies have analysed the presence of child trauma in males and their possible correlation with the development of an ED.

A recent study showed that boys with a history of sexual abuse presented a higher risk of EDs than girls [27].

In a study on a large sample of male students [28] it was found that about 4% had had sexual traumatic experiences caused by male abusers. In these subjects the abnormal eating behaviour was more common in those who reported an adverse family background.

It therefore appears that there is a complex interaction between ED development and traumatic experiences also for male patients and a key role is probably played by the family context that is often characterized by dysfunctional aspects leading the patient to develop low self-esteem, a low tolerance to frustration and greater vulnerability (Part 1 Chapter 6).

The development of an ED seems to be the attempt to manage the vulnerability and the emotions related to traumatic experience.

The increased presence of depression in male patients with EDs and a history of sexual abuse were also seen as an attempt to regulate negative internal states [29].

A recent study run on a large sample of men examined the association between EDs and a history of childhood abuse in gay and bisexual men [30]. The results showed that gay and bisexual men with a history of childhood sexual abuse were more likely to have a sub-clinical ED or a full syndrome. The type of ED more often associated with sexual abuse was bulimia or the binge-purging form of AN.

Binge-purge symptomatology was considered an attempt to cope with anxiety or depression following traumatic episodes.

In conclusion, there are several factors that may mediate the link between traumatic experiences and ED development, such as the type and the severity of the abuse, the initial reaction to the abuse both by the child and by the family, the functioning of the child before the abuse and the family background.

It is therefore important to investigate the presence of a physical or sexual abuse in childhood because, although there isn't a specific connection between the presence of trauma and the development of an ED, a traumatic event makes the individual highly vulnerable to developing psychiatric disorders, particularly EDs, and worsens ED prognosis [31].

Family as a Resource

If it is true that some roots of an ED can be found in the family history and dynamics it is also true that the presence of an ED can be profoundly distressing for all the family members. Families have an undisputable impact on their children and consequently on their ED course. Therefore the family needs to be involved in their children's treatment. In this sense, parents need to be empowered to help their children and cope with difficulties. They need to be supported as they can be in a trouble with their parental role. They can really represent a great resource in the therapeutic process and the more they collaborate the more likely a good outcome can be achieved.

References

[1] Bruch, H. Eating Disorders: Obesity , Anorexia Nervosa, and the Person Within. Routledge and Kegan, London, 1973.

[2] Minuchin, S; Rosman, BL; Baker, L. Psychosomatic Families. Harvard University Press, Cambridge (Massachussetts), 1978.

[3] Selvini Palazzoli, MP. Self Starvation. Chaucer Publishing Company, London, 1974.

[4] Strober, M; Yager, J. A developmental perspective on the treatment of anorexia nervosa in adolescents. In Guilford Press . Anorexia Nervosa and Bulimia Garner DM and Garfinkel PE, New York, 1985.

[5] Schmidt, U; Humfress, H; Treasure, J. The Role of General Family Environment and Sexual and Physical Abuse in the Origins of Eating Disorders. *European eating Disorder review*, 1997 5 (3), 184-207.

[6] Perdereu, F; Faucher, S; Wallier, J; Vibert, S; Godart, N. Family History of Anxiety and Mood Disorders in Anorexia Nervosa: Review of the Literature. *Eating and Weight Disorders*, 2008 13, 1-3.

[7] Logue, CM ; Crowe, RR ; Bean, JA. A Family study of Anorexia and Bulimia.*Comp. Psychiatry*, 1989 30, 179-188.

[8] Halmi, KA; Eckert, M; Marchi, P; Sampugnaro, V; Apple, R; Cohen, J. Comorbidity of Psychiatric diagnoses in Anorexia Nervosa. *Arch. Gen. Psychiatry* , 1991 48, 712-718.

[9] Beato-Fernandez, L; Rodriguez-Cano, T. Gender differences regarding psychopathological, family and social characteristics in adolescents with abnormal eating behavior. *Eat behaviors*, 2005 6, 337-344.

[10] Jammet, Ph; Gorge, A; Zweifel, R; Flavigny, H. The family environment of patients with Anorexia Nervosa. Effect on treatment. *Ann. Med. Interne*, 1973, 124, 247-252.

[11] Blissett, J; Meyer, C; Haycraft, E. Maternal mental health and child feeding problems in a non-clinical group. *Eat Behav*, 2007 8, 311-318.

[12] Tiggeman, M; Lowes, J.Predictors of maternal control over children's eating. *Appetite*, 2002 39, 1-7.

[13] Stein, A; Murray, L; Cooper, P; Fairburn, CG. Infant growth in the context of maternal eating disorders and maternal depression. *Psychological Med*, 1996 26, 569-574.

[14] Russell, GFM; Treasure, J; Eisler, I. Mothers with anorexia nervosa who underfeed their children: their recognition and management. *Psychological Medicine*, 1998 28, 93-108.

[15] Stein, A; Wooley, H; Cooper, SD; Fairburn, CG. An observational study of mothers with eating disorders and their infants. *J. Child Psychol. Psychiatry,* 1994 35 (4), 733-48.

[16] Agras, S; Hammer, L; Mc Nicholas, F. A perspective study of the influence of eating disordered mothers on their children. *Int. J. Eat Disord.,* 1999 25, 253-262.

[17] Patel, P; Wheatcroft, R; Park, RJ; Stein, A. The children of mothers with eating disorders. *Clinical Child and Family Psychology Rewiew*, 2002 5 (1), 1-19.

[18] Smolak, L; Murnen, SK. A meta analitytic examination of the relationship between child sexual abuse and eating disorders. *Int. J. Eat Disord.,* 2002 31, 136-150.

[19] Garner, DM. Pathogenesis of anorexia nervosa . *Lancet*, 1993 341, 1631-1635.

[20] Oppenheimer, R; Howells, K; Palmer, L; Chaloner, D. Adverse sexual experiences in childhood and clinical eating disorders: A preliminary description. *Journal of Psychiatric Research,* 1985 19, 157-161.

[21] Palmer, R; Oppenheimer, R; Dignon, A; Chaloner, D; Howells, K. Chilhood sexual experiences with adults reported by women with eating disorders: An extended series. *British Journal of Psychiatry*, 1990 156, 699-703.

[22] Folsom, V; Krahn, D; Nairn, K; Gold, L; Demitrack, MA; Silk, KR. The impact of sexual abuse and physical abuse on eating disordered and psychiatric symptoms: A comparison of eating disorder and psychiatric inpatients. *Int. J. Eating Disord.,* 1993 13, 249-257.

[23] Molinari, E. Eating disorders and sexual abuse. Eating Weight Disord, 2001 6, 68-80.

[24] Vanderlinden, J; Vandereycken, W. Trauma, dissociation and impulse dyscontrol in eating disorders. Brunner, Mazel Inc. 1997.

[25] Favaro, A; Dalle Grave, R; Santonastaso, P. Impact of a history of physical and sexual abuse, in eating-disordered and asymptomatic subjects. *Acta psychiatr Scand,* 1997 97, 358-363.

[26] Root,MPP; Fallon, P. The incidence of victimization experiences in a bulimic sample. *J. Interpersonal Violence*, 1988 3, 161-173.

[27] Neumark-Sztainer, D; Story, M; Hannan, PJ; Beuhring, T; Resnick, MD. Disordered eating among adolescents: association with sexual/physical abuse and other familial/psychosocial factors. *Int. J. Eat Disord.* , 2000 28, 249-258.

[28] Kinzl, JF; Mangweth, B; Traweger, CM; Biebl, W. Eating disordered behaviour in males: the impact of adverse childhood experiences. *Int .J. Eat Disord.,* 1997 22, 131-138.

[29] Mitchell, K; Mazzeo, S. Mediators of the association between abuse and disordered eating in undergraduate men. *Eat Behav.*, 2005 6, 318-327.

[30] Feldman, MB; Meyer, H. Childhood abuse and eating disorders in gay and bisexual men. *Int .J. Eat Disord.*, 2007 40 (5), 418-423.

[31] Atti del Seminario Internazionale: Abuso precoce e disturbi del comportamento alimentare, Perugia (IT), 23 marzo 2003.

Chapter 8

EATING DISORDERS IN MEN AND PSYCHIATRIC COMORBIDITY

E. Manzato

ABSTRACT

In this chapter we focus on psychiatric comorbidity in EDs.

In general, most EDs are burdened by the presence of another psychiatric disorder which should be correctly diagnosed to plan an appropriate treatment.

The presence of psychiatric morbidity in patients with Eating Disorders is an unfavourable prognostic factor because it has negative implications on the clinical behaviour of the Eating Disorder, on patient compliance and therefore on the disease's course.

We therefore consider, with some interest, to devote a chapter to the description of psychiatric comorbidity, highlighting the differences between genders.

We will briefly introduce the concept of comorbidity and we will go deeper on psychiatric co-morbidity.

We will mention the main difficulties for a proper evaluation of psychiatric comorbidity in thc coursc of an Eating Disorder.

We will then treat psychiatric disorders which could be most frequently found in Eds, giving a brief clinical definition and subdividing them into four sections: mood disorders, obsessive-compulsive disorders, substance abuse disorders and personality disorders.

Finally, a survey of the most important studies about psychiatric co-morbidity in Eating Disorders, with particular attention to the gender differences, will be presented.

It is widely reported in the literature the existence of mental health disorders comorbidity in patients with EDs.

The concept of "comorbidity" was introduced in general medicine in the '70s and it is defined as any distinct lifetime additional clinical entity or a clinical entity that may occur during the clinical course of a patient.

The term comorbidity was also adopted in psychiatry and it is used to describe the coexistence of two or more psychiatric syndromes or personality disorders .

In dealing with psychiatric disorders comorbidity we will refer to the classification of the Fourth Edition of the Diagnostic and Statistical Manual of Mental Disorders (DSM IV-TR) [1], which distinguishes them as Axis 1 disorders (psychiatric syndromes) or Axis 2 (personality disorder).

Psychiatric comorbidity in EDs can be interpreted in different ways and the main hypotheses are summarized as follows:

- comorbidity, especially mood and anxiety disorders, may be a consequence of EDs
- EDs could be a consequence of a pre-existing psychiatric disorder (i.e. a secondary manifestation of the pre-existing psychopathological disorder)
- both EDs and psychiatric disorders belong to the same spectrum and also have in common the aetiology and some aspects of cerebral functioning mediators

The diagnosis of comorbidity has clinical implications because it may give an important contribution to the prediction of general functioning, clinical phenomenology, prognosis and treatment outcome.

Psychiatric comorbidity seems to be correlated with longer disease episodes, with a more unsatisfactory clinical course and with a greater frequency of relapses.

Psychiatric comorbidity influences several aspects of the therapeutic project: it may reduce patient's compliance, it may require a specific drug treatment (and in this case patient physical condition must be carefully evaluated), hospitalization or a specific psychiatric outpatient treatment.

Psychiatric comorbidity also has a prognostic value on ED outcome: the data coming from scientific literature reports an unfavourable prognosis if another psychiatric disorder coexists.

Therefore, owing to the importance of psychiatric comorbidity on ED severity, the professional figure who has a diagnostic suspect of an ED in a patient has to promptly consult a psychiatrist in order to achieve a correct psychopathologic arrangement and an anamnesis concerning the presence of lifetime psychiatric disorders.

The diagnosis of psychiatric comorbidity pertains to the psychiatrists. We now report a survey of the most important studies about psychiatric comorbidity in EDs, with particular attention to the gender differences. Also, notices about DSM definitions in the psychiatric field will be reported in order to give to all clinicians some guidance points.

The literature data about the presence of psychiatric comorbidity in EDs is rather variable because the correct diagnosis of the comorbid psychiatric disorder may sometimes be very difficult.

Moreover, most of the studies about psychiatric comorbidity in EDs have some limitations such as non-inclusion of a psychiatric control group, recruitment of community samples, lack of longitudinal designs, differences in the diagnostic criteria, and the exclusive use of tests without the validation of a clinical evaluation.

Comorbidity in ED patients may vary along the therapeutic course. Psychiatric disorders may in fact often be present in the acute phase and regress during treatment or in the regression phase of the ED. For example, depressive symptoms may be secondary to malnutrition and may spontaneously regress with refeeding and weight gain.

For this reason some researchers have suggested that, due to the negative effects of chronic malnutrition on mood, treatment for persisting comorbid conditions should be directed only towards the patients who have attained a more healthy weight.

Psychopathological changes during ED course complicates a correct evaluation of the comorbid axis II disorder. We know in fact that a personality disorder should be constant in the course of time.

The screening for personality disorders is therefore important because, providing a more comprehensive assessment, it may help in the treatment planning and improving the overall effects of treatment.

The data reported in ED patients demonstrate that the most frequent comorbidity is comorbidity with Axis I mood disorders, particularly major depressive disorder.

The presence of a comorbidity with anxiety disorders- especially obsessive and compulsive disorders- and with substance abuse disorder has also been reported.

For Axis II personality disorders the most common comorbidities are respectively distributed in cluster C, B and A.

Moreover, comorbidity can differ in the various subtypes of EDs.

For instance, restricting type AN has been found to be associated with Cluster C, particularly with obsessive-compulsive and avoidant personality disorders, whereas bingeing-purging AN and bulimia nervosa have been associated with Cluster B, particularly with borderline personality disorder.

We also know that EDs may be subject to diagnostic fluctuations and they may change during the course of illness in the same patient. For example AN can evolve into BN; less often does the opposite shift occur.

Psychiatric Comorbidity among Males with EDs

Most of the reports of the literature do not differentiate among the genders or include mixed samples with a prevalence of females. This little empirical attention devoted to examining the comorbidity of eating disorders in men is due to the low rate of EDs in males.

Given the relative rarity of men affectd by EDs, it has been a challenge to generate samples with a sizable number of male cases. The literature, in fact, includes case reports or samples with few participants and only few studies have a large sample of men with EDs.

For the most part, studies have found high rates of psychiatric comorbidity for both females and males with an ED.

It seems that males with EDs report a higher percentage of comorbidity than control samples.

On the contrary, it seems that there are not significant differences in comorbidity between males and females with EDs.

In one of the first studies concerning a large group of 135 males affected by EDs, Carlat et al reported a high prevalence of comorbidity in particular with a depressive state (55%), substance abuse (17%), personality disorders in cluster A,B,C (24%), or alcohol dependence (14%) [2].

Striegel-Moore et al. [3] examined the psychiatric comorbidity of eating disorders in a national sample of hospitalized male veterans. The initial study sample was comprised of 466 men; on routine clinical assessment 98 male patients received a diagnosis of a current ED, using ICD criteria.

For the comorbidity analysis ED cases were individually matched with randomly selected male patients without EDs. The 98 cases with EDs included: 25 men with AN, 17 men with BN and 56 men with EDNOS.

Psychiatric comorbidity was high: 92% of AN cases, 100% of BN cases and 89% of EDNOS cases had at least one comorbid psychiatric diagnosis.

Men with AN in the same study were characterized by high rates of mood disorders, substance abuse (particularly alcohol abuse or dependence) or dependent disorder, schizophrenia and other psychotic disorders.

In eating disordered men there was a strong association between AN and schizophrenia.

Men with BN had high rates of comorbid substance abuse, mood and personality disorders.

The high rates of substance abuse, if chronic, result in a significant impairment in social functioning and the high rates of personality disorders, which are also generally associated with poor prognosis, suggest the presence of a subgroup of BN men who are at considerable risk and may require intensive interventions.

The EDNOS cases in this study represented the largest subgroup and they were also characterized by high rates of psychiatric comorbidity.

The pattern of comorbidity for EDNOS and AN cases was remarkably similar, both groups showing high rates of substance abuse, schizophrenia and mood disorders.

Bean e coll. investigated gender differences in the progression of comorbid psychopathology symptoms of ED patients [4].

This study screened the comorbid psychopathology in eating disordered males and females undergoing residential treatment using Personality Assessment Inventory (PAI).

The results showed that both males and females patients exhibit several comorbid disorders at admission to residential treatment and the severity of these symptoms was statistically significantly reduced over the course of treatment confirming the variability of comorbid psychiatric symptoms during treatment. At admission, the mean raw scores for females were statistically significantly higher than the mean raw scores for males on 4 of the 11 clinical scales of the PAI, mainly the ones in the " neurotic" spectrum of disorders.

Anxiety and depression scales as well as borderline personality disorders features were higher in women. At the time of discharge the only statistically significant difference between genders was that females continued to score higher than males on borderline features.

The study showed that, in general, males have less severe symptoms of comorbid pathology than females at admission but females make better progress at reducing depressive and anxiety-related symptoms over the course of treatment.

After this introduction, we will focus now on four specific psychiatric pathologies often found in comorbidity with EDs and then, respectively, mood disorders, substance abuse, obsessive symptoms and personality disorders.

We will give a short definition of each psychiatric disturbance, as it is impossible to discuss all the different types of mental disease in a completely thorough and exhaustive way.

We will report some scientific studies with the aim of giving PCPs useful information about this argument.

MOOD DISORDERS

Mood disorders are characterized by a disturbance in the regulation of mood and behaviour.

They include disorders characterized by:

- presence of one or more major depressive episodes (persistent feelings of sadness, fatigue and loss of interest in usually enjoyed activities, weight changes, disturbances in sleep, lack of motivation, guilt, effect on powers of concentration, death-related thoughts; all these symptoms for at least two weeks)
- dysthymic disorders characterized by depressive symptoms similar to depressive episodes but less severe
- depression in association with medical illness or alcohol and substance abuse.

In addition, there are bipolar disorders in which people experience abnormally elevated (manic or hypomanic) and abnormally depressed states for short, or significant periods of time.

It is important to emphasize that mood disorders are frequent in EDs and that it can be difficult to diagnose the mood disorder during the acute phase of an ED.

In severe AN, malnutrition may often induce depressive symptoms but these are likely to disappear with refeeding and weight gain.

According to a review made by Godard et al. [5] there are several factors that may influence the evaluation of comorbidity of mood disorders: one of the most important concerns in the phase of the ED.

In fact, the data is very different depending on whether the ED is in the acute phase, and thus the morbidity is evaluated in hospitalized patients, or if it is in partial or total remission, meaning, concerning outpatients.

The findings in the scientific literature about the prevalence rates of mood disorders in EDs are not consistent. This can be due to the accuracy in evaluating the different types of mood disorders. It is in fact important to take into consideration the whole mood disorders spectrum and not only the Major Depression Disorder.

Godard et coll. reported that, despite the fact that most of the reports had some method inaccuracy, in AN the overall lifetime prevalence of mood disorders is around 40% in restricting AN and over 60% in bingeing-purging AN; in BN the prevalence ranges from 50% to 90%.

Therefore, the prevalence of mood disorders is higher in ED patients than in the general population.

The presence of mood disorders in ED changes in time. Herpetez- Dahlmann [6] studied a small sample of 34 patients with AN followed up for 7 years to evaluate their depressive disorder. In the first 3 years after the treatment there was an improvement in depressive symptoms but they relapsed in the following years.

Another aspect that has been scarcely considered in the literature is the sequence of presentation of MD in respect to the onset of the ED.

It is interesting to note that in studies which consider the year before the onset of an ED, the data shows that a MD precedes the onset of AN in 25% of cases [7] while MD precedes the onset of BN in 36% to 61% of cases [8,9].

Among mood disorders the Major Depressive Disorder (MDD) is the most frequently found and the MDD prevalence rates in AN and BN are significantly higher than in control groups. The lifetime prevalence of Major Depressive Disorder in AN-R is reported between 9.5% and 64.7% and in AN-BN is between 50% and 71.3%.

This wide prevalence range may be ascribed to the presence of methodological differences among the considered studies.

A correlation between the presence of a familial depressive disorder and a vulnerability to EDs has also been confirmed (see Part 1 Chapter 7).

Most clinical studies show that patients with Bipolar Disorder have elevated rates of ED and vice versa [10].

Nonetheless, after a review of the literature, few doubts persist about the fact that Bipolar Disorder and EDs, particularly BN and Bipolar Disorder, are related.

The comorbidity prevalence range between EDs and Bipolar Disorders may vary among the different studies according to the methods and the classifications used with an average that seems to be about 7.25% [11].

This association might be more frequent in bulimic patients presenting with a severe chronic type of EDs. The relatives of bulimic patients also display an increased morbid risk for Bipolar Disorder. Although the comorbidity between bulimia and Bipolar Disorder does not appear coincidental, the nosological relationship between these two disorders are not perfectly clear [12].

Also in AN however, the presence of a Bipolar Disorder [13] or of a sub-threshold bipolarity has been reported [14] with symptoms such as impulsiveness, irritability, elation, etc., having a probable impact on the course and the treatment of AN.

We want now to emphasize some common characteristics between EDs and Bipolar Disorders: both include alterations of food and weight, they both can have their onset in adolescence or in early adulthood and they both have the tendency to be chronic in their course with episodes of relapses.

The theoretical models proposed in Mc Elroy's review [11] to explain the association between the two disorders are the following:

"In the first model, bipolar and eating disorders are pathophysiologically distinct entities which overlap by chance, but with significant frequency…in the second model bipolar disorder and ED overlap because they share the same fundamental pathophysiology of dysregulation in mood, eating behaviour etc…the third model is that bipolar disorder and eating disorders co-occur because they are separate but pathophysiologically related disorders."

From a clinical point of view, the comorbidity of EDs with Bipolar Disorders can create problems in the compliance to the treatment.

Obsessive Compulsive Disorder

Obsessive-compulsive disorders belong to the area of anxiety disorders. Comorbidity of EDs and the spectrum of compulsive disorders may include: the obsessive-compulsive disorder, the obsessive-compulsive personality disorder and personality traits like perfectionism, rigidity, hypercontrol etc.

The DSM IV-TR defines the obsessive compulsive disorder as either the presence of obsessions or compulsions, recognition that the above are excessive or unreasonable and that obsessions or compulsions cause marked distress (the obsessions are parasitic ideas in an intact intellect, the compulsions are strong ideational or motor urges that must be satisfied).

The personality obsessive compulsive disorder is "a pervasive pattern of preoccupation with orderliness, perfectionism, mental and personal control" that leads the person to have an high preoccupation with details, list, order and perfectionism that interferes with completion of tasks.

Many studies emphasize the links between EDs, in particular AN, and disorders in the obsessive-compulsive (OC) spectrum due to the high prevalence of OC in AN.

In clinical samples the lifetime prevalence of OCD is highly variable as it ranges from 9.5% to 62% in ANR and from 10% to 66% in ANB, while in BN it varies from 0% to 42%: these large variations are determined by the methodologies used and the diagnostic difficulties because the two disorders have several symptoms in common [15].

In patients with AN, in fact, the described perfectionistic, rigid and inflexible personality traits can get worse during the acute phase of the ED.

The similarities of the two disorders suggested a clinical as well biological sharing hypothesis i.e. a dysregulation of the serotononergic system both in ECD and in OC [16].

The perfectionism and the obsessive symptoms greatly affect the AN symptoms: a strong perfectionism is correlated with both the need to adapt as much as possible to the ideal of body image and with the control in eating behaviour.

Also to be noted in the field of anxiety disorders in general, studies don't always make a distinction of gender and are mostly conducted on samples of AN women.

Kaye et al. found that about two-thirds of the individuals with EDs had one or more lifetime anxiety disorders and the most common were obsessive-compulsive disorder and social phobia. Furthermore, the presence of anxiety disorders was higher in samples with EDs than in the non-clinical group, and finally, the anxiety disorders commonly had their onset in childhood before the onset of the ED [17].

For the most part of the studies, the presence of obsessive traits is significantly associated with a poor prognosis [18].

OCD and ED also have a peak age of onset in adolescent years and, regardless of the sequence of onset, OCD symptoms significantly affect the ED treatment because they make it more difficult for patients to return to normal nutritional styles and also makes it harder to introduce them to new foods [19].

In a large sample of male and female patients Weltzin et al. [20] have analyzed the presence of OCB and of ED, the gender differences between the groups and the severity of ED symptoms between patients with and without OCB. They found that the groups of males with ED and OCB were slightly younger than the other groups, the diagnosis of AN occurred four times more frequently than BN and the diagnosis of EDNOS was negligent. The sample group who had a comorbility with OCB had a greater length of treatment (both male and female), males with OCB had a lower severity of ED symptoms as compared to females with OCB.

SUBSTANCE ABUSE

The essential characteristic of substance abuse is the pathological way of use of a substance that leads to significant disruption and results in cognitive behavioural physiological symptoms.

The comorbidity between ED and substance abuse has been widely demonstrated.

The data showed that about 12-18% of patients with AN and 30-70% of patients with BN are alcohol, tobacco or other drugs abusers [21].

It is evident that patients with BN or belonging to AN binge/purging subtype exhibit more comorbidity with substance abuse than patients with restricting AN or patients without ED.

Thompson-Brenner et al.[22] tried to link the substance abuses with specific types of personality (see section on personality disorders).

They identified a fifth subtype, a variant of "emotionally dysregulated" which showed more impulsive and antisocial behaviour called "behaviorally dysregulated" which is probably the type of personality most associated with substance abuse.

In fact, data collected by the authors stresses how the individuals with behavioural dysregulation and not those with emotional dysregulation may show specific vulnerability to alcohol or drug abuse.

Substance abuse in adolescents has been studied in the YRBSS project (Youth Risk Behavior Surveillance System) with a sample of over 13,000 adolescents that included a large sample of male high school adolescent students in the United States [23].

This study found elevated use of tobacco, illicit substances, alcohol and inhalant in adolescents with EDs (as it can be found in studies on eating disordered adult samples) and especially in those patients with bulimic symptoms.

The use of illicit substances may be related to several factors: the anorexic properties, their potential capability to alter body shape and size (like for instance a steroid) as one way to escape the aversive emotional experiences or as a clinical correlate of impulsivity.

Substance abuse, binge drinking and the use of tobacco had a very high prevalence in the whole sample suffering from an eating disorder, and it was higher in the adolescent male sample than in the female sample.

The lifetime use of steroids was more common in males with disordered eating. Besides the use of alcohol, the use of cocaine was also moderately strong in males (cocaine is a strong suppressor of appetite) and this could be linked to the anorectic effect of these substances together with the fact that cocaine and alcohol can "help" people coping with negative emotions.

The inhalant have been shown to cause loss of appetite and thus weight control.

The abuse of alcohol was used as appetite suppressor as well as "self-medication" useful to manage states of mind characterized by anxiety and depression. The study evidenced how in male students all association between disordered eating and use of each specific substance were statistically significant.

These results led the authors to hypothesize that males with both eating and substance abuse disorders may have wider disorders in the area of impulsivity.

PERSONALITY DISORDERS

Personality disorders are defined as an enduring pattern of inner experience and behavior that deviate markedly from the expectations of the culture of the individual who exhibits it.

The onset of these patterns of behavior can typically be traced back to late adolescence and the beginning of adulthood, and persist throughout a person's lifetime, which induce impaired social and/or occupational functioning.

Research examining links between personality and EDs proliferated in the past two decades because personality traits have been implicated in the onset, in the symptomatic expression and maintenance of EDs.

A recent study [24] reported that the presence of Personality Disorder was one of the best predictors of treatment utilization among women with AN and BN.

At the beginning we reported that the personality disorders more frequently associated with EDs belong to DSM Cluster B (Borderline, Histrionic and Narcissistic personality disorders) or Cluster C (anxious-fearful, obsessive-compulsive personality disorders).

But, if we go deeper in the literature about personality disorders, we can notice that the results of the studies regarding personality and ED are sometimes contradictory because it is difficult to identify a specific personality disorder as ED patients show heterogeneous patterns and because BN and AN diagnosis may sometimes coexist in the same patient in different moments of the ED course. In some cases, when DSM-IV diagnostic criteria are strictly applied, the diagnosis of a personality disorder in an ED patients is not so easily attained.

For these reasons, some of the studies aim to identify some personality traits that could represent risk factors for the onset of an ED.

Western et al. suggested that there may be distinct personality constellations that represent separate diatheses for the development of EDs [25].

They identified three personality subtypes: the High-functioning/ Perfectionistic prototype (characterized by personal and interpersonal strengths as well as a tendency to be self-critical, perfectionistic and guilty); the Emotionally Disregulated/Uncontrolled prototype (characterized by intense, labile emotions, emotional interference in thinking and impulse control, instable and self-destructive relationships, rejection sensitivity and suicidality, parasuicidality); the Constricted/Overcontrolled prototype (characterized by emotional constriction, feeling of depression, inadequacy, anxiety and social avoidance).

Dysregulated patients show a high level of comorbidity with post-traumatic and substance abuse disorders; constricted patients have other comorbid anxiety diagnosis; dysregulated patients show the worse treatment outcome.

Thompson–Brenner et al., by contacting clinicians treating eating disordered adolescent patients, investigated whether similar personality prototypes exist in adolescents with ED. [26]

Consistent with the findings from the adult literature, this study pointed out the same three types of personality pathology: High Functioning/Perfectionistic, Emotionally Disregulated, Avoidant /Depressed. The correct assessment of the personality style in adult and adolescent patients with EDs may be important because there are differences in symptomatology and clinical response.

REFERENCES

[1] American Psychiatric Association. *Diagnostic and Statistical Manual of Mental Disorders* Fourth Edition, Text revision, 2000.

[2] Carlat, DJ; Camargo, CA; Herzog, DB. Eating disorders in males: a report on 135 patients. *Am. J. Psychiatry,* 1997 154, 1127-1132.

[3] Striegel –Moore, R; Garvin, V; Dohm, FA; Rosenheck, RA. Psychiatric comorbility of ED in men: a national study of hospitalized veterans. *Int. J. Eat. Disord.,* 1999 25 (4), 399-404.

[4] Bean, P; Maddocks, MB; Timmel, P; Weltzin T. Gender differences in the progression of co-morbid psychopathology symptoms of eating disordered patients . *Eat Weight Disord,* 2005 10 (3), 168-174.

[5] Godart, NT; Perdereau, F; Rein, Z; Berthoz, S; Wallier, J; Jeammet, Ph; Flament, MF. Comorbility studies of eating disorders and mood disorders. Critical review of the literature. *J. Affect. Disord.*, 2007 97, 37-49.

[6] Herpetez-Dahlmann, BM; Wewetzer, C; Ramscmitz, H. The predictive value of depression in in anorexia nervosa. Results of a 7 years follow-up study . *Acta Psychiatrica Scandinava,* 1995 91 (2), 114-119.

[7] Smith, C; Feldman, SS; Nasserbakht, A; Steiner, H. Psychological characteristics and DSM-III-R diagnosis at 6-year follow-up of adolescent anorexia nervosa. *J. Am. Acad. Child Adolesc. Psych.* , 1993 32, 1237-1245.

[8] Schwalberg, MD; Barlow, DH; Alger, SA; Howard, LJ. Comparison of bulimics, obeses, binge eaters, social phobics and individuals with panic disorders on comorbility across DSM-III-R anxiety disorders. *J. Abnorm. Psychol.* , 1992 101, 4675-4681.

[9] Brewerton, TD. Toward a unified theory of serotonin dysregulstion in eating and related disorders. *Psychoneuroendocrinology,* 1995 20, 561- 590.

[10] Murry, M; Verdoux ,H; Burgeois, M. Comorbility of bipolar and eating disorders. Epidemiologic and therapeutic aspects. *Encephale,* 1995 21(5), 545-53.

[11] McElroy, SL; Kotwal, R; Keck, PE; Akiskal, HS. Comorbility of bipolar and eating disorders: distinct or related disorders with shared dysregulations?*J Affect Disord.*, 2005 86 (2-3), 107-27.

[12] Wildes, JE; Marcus, M; Fagiolini A. Eating disoerders and illness burden in patients with bipolar spectrum disorders.*Compr. Psychiatry,*2007 48 (6), 516-521.

[13] Halmi, KA; Eckert, E; Marchi, P; Sampugnaro, V; Apple, R; Cohen, J. Comorbility of psychiatric diagnoses in anorexia nervosa . *Arch Gen Psychiatry*, 1991 48,106-110.

[14] Wildes, JE; Marcus, MD; Gaskill, J A; Ringham, R. Depressive and manic-hypomanic spectrum psychopathology in patients with anorexia nervosa. *Compr. Psychiatry*, 2007 48, 413-418.

[15] Godart, NT; Flament, MF; Perdereau, F; Jeammet, P. Comorbility between eating disorders and anxiety disorders: a review. *In.t J. Eat Disord.,* 2002 32 (3), 253-70.

[16] Thiel, A; Broochs, A; Ohlmeier, M; Jacoby, GE; Schuller, G. Obsessive-Compulsive Disorder among patients with anorexia nervosa and bulimia nervosa. *Am. J. Psychiatry*, 1995 152, 72-75.

[17] Kaye, WH; Bulik, CM; Thornton, L; Barbarich, N; Masters, K. Comorbility of anxiety disorders with anorexia and bulimia nervosa. *Am. J. Psychiatry*, 2004 161 (12), 2215-21.

[18] Halmi, KA; Tozzi, F; Thornton, LM; Crow, S; Fichter, MM; Kaplan, AS; Keel, P; Klump,KL; Lilenfeld,LR; Mitchell,JE; Plotnicov,KH; Pollice,C; Rotondo, A; Strober, M; Woodside, DB; Berrettini, WH; Kaye, VH, Bulik, CM. The relation among perfectionism, obsessive-compulsive personality disorder and obsessive-compulsive disorder in individual with eating disorders. *Int. J. Eat Disord.*, 2005 38 (4), 371-374.

[19] Fisher, M; Fornar, V; Waldbaum, R; Gold, R. Tree case reports on the relathionship between anorexia nervosa and obsessive compulsive disorder. *Int..J. Adolesc. Med Health*, 2002 14, 328.

[20] Weltzin, T; Cornella Carlson, T; Weisensel, N; Timmel, P; Hallinan, P; Bean, P. The combined presence of obsessive compulsive behaviors in males and females with eating disorders account for longer lenghts of stay and more severe eating disorder symptoms. *Eat Weight Disord*, 2007 13, 176-182.

[21] Holderness, CC; Brooks-Gunn, J; Warren, MP. Co-morbidity of eating disorders and substance abuse review of the literature. *Int. J. Eat Disord.*, 1994 16, 1-34.

[22] Thompson-Brenner, H; Eddy, KT; Franko, DL; Dorer, D; Vashchenko, M; Herzog, DB. Personality Patology and Substance Abuse in eating Disorders: a longitudinal study. *Int. J. Eat Disord.*, 2008 41 (3), 203-208.

[23] Pisetsky, EM; May Chao, BAY; Dierker, LC; Alexis, MM; Striegel-Moore, RH. Disordered Eating and Substance Use in Hight School Students: Results from the Youth Risk Behavior Surveillance Systtem. *Int. J. Eat Disord.*, 2008 41 (5), 464- 470.

[24] Keel, PK; Dorer, DJ; Eddy, KT; Delinsky, SS; Franko, DL; Blai, MA; Keller, MB; Herzog, DB. Predictors of treatment utilization among women with anorexia and bulimia nervosa. *Am. J. Psychiatry*, 2002 159, 140-142.

[25] Westen, D; Harnden-Fischer, J; Personality profiles in eating disorders: rethinking the distinction between axis1 and axis 2. *Am. J. Psychiatry,* 2001 158, 547-562.

[26] Thompson-Brenner, H; Eddy, K T; Sati, DA; Boisseau, C; Westen, D. Personality subtypes in adolescents with eating disorders: validation of a classification approach. *Clin. Child Psycho.l Psychiatry,* 2008 49 (2), 170-180.

PART II. CLINICAL ASPECTS

PREFACE PART TWO

After the first theoretical part, useful to frame EDs in males, part two deals with more clinical issues. The following chapters offer some practical suggestions for working with male patients affected by EDs.

This second part is divided into three different chapters: one treats practical aspects related to the first approach, the second one, medical aspects, and the last one concerns skin features.

In the first chapter the attention was put on the difficulties in approaching and understanding patients with EDs, in particular if they are males.

Men are in fact less likely than women to identify themselves as suffering from an ED for both socio-cultural and psychological reasons.

Factors which make the diagnostic assessment in males difficult are outlined and discussed.

During the first assessment, it is fundamental to put the right questions in the right way in order to get closer to the patient and to make a correct diagnosis. In this context, a warm and empathic approach is essential to build up a relationship in which the patient can collaborate and be helped in his therapeutic path.

Actually, all guidelines emphasize the importance of the first visit as an opportunity for initiating a trustful relation: a good quality of this approach will allow the patient to rely upon the health care professional and accept a diagnostic and therapeutic course.

ED patients are generally characterized by low levels of awareness about their illness and unlike patients with other psychiatric conditions they do not experience their symptoms as distressing. Consequently, they may not be ready and motivated to change.

A motivational approach can be required to obtain patients' collaboration so that both the psychological assessment and the physician's evaluation can take place for better involvement and a complete understanding of the patient and his illness.

The second chapter dealing with medical complications is somewhat wide as it takes into consideration the variety of medical complications related to EDs. Step by step it will be explained how to proceed for a correct medical assessment and "staging" of the patients.

This is the only chapter dedicated to medical aspects in this book so the author aimed to explain the main medical complications in a more exhaustive way trying to be clear and practical at the same time.

The last section is dedicated to skin signs due to the malnutrition, self-starvation and purging practices which can be found in ED patients.

As skin conditions are perceptible and visible, well recognized dermatological problems may help in the identification and disclosure of an ED among those patients who deny their illness. We have devoted a specific chapter to dermatological aspects of EDs because at least 40 skin signs have been reported in these diseases. Some of them are considered "guiding signs" because they allow to suspect the presence of a hidden disorder. Skin signs are due to starvation, self-induced vomiting, drug consumption and concomitant psychiatric illness. A body mass index of 16 or less can be considered a critical value at which skin changes are more frequent.

Chapter 1

THE FIRST APPROACH TO EDS IN MALES

E. Manzato

ABSTRACT

This second part of the book has the purpose of addressing practical issues and to provide caregivers with some tools for the clinical management of males affected by EDs.

The Primary Care Physician (PCP) is, in most cases, the first professional figure to come in contact with the subject, therefore he has a very important role in the detection and management of an ED; at the same time he faces many difficulties in Eating Disordered patients in general, particularly in the case of males.

This chapter will talk about these concerns, focusing on two main problematic areas: early diagnosis and referral to a multi-professional ED team for validation of diagnosis and treatment plan.

PCPs should consider some important steps for an adequate proceeding: first they should create a trustful relationship with the subject, they should communicate that an ED is a psychological problem with severe medical consequences.

At the end of the physical evaluation and minimal diagnostic procedures the PCP should inform the patient about the results of this assessment: when a likely ED is present, the PCP should motivate the subject to be evaluated by a psychiatrist with experience in the field of Eating Disorders, possibly inside a multi-professional team concerned with somatic, nutritional and psychiatric aspects according to the main guidelines.

In this chapter, we will focus on some problematic issues of this process and we will report useful indications of these guidelines, feasible also in primary care setting.

The need for other specialists such as dentists, gastroenterologists, and diabetes specialists to be trained about EDs for secondary prevention purpose is stressed.

EDs are complex and multi-factorial disorders that require multidisciplinary and integrated care strategies. EDs can lead to severe physical complications, sometimes fatal, and tend to be persistent and prone to relapses.

Early diagnosis of EDs may have a positive prognostic value in both sexes, may prevent severe complications and may improve the global outcome (secondary prevention).

In males, early diagnosis is unfortunately still difficult: some reasons are related to the subject himself, such as the difficulty in recognizing the disorder, in accepting it without shame and in seeking professional help. Other reasons are related to the possibility that physicians, particularly PCPs, are not skilled enough in recognizing the new warning signs and symptoms of EDs in males and therefore are unable to engage the patients in a diagnostic and therapeutic process.

Even if males are at low risk to develop an ED they are not immune, and when an ED is present males too suffer physically and psychologically: it is therefore important for the PCP to be aware of this complex psychopathology .

Moreover, as a long duration of the disorder is associated with a worse prognosis it is important to make the correct diagnosis as soon as possible, improving secondary prevention strategies.

The correct sequence of these different steps -early diagnosis, adequate referral and treatment - may help the approach of the male patient.

The PCP is usually the first to be consulted and the first medical figure who can suspect the diagnosis. In this case he has to refer the patient to a specialist multi-professional center.

He has a key role, achieved through a long history of trustful relations with the patient and his family, and the way in which he approaches the patient will become the first important element of care.

The PCP is also a crucial figure in the process of treatment and in the further monitoring in the remission stage.

The PCP is also involved in coordinating treatment, in managing the medical complications, and to indicate the need for inpatient hospitalization together with other professional figures in mental and nutritional fields.

If the patient is unwilling or unable to refer to a mental health professional or nutritionist, the role of PCP is to monitor weight, nutritional intake, and physical condition and to help the patient in recognizing the need for treatment [1].

The main problem in approaching a suspected ED subject is represented on one side by the subject's denial of the disorder and his difficulty in seeking help, on the other side by the fact that PCPs seem to still be lacking experience in training and treating male ED patients.

A vigilant awareness of new warning signs and symptoms in EDs may be of great help in facing a "difficult" patient .

False Beliefs as Obstacles to an Early Diagnosis

A brief preface has to be done about the influence of the media and the related "false beliefs" associated with EDs in delaying a correct diagnosis, in particular, when the patient is a male.

The results of a survey commissioned by the National ED Association indicate that American people consider dieting (66%), media (64%) and families (52%) as the main causes of ED and that they don't consider these disorders as a medical condition [2].

Similar studies performed in UK highlight the same results: English people tend to consider AN as an extreme form of diet [3], despite AN having the highest percentage of mortality among psychiatric disorders.

Even if people believe that EDs are exclusively female disorders, males represent approximately 10% of all EDs (and the percentage is likely underestimated).

This detachment between physicians' perception and people's perception of EDs could negatively influence the ability to prevent, detect and treat an ED, particularly in males.

In fact, family members and friends participating in this stereotyped vision of ED could disregard the trouble and delay the seeking of care.

But the impact of these public constructs may also affect the PCPs and specialists: it is estimated that approximately 50% of ED are not recognized in clinical settings and when they are correctly diagnosed the patients do not always follow the adequate treatment.

The main responsibility of this stigma, regarding Eds and particularly EDs in males, is attributed to newspapers, one of the most important source of public information about mental illness, where EDs are not described as a true psychiatric disorder, but only as the result of low self-esteem, stressful situations or family issues.

In particular, AN is regarded by people as a "self-inflicted illness" and this may increase a sense of anger and refusal toward the patient [4].

Moreover, the articles about EDs often regard well known persons involved in show business encouraging imitative behaviours in adolescents.

When newspapers report cases of males affected by an ED they often describe them as having other psychiatric disorders pointing out the severity, more than for females [5].

The stigmatization of EDs constitutes a significant barrier against seeking treatment: "stigma" as discriminatory judge may lead affected subjects to be ashamed of their disorder and to hide it .

This vision has prevented men to consider EDs like other major psychiatric disorders: for example, social movements trying to decrease stigmatization against mental illness put EDs in a marginal position inside their struggle .

Furthermore, in the United States, EDs often are not considered by insurance companies to be as serious as other severe psychiatric disorders like schizophrenia.

Indeed, in the United States law groups and professional organizations are advocating for the inclusion of ED into the category of "serious mental illness," aiming to obtain insurance coverage for medical treatments.

Treatment costs and lack of insurance are reported, in fact, as another major barrier against the access to ED treatment.

In the Italian Public Health Service, treatment of EDs is now not charged to patients (legislative decree 29-4-1998) and this is considered by Italians specialists of EDs a significant step in recognizing the seriousness of these diseases.

Gender as an Obstacle to an Early Diagnosis

Another barrier against the access to adequate medical care seems to be the gender difference itself.

Beyond the typical features related to EDs, some studies point out how, in general, there are significant differences between the attitudes of men and women towards health services-so that it might be useful to develop more sensitive male health services [6].

In fact, males have difficulty in identifying themselves as patients and accepting the impact of their disease on everyday life; they want to maintain their identity in their work and family, their autonomy and self-determination far more than female patients.

A British review about the request of medical care by males, revealed men's reluctance to access health services: men are less likely to visit a doctor when they are ill and they are less likely to report on symptoms of disease [7].

Often men are also unlikely to be the first to seek help when they are married or have children: the family is seeking help for "the absent man" [8].

Finally, the reluctance of males to seek help when they are sick, combined with typical characteristics of ED patients (lack of awareness of illness or shame) results in a further delay between the onset of the disease and the demand for care.

The fact that the structures specialized in the care of EDs are addressed primarily to women could limit male patient's compliance. Therefore, it could be important to create specific pathways focused on the need of males.

The Difficulty For The PCP in Making a Correct Diagnostic Pathway

As already said before one of the first obstacles in the care of EDs is the difficulty of ED detection by family doctors.

We have already mentioned that some studies show a failure of physicians in recognizing EDs so that EDs may be undetected in about 50% of the cases [9].

To confirm this finding a study done by Hoek [10] in Holland revealed that, in an estimated number of EDs in the population, only 43% of patients with AN goes to their PCP and only 79% of these arrives to specialized centres.

In regards to BN, the percentages are even more dramatic: only 11% see a PCP and only 51% of these reaches a specialized centre.

The majority of patients are " lost in the street."

Even a U.S. study on the ability to diagnose BN demonstrated that 30% of family physicians had never diagnosed an ED and in any case, younger, female physicians were more likely to have bulimic patients[11].

The causes of this lack of recognition of EDs have been reported by physicians themselves to poor training in EDs: most physicians rated the quality of their undergraduate and postgraduate training in EDs as poor.

It seems that PCP's gender and the duration of medical practice affect their ability to identify EDs [12].

Female physicians seem more likely to screen often or routinely for EDs during periodic health examinations; in fact studies confirm the trend for younger female physicians to see a higher number of patients with EDs.

Male physicians are generally less prone to make a routine screening of ED or to even look for them unless they see important signs.

It was also found that, although patients with EDs often consult their PCP because of a great variety of symptoms including psychological, gastrointestinal and in women gynaecological complaints, EDs are diagnosed with difficulty. This underdiagnosis is particularly present when patients persist in denying their disease or the ED is present in a mild clinical picture.

In all these situations, if the PCP is not particularly trained to recognize all the aspects of this disorder, he may be unable to make a correct diagnosis.

Therefore, even if the PCP is in the best position to early identify the ED, he may have a low index of suspicion of EDs and hardly make a link between psychological or medical problems and ED, thus preventing early diagnosis and effective treatment [13].

Families with children or adolescents with EDs may spend a lot of time consulting PCPs or a variety of health professionals before being referred to specialist centres for EDs.

It is estimated that there is an average latency of about 7-4 months between parents' first seeking advice about EDs and their ultimate referral to specialists [14].

The methods of approach and the ability to identify the psychiatric disorder can have a substantial influence on patients' access to and pathways through care.

Weight as Diagnostic Key Point

Family physicians are important in the first line treatment of eating disorders but as we said the identification and the accurate diagnosis of an ED in primary care are still difficult.

Often, very simple indicators such as the evolution of weight are not correctly used [15]: outcomes studies suggest that low body mass index (BMI) at referral is predictive of poor ED prognosis and it is associated with significantly higher chronicity and mortality. The body mass index, obtained through a simple calculation (weight divided by height squared), allows PCPs to define the severity of underweight and therefore to propose the correct type of care.

The measurement of patient's weight and height is a simple way to check at least one of the diagnostic criteria of AN and it is also an objective method to verify the status of general malnutrition.

Additionally, although BMI is properly measured, adequate indications may not be given to the patient: American guidelines for the treatment of EDs [16] suggest that for patients with AN weighing less than 75% of their expected body weight or in presence of a rapid weight loss, treatment in a hospital is requested.

A study about the use of data concerning the weight of the National Eating Disorders Screening Program done in 1996 in the United States (counsellors were provided with versions of Body Weight Assessment Tool for women and men) showed that "despite clear instructions in the procedure manual, counsellors may have been confused in referring extremely underweight men because the formula and BWAT for determining the cut off of 75% of expected body weight that demarcated this weight category differed for men and women."

Therefore the male patient with an ED could be more easily unrecognized than female patients in primary diagnosis even when BMI is used correctly as an index reference.

One study, examining the influence of clinical and non-clinical features of case presentation, has showed that in the primary care setting male patients, even when presenting the same symptoms as females, were less likely to receive appropriate diagnosis of an ED. In males ED diagnoses were frequently exchanged with depression, particularly when the patient had a bulimic disorder.

The patient's gender (much more than ethnicity) was found to be one of the most influential non-clinical variables in limiting the diagnosis and consequently the possibilities of treatment [17].

Obstacle to Treatment

Even when the symptoms are recognized in the primary care setting the transition from diagnosis to adequate treatment is not so automatic. In fact, a significant percentage of patients with a correctly diagnosed ED are treated without referral to specialist services, despite the severity of the disorder.

In the UK 20% of identified cases with anorexia nervosa and 40% of cases with bulimia nervosa are treated exclusively in primary care [18].

So, even if severe symptoms should function as "triggers" for clinicians, and practical guidelines are available for the treatment, clinical or patients' variables may represent an obstacle preventing the correct therapeutic path.

Since many cases of EDs are treated only in a primary care setting, a number of clinical guidelines have been developed to help monitor the patient's physical situation and to indicate useful therapeutic strategies.

In addition, clinical guidelines provide indications for severe cases in which referral to specialists' care is mandatory.

These indications, however, are not routinely followed by PCPs for different reasons: the PCP may be unaware of these recommendations or guidelines might be required for simplification for use in primary care setting also consistent with time availability of PCPs [19].

The steps that one must cross to get to a proper care seem more complicated for males when they suffer from a disorder generally thought of as a "female" disorder.

A study run in the United States on the use of medical facilities by ED patients [20] showed that males received less treatment than females and, when treated, they had fewer days of hospitalization. In this study the percentage of BN males treated in-hospital was significantly lower than the expected rate (according to the projections of the incidence of BN); the study suggested that there may be gender-specific barriers to receiving care or accessing treatment for BN.

In outpatient care settings, male AN patients also received significantly less care than female anorectic patients.

About this difference, it was not clear whether it reflected gender differences in clinical severity or whether it was due to gender biases in the treatment of AN.

The conclusion was that males with EDs had a double disadvantage: they were diagnosed to a lesser extent and also received less care [21].

The Role of the other Specialists

In addition to the PCP, other specialists may come in contact with EDs.

There are, for example, diseases like diabetes that can promote the development of an ED, particularly in adolescence and adulthood, so that diabetes specialists should be aware of the possibility of this comorbidity.

Issues that may predispose adolescents and young adults with diabetes Type 1 (DM-1) to EDs may include weight gain, dietary restrictions and a co-existing continual preoccupation with food.

It is not rare that a young subject diagnosed with DM-1 may have prior weight loss; once insulin therapy begins weight gain usually ensues and this could lead to or increase body dissatisfaction.

Even if data on the general prevalence of EDs in DM-1 are inconsistent, some authors report that among boys those with diabetes were nearly four time as likely to vomiting for weight control and five times as likely to engage in dieting than those without diabetes [22]. Therefore ED guidelines advise: "Young people with type 1 diabetes and poor treatment adherence should be screened and assessed for the presence of an ED" [23].

In young people, body dissatisfaction and weight gain may lead to the development of an ED or to the use of unhealthy weight control behaviours, such as a change in insulin dosage.

It has been reported that 15% of males with DM-1 use unhealthy behaviours to control their body weight, and often the handling of insulin is made without reference to a diabetologist [24].

In these patients, the insulin omission as a means of weight loss is more common than self=induced vomiting or laxative use. Altering the insulin regimen may lead to poorer metabolic control and cause micro vascular complications as it will be more thoroughly explained in the following chapter.

Increased rates of mortality in DM-1 patients with AN are reported [25].

Other specialists who may come into contact with patients with EDs and may help to improve secondary prevention are the dentists.

They have an important role in the assessment of oro-facial manifestations of EDs, but despite this opportunity, few dentists are skilled in recognizing specific signs.

A study on a sample of dentists investigating their ability to correctly diagnose the patients with EDs showed that less than half of dentists reported currently assessing patients for EDs and only 19% reported that they communicated with the patient's PCP about suspected ED [26].

The fear of offending a patient, the lack of training in patient approach and lack of interdisciplinary communication were considered by dentists as obstacles in investigating the presence of EDs.

The dental hygienist, due to the length of time spent with the patient, could be in a favourable condition to develop a strong relationship so should be encouraged to motivate the patient to seek care [27]. But often this important opportunity to improve the secondary prevention is lost.

In regards to dermatological problems, which can help a PCP to suspect an ED see Part 2 in Chapter 3.

Obstacles to Treatment Compliance

Once a correct diagnosis is made, the physicians have to face a serious difficulty: the compliance to treatment.

In fact, patients with AN are often "carried" by the family. They may not have a real awareness of the disease and therefore have no real motivation to seek treatment.

On the contrary, patients with BN are hindered by feelings of guilt with respect to their ED and try to hide it. They are frightened by the fact that family members could potentially find out their symptoms.

Men with EDs are often in a critical medical condition even if their BMI is just below the limit of the normal value and their situation of under nutrition and weight loss can be easily concealed.

This situation can represent an obstacle both for the family and for the PCP to recognize the danger related to the presence of anorexia until a complete medical evaluation is done.

It is important to consider that ED are diseases involving both the body and the mind and that AN and BN present a great therapeutic challenge because of the risk of chronicity and the danger of mortality.

From the beginning, a trustful relationship should be established with the patient, and it is necessary to develop a therapeutic relationship and to motivate the patient to accept the referral to ED specialists and a treatment plan.

Treatment programs of EDs, especially in severe forms, should be performed inside a multidisciplinary team addressing all involved areas (psychological, somatic, nutrition): therefore after the diagnostic evaluation, it is necessary to motivate a patient to be taken to specialized centres.

AN is characterized by ego-syntonic self starvation, denial of illness and ambivalence towards treatment: these features make it difficult for patients with AN, who rarely turn spontaneusly to the doctor for their ED, in spite of the presence of serious medical and psychiatric comorbidity.

Most patients do not show any desire to change or they accept the treatment on their own terms, ideally with minimal or no weight gain.

Motivation for treatment may be one of the first problems faced: in most cases, the ED is ego-syntonic and “helps” to maintain a psychological and relational balance that otherwise would be broken. The therapy is a request to the patient to abandon behaviours and eating habits that gave him security.

The ego-syntonic nature of AN leads to an ambivalent attitude in which the motivation to treatment is due only to the desire of obtaining temporary relief from physical and/or psychological problems.

In fact, as soon as the weight increases patients with AN return to fight for food and weight control: the only possibility of a successful therapy is to help them abandon their vision of "weight control" as the only solution to their problems.

To do this it is necessary to establish, from the very beginning, a strong therapeutic alliance with the subject.

Often, patients with AN are brought to the doctor by the parents or partners, concerned about their physical health, and they accept the medical examination only to please the family while retaining their ambivalent attitude towards the care: on one side they ask (or are pushed to ask) for treatment, on another side they are initially unable to accept changes of food and are still frightened by weight gain.

So, keeping in mind that the treatment goes toward a direction that is opposite to the need of weight control and nutrition of AN patients, the first challenge is to create a therapeutic relationship that at the same time respects the fears of the patient.

In order to avoid a conflict with an AN patient it might be useful at the beginning not to propose a therapeutic program with definite goals but to require his availability for a "diagnostic framework": the PCP should explain to the subject that an assessment of his physical, mental and alimentary situation will be necessary for establishing whether an ED is present or not and, if present, the degree of its severity.

Not immediately engaging a fight on weight when the patient is not in a medical emergency allows the PCP to have a realistic chance to make all necessary investigations to confirm the diagnostic suspicion of an ED and to have the time to create a therapeutic alliance and a trustful relationship with the patient.

BN is less visible from the physical point of view because it is not associated with the severe weight loss typical of AN and generally creates less anxiety in the family.

The bulimic patients may live for years in solitude with their symptoms, sometimes even managing to hide it to the partner: this is a serious problem because bulimia is also associated with severe medical complications which can be associated with a poor outcome.

An early treatment represents the first step for a good prognosis in ED; nevertheless it has been demonstrated that in BN the time between the onset of the disorder and the demand for care is about 4 years longer that in AN.

This long latency before the request for treatment is attributable to the great sense of guilt and shame that characterizes BN patients preventing them to consider their altered behaviour as a disease.

Also for BN, it is important to remember that treatment goes in a direction that is opposite to the patient's need: standardization of food and suspension of compensative behaviours are perceived as dangerous by the patient who is afraid to gain weight and afraid to lose his control over weight once he stopped his usual compensatory practices.

These difficulties in the approach related to the nature of ED are even more exaggerated in males and make it even more difficult to detect and provide treatment.

The Relevance of the First Approach with the Patient and His Family

In the last few decades, many guidelines for the treatment of EDs have been drawn up. The most recent ones [16, 23,28] stress the importance of a "lenient" approach with the patient with an ED.

The APA guidelines suggest a cooperative attitude: "At the very outset, clinicians should attempt to build trust, establish mutual respect, and develop a therapeutic relationship with the patient that will serve as the basis for ongoing exploration and treatment of the problems associated with ED" [16].

The indications provided to psychiatrists who are involved in ED treatment may be valid also for the PCP: "The patient's understanding of how the illness developed and the effects of any interpersonal problems on the onset of the ED should be obtained regarding ED and other psychiatric disorders, obesity, family interactions in relation to the patient's disorder, and attitudes toward eating, exercise and appearance. It is essential not to articulate theory in order to blame or permit family members to blame one another or themselves"[16].

Finally, we want to remind ourselves of the need to involve the family when facing an ED patient.

First of all, it is necessary to provide adequate information about all the aspects of the ED as suggested in one of the main guidelines: "Patients and, where appropriate, caretakers should be provided with education and information on the nature, course, and treatment of EDs. In addition to the provision of information, family and caretakers may be informed of self-help groups and support groups, and offered the opportunity to participate in such groups where they exist" [23].

We remember that caring for a person with an ED has been associated with psychological distress and poor life quality of caregivers, especially in the case of associated psychiatric morbidity.

The only social support for families of patients with EDs are given is by friends or relatives, but in general many caregivers feel isolated and alone due to the high stigma and lack of understanding surrounding EDs.

Mothers in particular report high levels of emotional stress.

Meeting the needs of caregivers is of great importance in the treatment: it lowers the level of the stress, it makes the family a resource in patient's compliance to treatment and it can improve the outcome. It also has an important prognostic significance as it may help to reduce relapses [29].

The work on the family's part starting from the first contact with patients with EDs is mandatory when we are facing an adolescent: in this case the ED is a strong element of distress in family relationships and often has a meaning within the balance of the family.

For children and adolescents, evidence data indicates that family treatment is the most effective intervention suggested by the main guidelines: "Since eating is a quintessential family activity, the opportunity to observe patterns of family interaction around the eating and particularly around the eating problems can be useful in assessment. Family members can provide useful perspectives on factors contributing to the onset of the disorders and issues that may aid or hamper efforts at recovery. Family members are often distressed by difficulties in understanding and interacting with the patient. Clinicians need to empathically listen to family members, advise them on their interactions with the patient, and, when indicated, involve them in conjoint or individual treatment so that the patient and family all stand the best chance of achieving a good outcome"[16].

Therefore, the best way to help the patient be treated is to create a climate of trust with him and his family. The PCP is usually the first therapist who, with his attentive and empathic listening, can help the ED patient in his difficult path toward healing.

References

[1] Walsh, J; Wheat, ME; Freund, K. Detection, evaluation, and treatment of ED. The role of the primary care physician. *J Gen Intern Med*, 2000 15 (8), 577-590.

[2] American public opinion on ED: poll conducted on behalf of the National eating Disorders Association (report on the internet) Seattle: GMI, Inc.; March 25, 2005.

[3] Crisp, A. Stigmatization of and discrimination against people with eating disorders including a report of two nationwide surveys. *Eur Eat Disord Rev*, 2005 13, 147-152.

[4] Stewart, MC; Keel, PK; Schiavo, RS. Stigmatization of anorexia nervosa. *Int J Eat Disord*, 2006 39, 320-325.

[5] O'Hara, SK; Clegg Smith, K. Presentation of eating disorders in the news media: what are the implications for patients diagnosis and treatment? *Patient Ed and Couns*, 2007 68, 47-51.

[6] Madsen, SA. Men's special neED and attitudes as patients. *J Mens Health Gend*, 2007 4 (3), 361-362.

[7] Galdas, PM; Cheater, F; Marshall, P. Men and health help seeking behaviour: literature review.*J Adv Nurs*, 2005 49 (6), 616- 623.

[8] Lewis, C; O'Brien, M. Constraints on fathers: research, theory and clinical practice. In Reassessing Fatherhood, Sage, 1-19, London 1987.

[9] King MB, Eating disorders in a general practice population: prevalence, characteristics and follow-up at 12 to 18 months. *Psychol Med* (Monogr. Suppl.), 14, 1-34, 1989

[10] Hoek HW. : The incidence and prevalence of anorexia nervosa and bulimia nervosa in primary care. *Psychol Med.*, 21(2), 455-460, 1991.

[11] Bursten MS, Gabel LL, Brose JA, Monk JS. Detecting and treating bulimia nervosa: how involved are family physicians? *J Board Fam Pract*, 9 (4), 241-248, 1996.

[12] Boulé CJ, McSherry JA. Patients with eating disorders. How well are family physician managing them? Can Fam Physician, 48, 1807-1813, 2002.

[13] Ogg EC, Millar Hr, Pusztai EE, Thom AS. General practice consultation patterns preceding diagnosis of eating disorders. *Int J Eat Disord*, 22, 89-93, 1997.

[14] Bryant-Waugh RJ, Lask BD, Shafran L, Fosson AR. Do doctors recognise eating disorders in children? *Archives of Disease in Childhood*, 67, 103-105, 1997.

[15] Becker AE, Thomas JJ, Franko DL, Herzog DB. Interpretation and use of weight information in the evaluation of eating disorders: counselor response to weight information in a national eating disorders educational and screening program. *Int J Eat Disord*, 37, (1), 38-43, 2005.

[16] American Psychiatric Association Practice guideline to the treatment of patients with an eating disorders. *Am J Psychiatry*, vol. 163, 7, 2006.

[17] Currin L, Schmidt U, Waller G. Variables that influence diagnosis and treatment of eating disorders within primary care settings: a vignette study. *Int J Eat Disord*, 40, 257-262, 2007.

[18] Turnbull S, Ward A, Treasure J, Jick H, Derby L. The demand for eating disorder care. An epidemiological study using the general practice research database. *Br J Psychiatry* 169, 705-712, 1996.

[19] Currin L, Waller G, Treasure J, Nodder J, Stone C, Yeomans M, Schmidt U. The use of guidelines for dissemination of " Best practice" in primary care of patients with eating disorders. *Int J Eat Disord* 40, 476-479, 2007.

[20] Striegel-Moore RH, Leslie D, Petrill SA, Garvin V, Rosenheck RA. One-year use and cost of inpatient and outpatient services among female and male patients with an eating disorder: evidence from a national database of health insurance claims.*Int J Eat Disord*, 27, 381-389, 2000.

[21] Striegel-Moore RH. Health services research in anorexia nervosa. *Int J Eat Disord* , 37, 531-534, 2005.

[22] Ackard DM, Vik N, Neumark-Sztainer D, Schmitz KH, Hannan P, Jacobs D. Disordered eating and body dissatisfation in adolescent with type 1 diabetes and a population-based comparison sample:comparative prevalence and clinical implications. *Pediatr Diabetes*, 9 (part 1) 312-319, 2008.

[23] National Collaborating centre for Mental health. Eating disorders. Core interventions in the treatment and management of anorexia nervosa, bulimia nervosa and related eating. National Clinical Practice Guideline. N.9. Leicester and London: British Psychological Society and Gaskell., 2004.

[24] Neumark-Sztainer D, Patterson J, Mellin A, Ackard D, Utter J, Story M, Sockalosky J. Weight control practices and disordered eating behaviors among adolescent females and males with type 1 diabetes. *Diabetes care* 25, 1289-1296, 2002.

[25] Nielsen S, Emborg C, Molbak A. Mortality in concurrent Type 1 diabetes and anorexia nervosa. *Diabetes Care*, 25, 309-313, 2002.

[26] DeBate RD, Plichta S, Tedesco LA, Kerschbaum WE. Integration of oral health care and mental health services: dental hygienists' readiness and capacity for secondary prevention of eating disorders. *J Behav Health Serv Res*, 33 (1), 113-125, 2005.

[27] DiGioacchino DeBate R, Tedesco L. Increasing dentists' capacity for secondary prevention of eating disorders: identification of training, network, and professional contingencies. *J of dental education*, vol 70, 10, 1066-1075, 2006.

[28] Beumont P, Hay P, Beumont D et al. Australian and New Zealand clinical practice guidelines for the treatment of anorexia nervosa. *Australian and New Zealand Journal of Psychiatry*, 38, 659-670, 2004.

[29] Kyriacou MA, Treasure J, Schmidt U. Understanding how parents cope with living with someone with anorexia nervosa: modelling the factors that are associated with carer distress. *Int J Eat Disord*, 41, 233-242, 2008.

Chapter 2

MEDICAL EVALUATION OF EATING DISORDERS: FOCUS ON GENDER DIFFERENCES

M. Gualandi

ABSTRACT

The medical aspects of Eating Disorders will be discussed in this chapter.

Many items will be considered: the request for help, the first approach to the patient, the physical assessment and the diagnostic procedures. Finally, the main medical manifestations of Anorexia and Bulimia nervosa will be reviewed and some hints about treatment and outcome of medical complications in Eating Disorders will be given.

The role of primary care practitioners and the contribution of the experts in internal medicine to the multidisciplinary team work will be reviewed as crucial points of the global intervention.

All of these aspects will be discussed in relation to the main guidelines, the literature scientific reports and the experience of our Unit for Eating Disorders.

Gender differences of Eating Disorders will be underlined with a specific focus on males, an intriguing low risk population.

INTRODUCTION

EDs are psychiatric conditions complicated by multiple organ dysfunctions due to malnutrition, binging, purging and excessive compulsive exercise, potentially leading to a variety of severe, life threatening medical consequences.

Because of the complexity of these disorders the optimal assessment and appropriate management of EDs should require different professional figures, able to recognize the relationship among psychological, physical and social aspects and to work together in a coordinated team.

This multidisciplinary model has been recognized as the best model of intervention and it is recommended by the main international guidelines based on evidence studies [1,2].

APA practice guidelines 2006 [1] on EDs indicate as a recommendation of first degree care- recommended with substantial clinical confidence - a model based on a team approach: "*in treating adults with ED, the psychiatrist may assume the leadership role within a program or team that includes other physicians, psychologists, registered dieticians, and social workers or may work collaboratively on a team led by others. For the management of acute and ongoing medical and dental complications, it is important that psychiatrists consult other physician specialists and dentists. When a patient is managed by an interdisciplinary team in an outpatient setting, communication among the professionals is essential for monitoring the patient's progress, making necessary adjustments to the treatment plan, and delineating the specific roles and tasks of each team member.*"

Epidemiologic data, reported in this book in Part 1- Chapter 2, shows how ED generally affects young people, in well developed countries, and in females much more than males. As it has already been reported in previous chapters, during the last two decades new and interesting data concerning EDs in males has been published: some authors [3] have reported an increased proportion of males seeking treatment, by analyzing the percentage of total admissions of males between 1984 and 1997, in an inpatient eating disorder service. In contrast with this study, a recent research, concerning a clinical cohort of 2,554 new patients evaluated during a period of 21 years (from 1987 to 2006) in a specialized ED Unit for adults, did not point out any increase over time of the proportion of males, and calculated them, on average, at 5 % of all patients [4].

Both of these studies were limited to a clinical male population: therefore it has been supposed that prevalence and incidence of EDs in males could be still underestimated in clinical settings because of underdiagnosis. Several factors may contribute to underdiagnose of an ED in a male patient; among these, cultural bias and the presence of new symptoms such as body dysmorphic symptoms, still poorly recognized as warning aspects in males [5].

Therefore greater attention should be paid to new risk factors and to new signs of EDs in this low risk population: their knowledge is particularly relevant because it is well known how early diagnosis and treatment are crucial for a good prognosis, especially in adolescents.

In the present chapter the different steps of medical intervention and the main somatic complications of anorexia, bulimia and ED-NOS (excluding BED) will be reviewed, focusing on peculiarities - if present - of male patients in comparison with females.

2.0. From Seeking Help to the Medical Evaluation

Medical assessment may be advised and required by different figures besides the subject himself, generally depending upon age.

Family members, teachers, coaches, friends may recognize and be alarmed by the presence in their son, friend or student of unhealthy behaviours or signs such as excessive exercise, altered alimentary patterns, weight fluctuations or growth retardation and consequently they may encourage a medical check.

In other cases, the subject himself may ask directly for a visit in the primary care setting or he may seek help with a variety of ED related symptoms to other specialists such as dentists, dieticians, gastroenterologists (for instance when dental erosions, constipation or abdominal pain are present).

Actually, the diagnosis may still be more difficult and delayed for a male [6] and this is a critical point if we consider that most medical complications of EDs are more treatable if diagnosed early.

This difficulty may be due to many factors limiting awareness of the actual risk of EDs in males such as:

- The stereotype that EDs are female illnesses: the diffusion of epidemioloic data concerning the major reported prevalence and incidence of EDs in females may limit a full understanding of the problems faced by a male patient; therefore the diagnostic suspicion may be delayed even in qualified settings.
- ED males are not represented in the media: TV, cinema, books reported very often the drama of young women engaged in a struggle against anorexia or bulimia. Men with similar problems are not generally represented in the media and therefore men are less present in the collective belief as potentially eating disordered patients.
- The lack of a dramatic and visible event such as the absence of menstrual cycle makes the diagnosis in males more difficult, besides representing a critical point of DSM-IV criteria.
- The shame and fear for a male subject to suffer from a typical "female illness."

In contrast with these stereotypes, male's concerns about weight and new trends about masculine body image are rapidly increasing.

A new and more muscular image of men is emerging in the media, suggesting a new body ideal to both men and young boys.

Men are now required to be shaped, as fair and fashionable as women.

This new model is becoming a cultural risk factor for the development of EDs in men.

An increased knowledge and consciousness about these new risk factors and warning signs such as dysmorphophobia [7] or compulsive exercise could help to detect an ED in a male and to avoid delays in diagnosis or underdiagnosis.

2.1. The Role of Primary Care

Most people suspected to be affected by an ED are likely to be evaluated for the first time by a PCP: therefore the PCP should be skilled in recognizing and managing an eating disordered patient and should be able to collaborate with other professional figures, experienced at diagnosis and treatment of EDs.

The PCP may deal with subjects who are not collaborative or not able to recognize their disorder.

A subject who denies the psychological nature of his behaviour represents a real challenge for the physician.Therefore, during the first approach it may be useful to start with unthreatening questions, not too specific, just to engage the patient.

Once a good relationship with the subject is established, further questions could clarify if the patient has an ED or not. These questions may be unstructured, focused on patient's weight and shape concerns or structured following, for instance, the SCOFF Questionnaire[1], a

[1] The SCOFF Questionnaire is considered one valid and reliable screening tool for detecting the existence of an eating disorder. The questions focus on some key characteristics of anorexia and bulimia:

tool well validated and frequently used in Great Britain, as well as DSM-IV Diagnostic Criteria.

After engagement it is possible to initiate the diagnostic phase.

The medical evaluation of a subject suspected to have an ED must be directed to define the clinical condition through an accurate physical examination and selected diagnostic tools. Emergent or critical aspects must be identified as soon as possible so that the type of care setting may be correctly indicated. It may be useless and dangerous to refer the patient primarily to a full psychiatric intervention if the subject is, for instance, severely emaciated and needs overall to be hospitalized for nutritional therapy and for control of medical complications (see Guidelines for Hospitalization). In this case, the experts in the mental area, preferably working inside a multi-professional team for EDs should be alerted and should be aware of the risk of mortality caused by malnutrition or other medical complications: they are required, in this phase, to be present and support the intervention of physicians utilizing collaborative teamwork.

If the subject is not severely ill, the PCP may have time to better investigate the presence of possible risk factors for an ED, the family and personal history and the co-existence with other diseases.

It may be also necessary to perform a differential diagnosis through additional tests.

At the end of this diagnostic phase, in presence of a possible ED subject, the referral to mental area specialists or, whenever available, to a multidisciplinary expert team for a final validation of diagnosis and an adequate treatment plan is mandatory.

The PCP should also play a central role in maintaining continuity of care even when the patient undergoes a sequence of different treatment settings.

All these steps of a full clinical evaluation will be now extensively described.

2.2. The Medical Assessment

The Family History

The patient's history must be accurately assessed, and focused on specific risk factors for EDs in males. As male patients are actually a population at low risk for developing an ED, it is particularly relevant to find out specific risk factors, even more than in the female population in which sex and age represent the major risk factors.

At first it is important to ask the subject about the presence of EDs in the family (mother, father and first degree relatives).

In most studies regarding primarily females both AN and BN are reported significantly more common among family members than in the general population and both genetic and environmental factors are involved in family clustering [8-14].

There is a growing evidence that males affected by EDs may also have a pattern of familial aggregation similar to females' patterns [15,16] or even stronger, as suggested by the

- Do you make yourself **Sick** because you feel uncomfortably full?
- Do you worry you have lost **Control** over how much you eat?
- Have you recently lost more than **One** stone in a 3 month period?
- Do you believe yourself to be **Fat** when others say you are too thin?
- Would you say that **Food** dominates your life?

results from a nationwide study of Finnish twins [17] focused on male AN. It has been suggested by these authors that "in order to develop an ED men require a stronger genetic predisposition and more adverse environmental factors than women." Another research [18] concerning a large number of both males and females has instead demonstrated that a maternal history of an eating disorder is a risk factor only in young adolescent females: in males only negative comments about weight by fathers were predictive of starting to binge at least weekly.

Another important issue in the family history is the presence of overweight and obese members of the family.

In a study involving 135 males affected by EDs (30 AN, 62 BN, 43 EDNOS) overweight/obesity was present in 53 % of the parents. Bulimic patients were more likely to have a parental history of overweight in comparison with anorectic patients [19].

In another study conducted on a small size sample of anorectic boys all the mothers and fathers were found to be overweight, even though obesity was present only in the fathers who also showed moderate to severe degrees of alcoholism [20].

Crisp reported in a research (1986), involving 36 AN male patients, 100 AN female patients and their families, that weight disorders were even more common in males' families than in females'. Males had a higher percentage of AN in the mothers and a higher percentage of obesity in the fathers when compared with the female group[21]. Many years later Crisp confirmed these earlier reports through the analysis of the overall data from a data base including 751 AN females and 62 AN males [22]. Psychiatric aspects in the family members have already been presented in Part 1 -Chapter 7.

Personal History and Lifestyle

The main areas to investigate in collecting the personal (previous and current) history of the patients are the following: presence at birth of a perinatal/obstetric trauma, pubertal development and growth patterns, history of weight, type of occupation, life style – exercise, alcohol- tobacco- substance use/abuse - alimentary patterns and eating unhealthy behaviours (binging, compensative and purging behaviours), sexual drive and medical co-morbidity.

Psychological characteristics such as perfectionism, attention to body image, life events, gender identity problems, psychiatric comorbidity should, instead, be assessed by specialists in the mental area, experts in EDs.

The physician should instead consider:

- **Obstetric complications**

There is a growing evidence that a variety of complications related to the health of offsprings and their mothers is associated to a higher risk of anorexia among girls [23]. A recent study in eating disordered females has demonstrated that pathological events related to their birth such as maternal anaemia, diabetes mellitus, pre-eclampsia, placental infarction, neonatal cardiac problems and hyporeactivity resulted in significant independent predictors of the onset of anorexia. Placental infarction, neonatal hyporeactivity, early eating difficulties, and low birth weight for gestational age were instead significantly associated to the risk of bulimia [24]. Therefore, it may be relevant to investigate such pathologic events even though, so far, no similar research including males has been performed.

- **Weight History**

Among children and adolescents, the most important indicators of an adequate caloric intake are represented by growth curves and standard deviation scores (Zeta score) for height and weight in a reference population [25].

In adults, Body Mass Index (BMI) is considered the most important and reliable anthropometric index in order to analyze the post pubertal weight fluctuations (see paragraph on "Anthropometric measurements").The weight assessment in the adult should be comprehensive of the following information: the pre-morbid highest and lowest weight, the weight maintained for the longest time and the desired weight. Also, weight loss or weight gain percentages of Ideal Body Weight (IBW) have been considered useful indicators of unhealthy weight.

Weight history can reveal a previous subclinical undiagnosed disease or unhealthy behaviours - such as restrictive dieting and overeating - that represent relevant risk factors for developing an eating disorder.

A history of overweight or obesity has been reported as more common in males than in females with EDs [26-28]. Also, the highest lifetime weight is higher in males than in females [3]: other authors confirmed these results, especially in bulimic males [19].

Nevertheless, overweight males seem to be less exposed than females to the risk of dieting because they have a different perception and a more positive idea of their weight.

In adolescence this difference between genders is less evident and the onset of an eating disorder may be triggered by dieting in overweight male adolescents when they perceive they are fat [5].

A two year follow up in an early adolescent school population found overweight to be antecedent to the development of some form of ED both in males and in females, probably due to dieting [29].

- **Life style**

Life style can have an impact on the development and course of an eating disorder. Therefore alcohol and substance abuse as well as smoking and exercise must be carefully analyzed.

The association between alcohol abuse and EDs has been deeply investigated through a multicenter research concerning only females [30]: the results of this study indicated that alcohol use disorder was significantly more prevalent in women with ANbp and BN than in women with ANr ($p = .0001$); the majority of subjects reported primary onset of the eating disorder; only one third reported the onset of the alcohol abuse before the development of ED.

Another interesting research performed in a non-clinical population of both males and females [31] has investigated the relationship between unhealthy eating attitudes and health related behaviours such as alcohol/ tobacco use and exercise.

According to the results of this study alcohol, smoking, and exercise were each associated with disturbed eating attitudes, particularly with specific items such as the drive for thinness, body dissatisfaction and perfectionism. Interactive effects of gender upon EDI scores were significant only in the use of exercise. In fact, women in comparison with males appeared to exercise for different reasons, such as to escape the negative consequences of weight gain, while men generally exercised for positive goals like fitness and muscularity.

Furthermore less frequent laxative abuse in males than in the females has been reported by different studies [3,5,21].

An important review of 51 studies concerning comorbidity of EDs and substance abuse has showed that substance abuse among eating disordered women was stronger in BN than in AN: similarly ANr subjects were less prone to substance abuse than ANbp subjects [32].

Attitude towards exercising must be investigated to understand whether the subject is engaged in healthy sporting activity or instead being driven or compelled to exercise in order to control his weight, to alter his shape and burn off calories (Part 1, Chapter 4).

- **Sexual drive**

Sexual drive represents a very important issue in the history of male patients where the lack of a visible and early symptom such as amenorrhea makes diagnosis more difficult than in females.

It has been reported that males with EDs have less sexual intercourses before the onset of the disease or at the time of first evaluation in comparison with females with EDs [33,34]. Gender identity concerns are considered important risk factors for the development of an eating disorder [35,36] and may be one of the reasons of sexual problems in a male subject (see Part 1-Chapter 5).

In some cases an early impairment of gonadal axis (effect of excessive exercise or altered alimentary patterns or both) may cause early symptoms such as a decreased sexual desire in a pre-diagnostic phase, similarly to early amenorrhea (when amenorrhea has its onset before weight loss).

In a study by Pope, males with BN appear to be more sexually active than males with AN, both before and during their illness [37].

- **Concurrent general medical conditions**

Diabetes Mellitus The comorbidity of Diabetes Mellitus type 1(DM-1) and EDs has been investigated by several researchers in females: in some cases no significant association was found between the two conditions [38,39]: on the contrary in other studies the prevalence of clinical EDs in young DM-1 females was reported to be much higher than in non-diabetic females, with a prevalence ranging from 5 to 15 % [40,41]: a meta-analysis of controlled studies on this argument, performed by Mannucci et al., showed that BN especially was significantly more present in females with DM-1, in comparison with non-diabetic subjects [42]. Nissim et al. have reported that both ED-NOS and bulimia were more than twice as common in adolescent girls with DM-1 in comparison with their non-diabetic counterparts [43]. General practitioners or diabetes specialists have to pay particular attention to the coexistence of eating disorders and DM-1 because this complex situation can actually lead to serious medical problems related to the poorer metabolic control in these patients compared with DM-1 patients without an eating disorder.

The main reason of this metabolic imbalance seems to be the insulin misuse (skipping insulin or taking less insulin than prescribed) that represents one of the most common weight loss behaviour in girls with DM-1 and ED. The duration of severe insulin omission has been found to be associated to an increased risk of long term complications such as retinopathy and nephropathy [44,45]. APA guidelines 2006 - see the paragraph about concurrent general medical conditions : Type 1 diabetes[2] - suggest that insulin omission should be considered as a specific type of purging behaviour in the next DSM revision. The majority of DM-1 patients seems to develop an ED after the onset of diabetes [46]: in fact specific aspects of DM-1 and its management (for instance weight gain associated with initiation of insulin treatment and dietary restraint) may trigger the body dissatisfaction and the drive for thinness that accompany eating disturbances.

Not only is diabetes worsened by the presence of an ED but ED itself, if associated with diabetes, may be persistent [47] and more refractory to treatment in comparison with an ED without comorbidity [48]. Mortality rates resulted higher in patients affected by DM-1 and Anorexia Nervosa in comparison patients DM-1 or AN patients without comorbidity [49].

The majority of the studies concerning comorbidity between DM-1 and ED have included only female patients so that gender specificity concerns have not been deeply investigated. Nevertheless, some interesting studies including both males and females have been published and we will discuss their results. A large multicenter research [46] studied the prevalence of EDs in DM-1 and diabetes mellitus type 2 (DM-2) in 663 patients, there were 307 men and 356 women. The results indicated that EDs in the subsample of females affected by DM-1 were significantly higher in comparison with the male patients, while no significant difference was observed between males and females in the DM-2 sample. The same research showed that bulimia nervosa and ED-NOS were the prevalent EDs in Type 1 diabetes while in Type 2 the prevalent ED in both sexes was Binge Eating Disorder (BED).

Differently from insulin dependent diabetes, eating disorder, specifically BED, was present before the onset of diabetes type 2 in 90 % of cases; therefore the authors hypothesized that being overweight and obese –as a consequence of BED- might lead to type 2 diabetes in some patients.

Friedman S. et al. reported in a study including 69 patients affected by DM-1 that ED-NOS (bulimic type) was significantly more frequent in women than in men (43 % vs 21%); in females only 4.8% had a full syndrome represented by bulimia [50] while full syndromes were not diagnosed in males.

Neumark -Sztainer D.et al investigated the prevalence of "weight control practices /disordered eating behaviours" among adolescent females (70) and males (73) with type 1 diabetes.

The results of this research indicated a higher prevalence of unhealthy weight control practices in females (37.9 %) in comparison with males (15.9%): insulin misuse was, together with skipping meals, a typical weight control practice only for females, in fact only one man reported this behaviour. These habits were associated with poorer metabolic control as demonstrated by higher HB A1 [2] [51].

Being a young male seems -in diabetes type 1- to represent a protective factor against the development of an eating disorder: if an ED is still present, being male seems to represent a protective factor against insulin misuse.

Celiac Disease The association between celiac disease and EDs has been poorly investigated. Celiac Disease (CD) is an inflammatory disorder of small bowel triggered by intolerance to gluten and diagnosed through the presence of antibodies to transglutaminase (TGA). It is a frequent disease (1/100), prevalent in women, that, in most cases, becomes symptomatic early, during childhood or adolescence. The manifestations of the disease are very different, ranging from a silent form to a full symptomatic one. Recent studies of the literature have reported some more data, both in adolescents and adults, about the

[2] HbA1c: measure of metabolic control that represents the mean glucose concentration for the 2 months preceding the test.

comorbidity of celiac sprue and eating disorder: an exploration of 10 cases has pointed out the clinical implications for the diagnosis and treatment of both illnesses [52]. In a case report of association between the two diseases the authors conclude that although the cause and effect relationship between anorexia nervosa and celiac disease is still unclear it may be relevant to rule out a celiac sprue particularly in subjects where nausea and bloating are prominent complaints [53]. A recent large systematic study assessed the current and lifetime rates of ED in adolescent celiac patients, looking also for sex differences: a higher rate of eating disorders, especially a higher rate of bulimia nervosa than expected, was found in celiac females and, in most cases, diagnosis of celiac disease preceded the onset of eating pathology by between 2 and 17 years: none of the CD affected males had an eating disorder. The same research compared the prevalence of EDs in CD subjects with the prevalence of EDs in DM-1 subjects: CD patients had lower prevalence rates of ED than DM-1 subjects but a statistical significance of this difference was not present except for subliminal ED (2.9% vs 9.4%) [54]. More and multicentric data are necessary in order to define whether the association between these two diseases, both prevalent in young females, is casual or has a pathogenetic relationship. The need for a gluten free diet in a adolescent female could represent a trigger for developing an ED, similarly to other chronic conditions, since it requires a particular focus on dieting for medical reasons. Could antigens passing through an impaired intestinal barrier be responsible for the psychiatric disorder? These questions are still unanswered and need more research in order to be clarified.

Current Symptoms

In some cases symptoms in EDs may be absent or, instead, present but not relevant for the subject or, finally, denied. These aspects are particularly present in males: they are less likely to seek treatment and this delay in diagnosis may result in a higher risk for developing medical complications [6].

During the first visit, it is important to help the patient recognize his discomfort with specific questions and to motivate him to go into the diagnostic phase, even though he apparently feels well. Symptoms are due to the functional/adaptative and organic consequences of malnutrition and unhealthy behaviours.

Although most symptoms of EDs are similar between men and women the absence of a visible and early symptom such as amenhorrea is one of reasons why diagnosing AN in males is frequently overlooked and delayed. A symptom due to the same origin of amenorrhea, the hypothalamic- hypopituitary-hypogonadism, is the decrease of sexual drive in men but this symptom does not have the same diagnostic value as the loss of menstrual cycle.

Most males affected by AN control their weight through intense exercise in lieu of purging behaviours, and laxative abuse is not frequent in males [5], therefore purging related symptoms are less frequent in males.

Most common symptoms of AN and BN are summarized in Tables I and II : in bold are potentially gender related differences.

Table I Prevalent symptoms in AN

- Anxiety, irritable mood
- Lethargy, poor concentration
- Fatigue, weakness
- Palpitation
- Dizziness, faintness, syncope
- Muscle aches ,cramps
- Head ache
- Constipation
- Cold intolerance
- Abdominal pain
- Dispepsia
- **Amenorrhea**
- **Decreased sexual drive (male)**

Table II Prevalent symptoms in BN

- Irritable mood
- Apathy, poor concentration
- Weakness
- Palpitation
- **Abdominal pain and discomfort in vomiting**
- **Heartburn**
- **Bloating in laxative abusers**
- **Bowel irregularities**
- **Throat ache**
- **Teeth ache**
- Headache, dizziness

Physical Examination

The physical examination is the most important step of the diagnostic phase.

Clinicians are required to promptly identify any sign indicating a severely ill subject, such as emaciation, altered hemodynamic status, excessive sinus bradicardia or abdominal pain. To do this, they have to to assess the subject with their eyes and with their hands but also they must get some objective measurements.

Anthropometric measurements and evaluation of physical signs are the two main steps of the physical examination.

1. ***Anthropometric measurements*** are necessary tools for the definition of normal growth and healthy nutritional status in adolescents and adults. The main nutritional index used for the evaluation of an adult subject is the *Body mass index (BMI): BMI* is a simple ratio of weight-in kilograms- divided by the square of the height in metres (kg/m^2): it is the most important and reliable anthropometric index in adults.

BMI is used to screen for weight categories (Table III) that may lead to health problems: the values associated with the lowest health risks, therefore to highest life expectancy, are the values between 18.5 and 25.

Table III Weight categories by BMI

BMI < 18.5	underweight
BMI 18.5-25	normal weight
BMI 25-29.9	overweight
BMI >29.9	obesity

In men the diagnostic value of BMI is more limited than in women: the presence of good muscularity may hide an abnormal decrease of fat mass. Excessive fat mass decrease is known to be related to major medical complications even in the presence of a BMI in normal ranges. In these cases the assessment of body composition may be more useful to define the risk of organic damage.

Woodside, in a review on clinical aspects of EDs in males, writes: "When using body mass index (BMI), a higher BMI should be used for defining normal in men, most often 22 to 27, than for women, where 20 to 25 is the standard. While there is no uniform agreement on the BMI that qualifies for a diagnosis of anorexia, most clinicians use an index of 17.5 for women and 19 to 19.5 for men" [55].

BMI is not a suitable indicator for children who have still to grow up and to reach their full, adult height.

Growth centile charts (height and weight charts) should be used in these cases: they provide a fundamental tool to determine whether children and adolescents are regular in growth [56].

Weight loss as percentage of ideal body weight (IBW) is becoming less frequently used in recent years because BMI ranges for men and women are now considered to be more reliable than IBW related formulas.

Weight loss as percentage of usual weight is the result of : usual weight – current weight, /usual weight x 100. This is an important parameter because even relevant medical complications may occur in case of an high degree and rapidity of weight loss even though BMI is still mantained into normal ranges. This aspect may be even more observed in males, particularly in overweight males.

The analysis of body composition also contributes to better define nutritional status: the human body is composed by two main compartments, fat mass (FAT) and fat free mass (FFM). Body composition may be assessed through several methods; the most commonly used are the measure of skinfold thickness, the bioelectric impedance analysis and Dual-energy X-ray absorptiometry. Skinfold thickness, representative of percent body fat, may be measured through plicometry: in men the three preferential sites are chest, abdomen and thigh, while triceps, suprailiac site and thigh are the three preferred sites in women; this index is strictly correlated with BMI but, in presence of obesity or severe underweight, it is not reliable. Bioimpedentiometry (BIA) is based on the differences in electrical conductive properties of human body tissues, depending upon the content in water and electrolytes: it represents one of the most commonly applied tools for determining body composition. Dual-energy X-ray absorptiometry (DXA)is generally used to determine bone mineral density but it is also increasingly used to measure body composition in its three components: body fat, muscle, and bone mineral. Radiation exposure is very low, therefore this procedure is considered safe.

*2.**Evaluation of physical signs**:* physical signs may be caused by malnutrition, by binging/purging behaviours and/or by adaptive responses to starvation and excessive exercise.

Vital signs should always be measured during the first visit: body temperature, blood systemic pressure, pulse rate and rhythm, postural changes in pulse or in blood pressure must be taken by the physician in order to assess the basic body functions.

The physical examination is performed by evaluating the patient's general appearance and by the assessment of main organ systems.

General appearance is comprehensive of depressed mood, cognitive impairment, dermatologic abnormalities, dehydration, emaciation, pallor, evidence of lymph nodes, jaundice etc..

Prevalent physical signs are summarized in Tables IV-V, in bold are potentially gender related differences.

The physical findings in AN and BN are, in general, highly similar in males and females, nevertheless some differences may be present and need to be underlined.

BMI in anorectic and bulimic males is generally higher in comparison with females at first presentation.

In adolescence, stature and growth may be more altered in AN males rather than in AN females.

In bulimic males typical compensatory behaviours for weight control such as vomiting and abuse of laxative/pills are less likely than in bulimic females so that symptoms and signs related to purging behaviour are less present.

On the contrary, excessive exercise is particularly relevant in male anorexia and it is used not only for weight control but also for positive goals such as fitness and increasing muscularity focused on trunk and shoulder muscularity.

In some cases males are affected by muscle dismorphia: it is a form of body dismorphic disorder typical of males caused by the idea that one's body is not lean or muscular enough.

(Part 1 Chapter 3).

This disorder can lead over-intensive exercise, focusing on muscle mass, and may be related to anabolic steroid use for improving muscle bulk. Clinicians should be prepared to assess this kind of patient from a different point view, looking not only at BMI but also evaluating patient's body composition.

Table IV Prevalent signs in AN

- **Arrested growth in adolescent/altered puberal development**
- **Short stature**
- **Increased lean mass/fat mass ratio**
- **High Muscularity**
- Emaciation
- Pallor
- Dehidration
- Bradicardia
- Systemic hypotension
- Acrocianosis
- Hypercarotenemia
- Other dermatologic signs
- Oedema (periorbital, at the extremities)
- **Erosion of dental enamel in purging subtype AN**
- **Enlarged salivary glands in purging subtype AN**

Table V Prevalent signs in bulimia

- Arrhythmias
- Hypotension
- **Oedema (periorbital, at the extremities)**
- **Periorbital petechiae**
- **Abdominal bloating/pain**
- Dermatologic signs
- **Dental caries with enamel's erosion**
- **Erythema of pharynx**
- **Enlarged salivary glands**
- **Glossitis, cheilitis**
- **Bleeding from the upper intestinal tract**
- **Increase of muscle mass**
- **Higher mean weight**

Laboratory and Instrumental Procedures

Laboratory and instrumental investigations should be generally limited to baseline investigations, helpful in assessing and diagnosing the medical condition; ruling out other diagnosis or the presence of severe clinical features which may require additional tests.

Baseline investigations are biochemistry routine tests (electrolytes, blood urea nitrogen, creatinine level, glucose, liver function tests), full blood count, calcium, phosphorus, magnesium, thyroid hormones in AN, gonadic hormones in AN, a baseline Electrocardiogram, DXA in AN if a severe underweight is present at least since 6 months.

In anorexia, even though in presence of severe weight loss, blood chemistry tests may result in normal ranges at the time of first evaluation: sometimes they apparently worsen after rehidration, such as haemoglobin level.

These normal laboratory results should not deceive clinicians and influence decisions about the need for a more intensive treatment if the patient is at risk.

The patient could use the negativity of laboratory tests in order to demonstrate his good health and try to avoid more intensive treatment: therefore it is useful that the clinicians provide correct information to the patient about the fact that adaptive mechanisms due to starvation such as the decrease of basal metabolism and hypervagotonia may be able to reduce caloric expenditure and create an apparent equilibrium.

Both patients and clinicians must be aware that a breakdown of these mechanisms can lead to potential lifethreatening consequences .

Leucopenia, particularly neutropenia and normocromic normocitic anemia, due to bone marrow depression, may be the first laboratory changes in restrictive anorexia, while electrolyte imbalance with hypopotassiemia may represent the first sign of purging anorexia or bulimia.

ECG 12 standard derivations can show a severe sinusal bradicardia in anorexia or arrhythmias in anorexia and bulimia; Dxa scan should be always be requested, independently from the current BMI, from gender and diagnostic class of eating disorder if current or postpuberal lifetime underweight has been present at least for six months in the history of the patient. In fact osteopenia and osteoporosis are very frequent and potentially irreversible complications and the old concept that only anorectic amenorrhoic females could be affected by these problems has not been confirmed by recent literature data .

Differential Diagnosis

Because changes in appetite and weight are commonly caused by many medical conditions, it is important to rule out cancer, endocrine disturbances, chronic infections as well as other illnesses causing a weight loss before assuming that the symptoms are of psychiatric origin. This is especially the case when weight loss or weight gain occur in conjunction with other ED unrelated symptoms and/or when psychopathological thoughts are resolutely denied by the patient.

The diseases more frequently involved in differential diagnosis are summarized in Table VI.

Table VI Main diseases to be considered in differential diagnosis

- Gastroenteric diseases such as inflammatory bowel diseases (IBD), malabsorption syndromes, intestinal parasitic infections, chronic pancreatitis, celiac disease, blood diseases (i.e lymphoma)
- Cancer
- Chronic infections (HIV infection, Tubercolosis)
- Cystic fibrosis
- Diabetes mellitus
- Cushing syndrome, Addison’s disease
- Neurologic disease (hypotalam lesions or tumors)

2.3. The Referral to Specialists

During the medical assessment, the diagnosis of an eating disorder may be highly suspected but its validation, in any case, must be done by the psychiatrist.

The referral to the psychiatrist may be hardly accepted by the patient: he might be frightened to face a specialist of mental diseases, even more if he has been so far denying symptoms or on the contrary he has been focused only on somatic manifestations of the disease without recognizing their psychological origin.

The physician should communicate that the clinical picture may be due to abnormal thinking patterns concerning weight and body image expressed through unhealthy and harmful behaviours: he should also give the patient correct information about organic complications and related risks in terms of morbidity and mortality of an untreated ED disease.

The multidisciplinary team is responsible for validation of diagnosis and an adequate treatment plan.

A registered dietician, skilled in dealing with ED, is another basic professional figure who must be included in the teamwork: he has to investigate about alimentary patterns, the history of the weight and its fluctuations, the degree of the restriction, of purging, binging and compulsive exercise.

The dietician needs to share all these pieces of information with the other components of the ED team: each intervention concerning nutrition and weight requires an agreement between all the professional figures.

The physician working in the team should complete the disease staging through second level investigations; he should treat and monitor the medical complications, cooperate with the team in indicating the level of care, the treatment site and the need and timing for hospitalization – see Levels of Care APA 2006[3]-due to medical complications and finally collaborate for safe weight restoration through a refeeding treatment plan, carefully monitoring the whole refeeding phase.

2.4. Main Medical Complications of EDs: Anorexia Nervosa

AN is a psychiatric disease characterized by a wide range of medical complications. Only half of patients have good outcome, the others have intermediate or poor outcome at risk for chronicity and death; the overall mortality rate is high, much more than in any other psychiatric disease [57,58]: Steinhausen reported in a meta-analysis of 119 studies globally including 5590 total patients a crude rate of mortality of 5% and 9% at a follow up of ten years [59]. In a very recent study Papadopoulos reviewed the outcome of six thousand and nine women who had an inpatient treatment for anorexia nervosa, finding an overall mortality

---

3 APA 2006 guidelines concerning the hospitalization : For adults: Heart rate <40 bpm; blood pressure <90/60 mmHg; glucose < 60 mg/dl; potassium < 3 mEq/L; electrolyte imbalance; temperature < 97.0°F; dehydration; hepatic, renal, or cardiovascular organ compromise requiring acute treatment; poorly controlled diabetes Weight as percentage of healthy body weight <85%, acute weight decline with food refusal even if not <85% of healthy body weight.The same guidelines suggest that" Hospitalization should occur before the onset of medical instability as manifested by abnormalities in vital signs…"

rate of 6.2%. This high mortality was attributable to suicide or to medical complications of AN, first of all to cardiovascular complications [60].

The main outcome data of AN, emerging from a wide body of studies performed during a decade (1980-1990), were reviewed by Pike [61]: the analysis showed an overall outcome - expressed as either good, intermediate or poor - ranged respectively from 27% to 58% (good outcome), from 20% to 40% (intermediate outcome) and from 16% to 37% (poor outcome).

Medical complications are obviously prevalent in full syndromes but they may be present and severe also in partial syndromes, which represent the major part of EDs [62]. The systemic and organ specific consequences depend upon the degree and duration of malnutrition, the rapidity of weight loss and the type of compensative behaviours (purging behaviours, compulsive exercise, fasting). Even adaptive mechanisms to starvation, especially concerning cardiovascular system, may provoke negative effects.

These adaptive responses may occur because malnutrition of EDs has different peculiarities in comparison with other types of malnutrition: it is generally due to a caloric deficiency more than protein deficiency, therefore vital functions are preserved for a long time; both fat mass and fat free mass are decreased; it generally arises in a healthy organism, being caused by a psychiatric disease. For all these reasons, if weight loss is not acute, the organism is able to organize a kind of metabolic defence through the decrease of resting metabolic rate. This homeostatic response may create an apparent metabolic equilibrium, even for a long time.

The main somatic changes allowing this equilibrium to exist in a common way is the decrease of resting metabolic rate.

Resting metabolic rate (RMR)[4] accounts for 50-70% of total energy expenditure and depends upon different factors:

-Body surface area: the more elevated height and weight are the higher RMR is
-Gender: females have a RMR 5-10 % lower in comparison with males.
-Body composition: fat mass is metabolically less active than lean mass
-Physical exercise: a regular physical exercise leads to an higher RMR. Athletes may have a RMR increase up to 20%.
-Age: RMR decreases of 2-5 % per decade after 25 years.

Anorectic patients have a variable decrease of RMR from 10% up to 50% in relation to a severe caloric restriction, due to a lower percentage of FFM together with the decrease of T3 [63,64].

Moreover, fasting induces a decrease of sympathetic tone and a consequent prevalence of vagal tone leading to bradicardia and orthostatic hypotension.

It is well known that a regular and intense exercise enhances vagal activity worsening bradicardia. These cardiovascular changes lead to minor caloric requirements through a decrease of RMR but at the same time put the patient at risk for negative cardiac events.

Despite these adaptive responses the persistence of severe malnutrition and of unhealthy behaviours may lead to damage to all vital organs such as the heart, bones, gastrointestinal

---

4 Resting MetabolicRrate (RMR) is the amount of energy expenditure at rest, in a neutrally temperate environment after twelve hours of fasting and eight hours of sleep. The release of energy in this state is sufficient only for the functioning of all the vital organs.

system, bone marrow, brain and reproductive system. Some of these complications, even severe, are completely reversible with weight recovery, but some others are not fully reversible.

We are now going to discuss the clinical picture of anorexia focusing on male subjects who are at a very low risk of developing this disease. The question is: is it possible that males in comparison with females have different consequences of the ED in relation to the same percentage of weight loss and despite the fact that they are facing the same disease? Actually the *disease itself* is different in males because it does not have the same behavioural features as in women (less purging behaviours, for instance), the *organism* of a male is different; male body composition, muscularity and hormonal responses are different. For instance, could the earlier decrease of lean mass in males in comparison with females provoke more severe medical complications on male organisms in comparison with females? Fat mass, which is less metabolically active in comparison with lean mass, is more physiologically represented in women's bodies and functions as an energy reserve.

Therefore, considering BMI in males may be less meaningful than evaluating the loss of fat mass.

Amenorrhea, one of the main symptoms in women whose presence discriminates the different diagnostic categories, does not have a corresponding symptom in males .

The decrease of testosterone has not the same diagnostic and categorical usefulness. This aspect, together with a different diagnostic value of BMI, may create assessment bias in disease staging of the same disease in the two sexes.

Finally *the time of onset and the time of diagnosis* are different in males, both delayed in comparison with females. As already reported it is possible that the higher diagnostic delay may determine a higher number of medical complications in males at first presentation [6].

For all these reasons we could expect different manifestations of the disease.

Crisp, one of the most reliable expert of ED in both sexes, concludes in a wide review of all studies that even though the disease is similar in the two sexes, age of onset, psychopathologic aspects, compensative behaviours, timing of diagnosis and effects of malnutrition may be different in men and "may be important in terms of incidence, prevalence and outcome" [21].

Now the main medical complications will be described in general and specific gender related differences will be discussed.

Cardiovascular Complications

Mortality in severe anorexia nervosa is due in most cases to a cardiac sudden death caused by a ventricular arrhythmia. Sudden cardiac death may represent the final event of a series of structural and functional alterations in the heart.

Thereby clinicians should be aware of these cardiovascular changes and skilled in recognizing, as early as possible, the high risk related to some of these alterations.

The pathogenetic mechanisms of the cardiovascular complications can be summarized in these main pathways:

- *Direct damage of starvation on cardiac muscle*: autoptic data has shown in anorectic hearts a reduced left ventricular mass and a multifocal myofibrillar degeneration with consequent atrophy.

- *Electrolyte imbalance:* it is prevalent in purging anorexia and bulimia and may lead to arrhythmias.
- *Excess parasympathetic activity*: it is related to percent weight loss and physical exercise and produces bradicardia and increased heart rate variability.
- *Dehydration and hypovolemia*: these factors contribute to hypotension and reduced cardiac output.

Standard 12- lead electrocardiogram is a baseline investigation, mandatory in all cases of ED. 24 hour ECG monitoring, echocardiography, and exercise ECG may be used for a full cardiac assessment in selected cases.

ECG Changes

One of the most common cardiovascular features in AN is sinus bradicardia defined as a day time heart rate (HR) under 50 beats/minute and a night time HR under 46 beats/minute.

Bradicardia in anorexia nervosa represents the effect of homeostatic responses to starvation such as increased cardiac vagal activity and decreased thyroid function: physical exercise, if intense and regular, may also contribute to increase bradicardia through the increase of parasympathetic activity.

Cardiac vagal tone in anorexia has been measured in a research by Kollai and resulted to be about 30% higher than in healthy subjects. Vagal tone values were directly related to weight loss percentage [65].

In a study of Misra et al., regarding girls with AN, heart rate correlated positively with BMI, fat mass and percentage of body fat, while it was inversely correlated with the duration of the disease [66].

Bradicardia is generally considered a benign physiologic response to starvation particularly when associated to intense physical exercise.

In different studies the prevalence of bradicardia in AN females ranges from 26% [66] to 43% [67]. Generally bradicardia is well tolerated and does not need a specific treatment.

Nevertheless it is important to consider that low pulse rate is positively correlated to weight loss and therefore bradicardia must be considered one of the markers of disease severity.

Hospitalization and monitoring of the subject, even if asymptomatic, is advised by main guidelines if heart rate drops below 40/minute [1,2], in order to avoid or to early treat cardiovascular complications such as haemodinamic instability, atrioventricular blocks or hyperkinetic arrhythmias.

Another indicator of equilibrium between sympathetic and vagal responses is the heart rate variability (HRV) that represents the natural variability of cardiac frequency to a variety of stimuli. An unbalanced sympathovagal modulation of heart rate variability, due to relative sympathetic failure and prevalent vagal activity, has been reported both in anorexia and in bulimia [68,69].

The increase of Qtc interval, expression of a delayed myocardial re-polarization, has been reported by many authors in ED subjects.

QTc prolongation is a well known risk factor for the onset of malignant arrhythmias, particularly for the onset of a form of polymorphic ventricular tachycardia called "Torsade de pointes." In the Rotterdam QT Project, a QTc interval >440 milliseconds was found to be associated with a 2.3 times higher risk for sudden death compared with a QTc of 440 msec or less [70]. Isner et al. studied necropsy findings and ECG, performed one week before their sudden death, in three AN women: QT intervals were over 460 milliseconds in all the cases and there was no anatomic cause of death [71].

There is still contrasting data in the literature about the prevalence of QTc prolongation in AN patients. In a group of 41 AN patients including two males Cooke et al. found a significantly longer QT interval in patients with anorexia nervosa than in age and sex matched controls; they demonstrated also that there was a significant tendency toward a normal QT interval after refeeding [72]. Lesiskiene in a Medline searched all of the English language studies from 1994 to 2005 and collected measurements of QTc and mean heart rate from patients with diagnoses of AN: the QTc interval resulted within normal range even if it was significantly longer than in controls and the author concluded that: "*Further investigations of sudden death in patients with AN due to cardiac arrest are needed and a model of clinical monitoring of cardiovascular system should be elaborated. If QTc prolongation is detected even in the normal range further cardiological examination for risk assessment and systematic clinical surveillance of the cardiovascular system should be considered*"[73].

Nevertheless in the single subject the length of QTc interval represents a very important parameter and requires a particular attention if drugs lengthening QTc are administered.

Monitoring ECG is an useful tool in these cases to prevent worsening of QTc and the occurrence of malignant arrhythmias.

QTc dispersion is another heart parameter that represents the difference between the maximum and the minimum QTc interval in the 12 lead ECG and indicates dishomogeneity of the repolarization phase, likely due to a damaged myocardium.

It is increased in a variety of heart diseases but also in other medical conditions and it is considered another important risk factor for malignant arrhythmias and sudden death [74].

QTc dispersion has been studied in AN patients compared with healthy controls: it resulted significantly greater in AN [75] and according to different studies it has been related to a low metabolic rate [76] and to a reduction of left ventricular mass [77], both well known effects of a self-induced starvation.

In another extensive research [78] including all subtypes of eating disorder both QT interval and QT dispersion were significantly longer than in the control in all diagnostic categories.

In multiple regression analyses low weight, low BMI and rapid weight loss immediately preceding the examination were the most important independent predictors of QTc interval prolongation and dispersion [79].

Most studies on ECG changes in ED are performed in females and/or in limited samples of males so that it is difficult to perform a reliable analysis of specific gender differences in cardiovascular changes induced by ED.

A study on a small group of anorectic males patients reported a median pulse rate within normal ranges with only forty percent of subjects having a pulse rate of 80 beats/minute or more, therefore contrasting with the data from females. This higher pulse rate was considered by the authors as a sign of an initial heart failure consistent with a more severe clinical picture [60] in males than in females at the time of first assessment

Nevertheless, in a non-clinical population, gender related electrocardiographic and electrophysiologic differences are well known and possibly related to hormonal factors.

Women have a higher intrinsic heart rate than men, a longer corrected QT interval and a shorter sinus nodal recovery time. QT prolonging drugs in women are therefore more dangerous than in men. On the contrary, sudden death has a higher incidence in men [80].

Echocardiografic Findings

Among the more common cardiac findings in women affected by anorexia nervosa an increased prevalence of abnormal motion [81] and a prolapse of the mitral valve has been reported [82]: other authors found a high prevalence of this cardiac finding both in anorexia and bulimia [83]. This abnormality, generally due to a myxomatous deposition and prevalent in women, in anorexia nervosa is, on the contrary, due to a discrepancy between the valve's apparatus and ventricular chamber. Mitral valve prolapse in ED is not generally associated to valve regurgitation and it can be reversible with weight gain.

Mild pericardial effusion, generally silent, has been described in anorectic female patients [84,85]. In the reported studies only in one patient the risk of cardiac tamponade required pericardiocentesis [86].

Etiopathogenesis of pericardial effusion is still controversial; hypoprotidemia does not appear to be involved. In a study involving 14 anorectic adolescent females with a silent pericardial effusion, ranging from mild to severe, a statistically significant negative relation with FT3 levels and calorimetry was reported while a negative relation with BMI was present but not statistically significant [87].

In one case report a pericardial effusion of moderate degree and a low T3 syndrome following an important weight decrease (from a BMI 25.2 to a BMI 14.2 in one year) turned to normality after weight recovery. In this case a slight increase of serum level of plasma brain natriuretic peptide (BNP) was also present, even in absence of symptoms of heart failure and returned to a normal value after weight recovery [88].

Left ventricular mass and volumes are often reduced in anorexia and regional wall motion abnormalities have been observed [89].

Nevertheless, heart failure is not a frequent event in anorectic patient at diagnosis, even if occasionally reported [90]. On the contrary, heart failure is often reported in the refeeding phase. In this case hypophosphataemia and rapid infusion of liquids and nutrients may potentiate the effect of the described anatomic and functional cardiac changes.

All cardiac manifestations seem to be reversible with weight recovery [91].

The main cardiovascular abnormalities are summarized in Table VII.

Table VII Main cardiovascular abnormalities in AN

Clinical signs
Hypotension, Hortostatic hypotension
Hortostatic increased pulse rate
Impaired exercise capacity
Decreased pulse rate
Peripheral vasoconstriction (acrocianosis)

Ecg changes :
Low voltage, QT prolongation, QT dispersion

ST segment abnormalities
Sinus bradicardia
Arrhythmias
- *Atrioventricular block*
- *Torsade de pointes*
- *Ventricular fibrillation*
- *Ventricular tachycardia*

Echocardiographic findings
Left ventricular changes (decreased mass and volume)
Pericardial effusion
Mitral valve prolapse
Reduced cardiac output

Hematologic Changes

Haematological changes are a frequent and well known consequence of malnutrition in anorectic patients. These alterations may be underestimated because of spurious normal results due to dehydration and haemoconcentration and they may become evident only after refeeding and rehydration.

A recent review on this argument reported that the more frequent changes in peripheral blood cell count are leukopenia (29-36%) and anemia (21-39%), while thrombocytopenia is reported to be less frequent (between 5 and 11%). 50% of patients with normal blood parameters showed signs of bone marrow atrophy so that the authors conclude that normal blood parameters are not reliable predictors of bone marrow impairment [92].

These abnormalities are not generally due to iron, B12 and folic deficiencies. In fact anemia is generally normochromic and normocitic with a normal or high level of iron and ferritin: actually AN girls save their iron stores more than healthy girls because of the absence of their menstrual cycle. Nevertheless iron deficiency due to malnutrition may also be present and, if relevant, it can cause microcytic anemia.

In vegetarian AN subjects B12 levels may be low and cause macrocytic anemia, which is more rarely due to a folic deficiency.

Except these specific deficiencies the haematological changes in AN have been generally ascribed to a decreased cellularity of the bone marrow. The degree of cellular loss may range from a mild hypoplasia, with a relative increase of fat tissue, to a gelatinous transformation of the bone marrow (GMT) with fat cell atrophy in the most severe cases.

Gelatinous bone marrow transformation, also called serous atrophy, is characterized by fat cell atrophy, focal loss of haematopoietic cells and deposition of extracellular gelatinous substance, which is composed of mucopolisaccharides. GMT has been extensively studied by Bohm [93]. This author made an archive research on 80,000 marrow biopsies and among them he found 155 cases of gelatinous transformation. Data from this study indicated that gelatinous transformation was twice as prevalent in males in comparison with females and that the GMT underlying diseases were gender and age related: among young people anorexia nervosa, acute febrile states and AIDS were the more commonly represented diseases.

Another similar study on this argument found 65 GMT bone marrow out of the total 1,498 examined marrows [94]. Infections (in 31 cases), nutritional deficiencies (in 5 cases), haematological disorders (in 17 cases), malignancies (in 3 cases), and miscellaneous (in 9 cases) were the underlying diseases.

According to these studies GMT seems to be an indicator of severe illnesses more than a specific marker of a particular disease.

Much evidence on bone marrow GMT in AN has been accumulating during the last few decades [95, 96] since Pearson in 1967 and Mant and Faragher in 1972 first described this particular finding in AN patients [97, 98].

Warren reported signs of bone marrow hypoplasia in 46% of AN patients presenting changes in their total blood cell count [99].

Abella et al. studied bone marrows, obtained through aspirate and biopsy specimens, in 44 AN patients and only in 5 cases (11%) did they find normal bone marrow, while in the remaining patients others alterations ranging from hypoplasia to GMT were present [100]. Bone marrow changes were correlated with the amount of weight loss and were not linked to proportionate changes in peripheral blood parameters. The pathophysiological mechanisms of these bone marrow changes are not yet fully clarified even though some hypotheses have been formulated and subsequently studied: marrow fat depletion could create an adverse environmental for hematopoiesis as demonstrated in studies in vitro in which fat cells played a crucial role in stem cells mantainance [101].

Magnetic resonance imaging (MRI), a useful and non-invasive tool in showing bone marrow changes [102,103] has been used by Lambert et al. to investigate the relation between hematologic changes and total body fat mass depletion. The authors studied body composition through DXA and bone marrow through MRI: a decrease in marrow fat and hematopoietic cellularity was revealed by a MRI water like signal. AN patients presenting this particular MRI pattern had the most severe hematologic abnormalities, the lowest BMI and the higher decrease of subcutaneous fat thickness [104].

A recent study of an Italian group showed a strong relation between leukopenia and IgF1 deficiency and therefore suggested a role of Gh-IGF 1 axis in the pathogenesis of leukopenia [105].

In spite of the relevance of haematological changes in anorexia nervosa a complete recovery after weight gain has been reported in the mentioned studies.

Males, in limited case reports, present the same haematological changes and fat marrow atrophy as females [106,107]. An increase of hematocrit and red cells in males practicing body building or resistance sports might suggest the use of androgenic-anabolic steroids and in some cases represent an important sign of "reverse anorexia syndrome" [108] .

As far as concerns about the susceptibility to infections of AN patients, contradicting results have been reported in the literature.

Golla et al. reported normal T-lymphocyte populations and proliferative lymphocyte responsiveness to mitogenic stimulation in nine cases of AN patients; on the contrary an impaired cell-mediated immunity was reported in protein-calorie malnourished patients [109].

Devuyst found that severe infectious complications occurred in 9% of AN patients vs 0% of controls ($p = 0.01$) and that they were more frequent in patients with neutropenia (relative risk, 15.1: 95% CI, 10-20.2) or low (< 12) BMI [110].

Hotta et al. published two cases of mycobacteriosis in AN girls [111].

Reduced cutaneous reactions were reported in a group of twelve AN girls: four of them were anergic; the patients presented mild leucopenia and a slight decrease of both T4+ and T3+ numbers [112].

An adaptive response in chronic anorexia could enable the immune system to be preserved in a long duration disease: differently from protein-energy malnutrition, infectious diseases are actually rare in AN [113].

Pubertal Delay and Growth Retardation

It is well known that an adequate caloric intake, a normal weight and fat mass gain are essential for the pubertal development and the growth progression. Facing an adolescent suspected of being an eating disordered subject it is important to analyze his stage of pubertal development and his growth curves.

The paediatrician or the PCP, depending on the patient's age, can easily get premorbid height and weight measurements from medical charts or family members and evaluate the decrease in the height standard deviation score.

Stunting of growth during the prepubertal and pubertal period is a very frequent sign of anorexia nervosa of 6 months duration or more and it may be considered an additional criterion for the diagnosis of an eating disorder in childhood and adolescence [114].

Males have a longer duration of bone growth and higher caloric requirements than females so that the effect of malnutrition may be stronger in adolescent males compared with females [115].

During normal puberty, the level of sex steroids increases and consequently determines an increased level of GH (Growth Hormone) and IGF-I (Insulin-Like Growth Factor-1), a bone trophic hormone that stimulates longitudinal bone growth and mediates the action of GH.

In anorexia nervosa several hormonal changes may be present, such as low thyroxine (T4) and triiodothyronine (T3), increase of cortisol, low level of sex hormones, GH resistance with high or normal basal levels of GH, inappropriately low levels of IGF-I and Growth Hormone Binding Protein (GHBP).

All these alterations may contribute both to a growth retardation- which is potentially irreversible if the disorder occurs before closure of the epiphyses- and to an impaired acquisition of peak bone mass during the second decade of life.

A linear growth retardation in 11 of 12 male AN adolescents has been observed in a recent research: weight restoration resulted in accelerated linear growth in all patients with growth impairment but a complete catch-up growth was achieved only in two of the eleven subjects [116]. In other studies a complete catch up growth [117] or a failure in gaining any height despite of weight gain [118] has been reported .

Once weight is restored in growing AN males, plasma leuteinizing hormone and testosterone levels return to normal levels so that puberty, with its concurrent physiological consequences, is rekindled.

Osteopenia and Osteoporosis

Osteopenia and osteoporosis are the main medical complications of anorexia nervosa both in women and in men. They represent an early consequence of anorexia and may persist despite of weight recovery. Severe bone loss puts adolescent and adult patients at high risk for kifosis, short stature- particularly in males- and fractures.

ED-NOS and bulimia too may produce a decrease of bone mineral density (BMD)[5] but prevalence and severity of bone loss are generally lower than in anorexia.

Some hints about definition and classification of osteopenia and osteoporosis will now follow.

Osteopenia and osteoporosis are medical terms indicating different degrees of bone mineral density decrease.

Differently from osteopenia, osteoporosis is a severe and progressive disease of skeleton characterized not only by a BMD decrease but also by a profound deterioration of bone microarchitecture.

Osteoporosis produces an increase of bone fragility and susceptibility to non-traumatic fractures.

This condition is considered scarcely reversible. Bone mineral loss is demonstrated through DEXA scan whose results are generally reported as:

1) Measured density in g/cm square (BMD)
2) z-score, the number of standard deviations (SD) above or below the mean for the patient's age and sex: this value is used in premenopausal women, in men under the age of 50 and in children.
3) t-score, the number of standard deviations above or below the mean for a healthy 30 year-old adult of the same sex as the patient: this value is used in post-menopausal women and men over 50 because it better predicts risk of future fractures. The relative risk of fractures increases 1.5-3 times for each SD below the mean BMD.

World Health Organization (WHO) [119] so defined the BMD related categories:
"Normal. A value of BMD within 1 standard deviation of the young adult reference mean (T-score $\geq$ -1)
Low bone mass (osteopenia). A value of BMD more than 1 standard deviation below the young adult mean, but less than 2 standard deviations below this value (T-score < -1 and > -2.5).
Osteoporosis. A value of BMD 2.5 standard deviations or more below the young adult mean (T-score $\leq$ -2.5).
Severe osteoporosis (established osteoporosis). A value of BMD 2.5 standard deviations or more below the young adult mean in the presence of one or more fragility fractures."

Bone loss is dependent by many factors of physiologic and pathologic origin: physiologic factors affecting BMD are age and menopause. BMD decreases of 1-2% every year after thirties, both in males and in females. Age dependent osteoporosis involves trabecular and cortical bone (typical fracture of femoral neck). In postmenopausal women there is an

[5] Bone mineral density is the areal or surface density expressed as g/cm square, generally measured using Hologic dual-energy Xray absorptiometry (DXA Scan) at lumbar spine (L1-L4 level) and neck of femur.

increase of bone turnover related to estrogens' deficiency and a consequent bone mineral loss prevalent in trabecular bones such as vertebrae (typical vertebral fracture). Age and menopause related osteoporosis is defined as primary osteoporosis.

Osteoporosis is defined as secondary when it is due to pathologic genetic or acquired conditions such as preexistent: endocrine diseases (hyperthyroidism, hyperparathyroidism, hypercortisolism, hypogonadism), undernutrition (i.e. EDs), neoplasms, hemopathies, reumathic diseases, gastroenteric diseases (celiac disease or inflammatory bowel disease), or steroid therapy.

EDs are one of the causes of secondary osteoporosis.

Actually, bone loss represents one of the most serious and potentially irreversible complications of EDs. This complication is particularly severe when ED affect adolescents: it is well known that one of the most important determinants of BMD in adults is the amount of bone present at the end of skeletal maturation, called "peak bone mass" and that adolescence is the crucial period for achieving a normal bone growth and an optimal peak bone mass. All causes that alter the achievement of a normal peak bone mass in the adolescence will predispose the subjects to osteopenia and osteoporosis.

Differently from other causes of osteoporosis - such as postmenopausal or hypothalamic amenorrhea unrelated to anorexia – the decrease of BMD in EDs is particularly rapid and severe, due to a low bone turnover [120]: in fact on one side osteoclastic cells, not inhibited by estrogens, destroy bone, on the other side osteoblastic function is impaired in relation to an altered nutritional status. In menopause and hypothalamic amenorrhea osteoblastic function is preserved so that a high turnover, allowing a slower decline in BMD, may be present.

In addition to malnutrition and estrogen or testosterone deficiency - which are the main causes of BMD loss in EDs - other factors may contribute to the development of osteopenia and osteoporosis such as hypercortisolemia, IgF1 deficiency, rare or excessive exercise, Vitamin D and/or Calcium deficiency, smoke, alcohol and familiarity for osteoporosis.

Deficiencies in bone mineral density have been well documented in AN females by Rigotti et al. since 1980 [121] and subsequently confirmed by a wide body of literature both in adult [122] and in adolescent [123] females. Osteopenia and Osteoporosis represent an early complication of the disease [123]. Trabecular bone is impaired by bone loss more than the cortical compartment and lumbar spine seems to be the more affected site [124]. The fracture risk in chronic AN had been reported to be sevenfold higher than in healthy matched subjects by Rigotti et al. [125]; later on Lucas et al. found a cumulative incidence of fractures of 57% in women affected by chronic anorexia after 20 years of illness [126].

The bone loss has been reported by Grinspoon et al. to be more severe in AN than in Hypothalamic Amenorrhea where estrogen deficiency is not associated with an altered nutritional status as in AN; according to this research malnutrition and decrease of lean mass were related to bone loss more than hypoestrogenism in AN patients [127].Therefore weight recovery appears to be the more important goal in the treatment of osteopenia and osteoporosis. A longitudinal study of BMD in 56 eating disordered women at point 0 and at point 1 (median=20.8 months) showed that the duration of amenorrhea, the low body weight together with vomiting, nicotine and alcohol use were significant predictors of severe BMD decrease [128].

In untreated AN patients bone loss /year continues and ranges from 4 to 10% [129].

Regaining a BMI>16.5 is reported to be a critical condition for the increase of markers of bone formation such as osteocalcin [130] but long-term and sustained weight recovery appear to be necessary before significant improvements may occur [131].

In most cases a full recovery of bone mineral density will never be achieved again [115, 132,133].

The treatment of osteopenia and osteoporosis in females, as said before, is primarily based on weight gain; estrogen therapy, if discoupled from weight gain, is not able to reverse bone loss or prevent it [134,135]. Another research by Miller et al. underlined that improvements in both reproduction function and weight, together with an increase in lean body mass, are necessary for skeletal recovery in women with AN, while oral contraceptives alone were not able to increase bone mass [136].

The effects of different therapeutic regimens applied to AN patients affected by osteopenia and osteoporosis have been reviewed by Mehler in a recent systematic analysis of the literature [137] and are summarized as follows:

-Recombinant IgF1 seems to be one of the most promising therapies: Mehler takes in consideration a well done study by Grinspoon [138] that reports how the administration of recombinant human insulin-like growth factor (IgF1) at low doses (30 Micrograms twice a day) is actually able to increase bone formation markers and to decrease resorption markers.

Biphosphonates, well known inhibitors of bone resorption, are very effective in postmenopausal osteoporosis but they are not recommended in premenopausal women as they are not safe for women at child bearing age as they accumulate in bones for a long time [139].

An adequate intake of calcium and Vitamin D is recommended (Calcium 1500 mg plus Vitamin D 400-800 IU/die), particularly in adolescence and weight bearing exercise may be advised even if there is no evidence that these strategies are really effective in restoring bone mass density.

The prevalence of osteopenia and osteoporosis have been studied in the different diagnostic subtypes of AN and in the other diagnostic classes of EDs: a prospective study showed that bone loss is prevalent in ANbp in comparison with ANr [140]: bone mineral density in BN and ED-NOS females has been less investigated and the existing data is contrasting. Both Zipfel and Andersen [140,141] reported normal values of BMD in normal weight BN without a previous history of AN and hypothesized that the presence of a significant bone loss in BN and ED-NOS subjects might be related to a previous history of weight loss.

Osteopenia and Osteoporosis in Males Affected by EDs

Generally speaking, osteoporosis occurs less frequently in men than in women in relation to a different accrual of bone during youth, a shorter life expectancy and the lack of a distinct endocrine event such as menopause.

Also for this reason the relevance of this condition in males affected by EDs has been for a long time under-recognized.

Recently, in relation to a major attention to EDs in males and a more careful evaluation of these patients, growing evidence of bone mineral loss in multiple sites has been reported in the affected males.

The onset of an eating disorder during adolescence has been recognized as more critical in males than in females with regard to the development of osteopenia and osteoporosis: actually the sex determines a different timing of peak bone mass, reached earlier in females than in males (most of the total gain reached at 11-15 years in females vs 13-17 years in males) and a different growth potential, persisting two years longer in boys [142]. Therefore, at the age of major risk for the onset of anorexia nervosa, adolescent girls may have completed their growth and peak mass accrual differently from adolescent boys who have generally a lower life-long peak mass and a shorter stature [115].

Gender related differences regarding frequency and degree of bone loss were also analyzed in an important research by Mehler: the subjects included in this study, admitted to an eating disorder program, were not significantly different with regard to admission age, BMI, length of stay from admission, number of previous hospitalizations or diagnostic categories while the median duration of EDs was shorter in males than in females. The author found a higher prevalence of osteopenia (36%) and osteoporosis (26%) in males than in females leading to the opinion that ED males were at higher risk for bone loss.

According to the results of Mehler, in ANr and ANbp but not in BN and ED-NOS, the severity of bone loss was significantly more pronounced in males than in females and ANbp males were the diagnostic subgroup with a major bone loss, similarly to females. Lowest BMI and longer duration of illness accounted for almost half of the variance at the lumbar spine [143]. Mehler did not find a significant relation between testosterone levels and BMD in contrast with Misra who found, instead, that a low lean mass and low testosterone levels predicted a low BMD in a group of AN males [144].

Andersen et al. found a worse but not significant bone loss at the lumbar spine in ANr and ANbp male subgroups in comparison with the female subgroups. Men with bulimia were significantly more deficient in BMD than women with bulimia [145].

Furthermore, healthy males, in general, fracture at a higher bone density level than females [146] therefore males with osteopenia and osteoporosis may have higher risk of fractures than females [143].

Recovery of weight is the best treatment of bone loss in both sexes. Calcium and Vitamin D may be helpful in both sexes. No statistically significant association between lifestyle, exercise and bone loss was found in males by Mehler [143].

In a study by Ringe [147] biphosphonates (alendronate and risedronate) show positive and safe effects in men with primary and secondary osteoporosis, similar to the effects obtained in postmenopausal osteoporosis.

Endocrine changes

Most of the endocrine changes occuring in AN represent the effect of a physiologic adaptation to starvation, are reversible after weight recovery and are similar in males and females except for gonadal axis [148].

Hypothalamic-Pituitary-Gonadic Axis

Amenorrhea is the typical diagnostic marker of female anorexia: amenorrhea is defined as primary if menarche is absent, secondary if the menstrual cycle is absent for at least three consecutive cycles in post-menarche age, according to the DSM IV- TR. Amenorrhea in AN is due to a dysfunction of hypothalamic-pituitary-gonadal axis leading to low or undetectable estradiol, decrease of luteinizing hormone (LH) spontaneous secretion both in the frequency and the amplitude of secretory bursts [149]. Hypothalamic dysfunction in AN patients is induced by starvation and consequent weight loss: stress and excessive exercise may also contribute to the onset of amenorrhea even before weight loss is established and may maintain it despite weight recovery. According to research by Crisp the response of LH to releasing factors gradually returns to normal values after weight recovery and represents a good predictor of restored gonadic function, both in males and in females [21]. Leptin, a hormone synthesized by adipose tissue, plays an important role as modulator of hypothalamic cascade: weight loss is directly related to a proportionate decrease of leptin, which, acting on the hypothalamus, regulates food intake and energy expenditure: a low leptin level stimulates food intake through neuropeptide Y and inhibits gonadal axis. When fat mass is increased a higher leptin level is produced with a consequent decrease of appetite, activation of GNRH and recovery of gonadal functioning. Nevertheless, different authors reported that amenorrhea may persist despite weight recovery. Komura [150] found persisting amenorrhea in 11% of the patients at a 10 years follow up.

Golden et al reported the persistence of amenorrhea in 14 % of a group of 100 AN adolescent patients at a 9 months (mean) follow up, despite of the fact that 91 % (mean) of standard body weight was achieved at this time. At a one year follow-up 68% of these persistently amenorrhoic patients had resumed menses, 32% remained amenorrhoic. In this last group, a lower level of FSH and LH was observed at baseline and lower estradiol and LH (statistically significant) were observed at the follow up.

The critical weight for resumption of menses was reported to be two kilograms more than the weight at which menses were lost [151]. A permanent damage of reproductive function has been described by Shomento in 30% of female patients when the disease lasted for more than one year [152].

Different factors have been put in relation to persistent amenhorrea due to a long-standing impairment of a normal neuroendocrine function: increase of CRF and consequent increase of cortisol, excessive exercise, inadequate intake of fatty nutrients, depression, stress, use of psychotrope substances.

In male patients LH, FSH and their responses to gonadotropin releasing hormones (GNRH) are decreased in comparison with healthy males even though not so significantly as in females: testosterone serum levels were significantly lower in anorectic patients than in healthy men [148]. Sex Hormone Binding Globulin (SHBG) is also increased in affected males and inversely related to BMI.

In males these endocrine disturbances do not determine a critical event similar to amenorrhea: anorexia in males may be associated to delayed puberty and stunting of growth in children and adolescents, to a decrease of libido and of sexual activity in post-pubertal subjects.

Fichter and Daser comparing males and females with anorexia found that males had more sexual anxieties than females and lower levels of sexual activity [153].

Premorbid sexual activity has been reported by Herzog [33] to be significantly lower in AN males than in females and this data has been partially confirmed by Crisp et al. [158] who, however, did not find a significant difference between the two sexes. Very little is known about fertility in affected males: research performed by Ayers [154] on resistance sports (marathon) athletes, not diagnosed as eating disordered patients, showed that, even though low total testosterone levels were present in the majority of subjects, only a small percentage of them had semen abnormalities consistent with infertility.

Males with bulimia were reported to be more sexually active than males with anorexia both before and during their illness in a study by Pope et al.[37].

Hypothalamic–Pituitary–Thyroid Axis

The majority of AN patients present the so called "Low T3 syndrome" characterized by low triiodothyronine (T3), normal or low thyroxin (T4) and normal TSH. Reduction of T3 levels in these patients is due to altered peripheral deiodination that preferentially transforms T4 into reverse T3, an inactive metabolite. These abnormalities represent an adaptive response to starvation by means of RMR decrease and do recover after weight gain. A specific treatment of low T3 syndrome is not recommended.

Hypothalamic–Pituitary–Adrenal Axis

It has been observed that plasma cortisol levels in AN adolescent females are often elevated, circadian rhythm is conserved and that dexamethasone partially suppresses hypercortisolemia [155]. Adrenocorticotrophic (ACTH) hormone has on the contrary normal levels. The cortisol increase may represent a protective mechanism against starvation, ensuring the production of glucose from alternative sites: it is due both to an elevated production of cortico-releasing factor (a possible reaction to stressors such as starvation) and to a decreased metabolic clearance of cortisol.

A high level of cortisol contributes to increase bone catabolism, thus worsening bone loss, and it may persist even after weight recovery, negatively interfering with remenorrhea through a decrease of LH.

GH–IGF-I axis

GH-IGF axis is profoundly altered in anorexia nervosa even if the pathophysiology of this alteration has not been fully clarified.

In a healthy subject GH has many different physiological actions: some of them, such as cartilage accrual and bone trophic action are mediated by IGF1, a peptide synthesized in liver and other organs. In addition GH acts also through a direct action on metabolism of lipids, glucides and proteins. In anorexia, IGF1 levels are decreased [66] and are inversely related to BMI, therefore IGF1 is considered a marker of malnutrition, reversible with weight gain.

On the contrary, GH increase has been reported by some authors, due to GH resistance [156, 157] or altered feedback on GHRH [158] while other authors have reported contrasting data such as different GH levels (GH hyper- or hyposecretors), independent from levels of IGF1 [159]. As a matter of fact an altered GH-IGF1 axis function during the years of active growth can result in bone mineral loss and in growth retardation or arrest that represent severe, long-lasting complications.

Electrolyte and Metabolic Disturbances

A significant number of electrolyte and metabolic disturbances are present in EDs.

Vomiting and laxative abuse are the main causes of electrolyte imbalance and therefore they are characteristic not only of purging anorexia and bulimia but also of ED-NOS whenever purging behaviours are present.

A careful monitoring and treatment of electrolyte imbalance is always required: actually electrolyte abnormalities may determine life threatening medical complications such as malignant arrhythmias.

Hypokalemia is one of the most well-known electrolyte disturbances in EDs: some researchers found it was a common finding in individuals with purging behaviours but relatively uncommon in the restrictive form of anorexia or in non-purging bulimia [160]. Others reported, on the contrary, that hypokalemia was present in 20% of patients with anorexia nervosa, half of them without declared purging behaviours [67].

Two main mechanisms may contribute to hypokalemia: a direct loss of potassium through emesis/stool/urine in relation to the type of purging behaviour or a loss of potassium due to the activation of renal renin-angiotensin system. The volume depletion induced by purging behaviours activates renin-angiotensin hormonal system causing sodium retention in exchange with potassium and hydrogen, a condition named pseudo-Bartter syndrome.

In both cases the result is an hypokalemic and hypocloremic metabolic alkalosis responsible of clinical manifestations such as weakness, muscular cramps, asthenia and in the more severe cases life threatening cardiac arrhythmias.

In treating these disturbances it is necessary to consider that kalemia is not always the mirror of the global potassium reserve, being that potassium is essentially intracellular; furthermore it must be considered that rehydration and correction of metabolic alkalosis are basilar because the activation of renin-angiotensin axis induced by volume depletion contributes to maintaining a low level of potassium, despite adequate oral treatment.

If purging behaviour suddenly stops, the pseudo-Bartter syndrome may cause salt retention and oedema. This effect does not require any treatment because gradually it is deactivated by a return to normal aldosterone levels. Nevertheless, patients may not be able to accept this effect, so they are at risk of a relapse into purging behaviours: in these cases a potassium-sparing diuretic could be used for a short period [161].

Hypomagnesemia and hypocalcaemia consequent to diuretic or laxative misuse may worsen cardiac risk for arrhythmias and may also be the cause of weakness, constipation, seizures and tethany. Magnesium deficiency is related also to inadequate dietary intake in chronic starvation that causes a severe progressive depletion of magnesium stores.

During the refeeding phase, nutrients administration must be slow and gradually increasing, otherwise magnesium will rapidly move into the cells together with glucose leading to a dangerous hypomagnesemia [162, 163].

Acute laxative misuse is responsible for the onset of hypocloremic metabolic acidosis and associated hypophosphataemia, while chronic abuse is associated with metabolic alkalosis.

We have already described the comorbidity of ED with diabetes 1 and 2 and the relationship between the two diseases.

A mild asymptomatic hypoglycemia represents another frequent metabolic consequence of starvation. On the contrary severe hypoglycemia, symptomatic of depleted hepatic glycogen, is an uncommon complication associated to a poor prognosis [164]. It has been recently described that a severe case of hypoglycemia wasassociated with impaired glycogenolysis, an increase of glucose-dependent insulinotropic polypeptide (GIP) and defective glucagons secretion [165].

Hypoinsulinism is one of the adaptive hormonal responses to a poor sugar intake and to low aminoacid levels in restrictive anorexia [166]. In the refeeding phase it is necessary to drip glucose infusion very gradually to avoid the onset of hyperglycaemia due to hypoinsulinism.

2.5. Main Medical Complications of EDs: Bulimia Nervosa

Bulimia has been classified into two types: the purging and non-purging type (DSM IV).

The purging type bulimia presents more medical complications related to inappropriate purging behaviours in comparison with non-purging type bulimia since in this case less severe compensatory behaviours such as episodes of fasting or excessive exercise are used.

Bulimia has a higher prevalence than anorexia, is generally less severe and has a better outcome due to the fact that weight is in normal ranges or sometimes slightly over upper limit. The mortality rate is lower than in anorexia, around 0.3% and the prevalent causes of death are arrhythmias due to electrolyte imbalance and suicide.

In general bulimia has a longer duration of illness prior to treatment and less physical signs than anorexia.

Bulimic patients are generally treated as outpatient, nevertheless electrolyte imbalance, arrhythmias and enteric complications may require an emergency medical treatment.

Gender Differences

In comparison with bulimic females, bulimic males present more compulsive exercise and less frequent purging behaviour [167], particularly less laxative abuse [4,5,21] and it has been reported a higher frequency of drug and alcohol abuse [168].

Furthermore, in comparison with females, males have also been reported to have a later age at onset of bulimia [169], a longer duration of illness prior to treatment, a higher level of premorbid overweight and a higher maximum and current weight [5].

Some medical complications of bulimia like electrolyte and metabolic imbalance and bone mineral loss have already been treated together with anorexia because the two diseases may often share a common history of malnutrition, excessive exercise and purging behaviour.

Other typical bulimic manifestations will be treated below and gender differences, whenever present, will be underlined.

Gastrointestinal Complications

Purging behaviours are associated with frequent gastrointestinal complications. The more involved sites are esophagus and colon.

Persistent vomiting can lead to esophagitis, esophageal ulcers, emathemesis or rarely to esophageal rupture - a life threatening event - and to severe chronic gastroesophageal reflux disease (GERD), that is the predisposing factor to the Barrett's Esophagus. In this condition a columnar epithelium of the intestinal type (intestinal metaplasia) replaces the normal squamous epithelium of the esophagus as a result of chronic irritation from gastric reflux. It represents a recognized risk factor for the onset of adenocarcinoma. In our experience chronic BN purging type patients, even though asymptomatic, should be advised to undergo to oesophago-gastro-duodenoscopy (OEGDS) when they receive their first medical assessment.

Binging can lead to gastric dilation and, rarely, also to the rupture of stomach.

Laxative abuse, as already underlined, is reported to be more frequent in females: it may potentially cause a variety of complications [170] ranging from melanosis coli (brown-black discoloration of colon's mucosa and submucosa) to atonic colon with consequent chronic constipation and laxative dependence. Finally a damage to neurological innervation can provoke a cathartic colonpathy: a permanently flaccid and dilated colon unable to function.

Oral complications such as tooth enamel erosions, cheilitis, sialoadenosis, erythema of oral mucosa are usual oral complications in the case of self-induced vomiting. Bulimia may sometimes be suspected by dentists or otolaryngologists, aware of the related oral signs; if the eating disorder is already diagnosed these specialists should be regularly consulted for a dental check.

Cardiovascular Complications

Volume depletion in purging bulimia may lead to hypotension, sometimes complicated by dizziness and syncope.

The ECG abnormalities due to electrolytes disturbances and arrhythmias have already been described in the specific paragraph concerning AN complications .

An irreversible and potentially life threatening cardiac complication of purging bulimia is the cardiomyopathy caused by the persistent use of ipecac, a drug used to induce emesis.

Renal Complications

Even though renal alterations are reported to be often present in ED patients [171], very severe renal complications are not generally considered as usual medical consequences of EDs: they have been reported prevalently in purging anorexia and bulimia with long duration of illness and long-term laxative abuse. Renal abnormalities may become evident through the presence of hematuria and proteinuria.

The main causes of renal dysfunction are:

- Chronic dehydration that may lead to prerenal dysfunction
- Severe hypokalemia: potassium depletion associated with long-term binge/purge type behavior may cause tubular damage and chronic interstitial nephritis through different mechanisms such as increased ammoniogenesis and activation of vasoactive mediators. This condition may (rarely) evolve into irreversible renal dysfunction [172, 173].

Rhabdomyolysis has been described as a rare cause of renal dysfunction in anorexia: the abnormal increase of serum creatine kinase activity (CK) may be induced by hypokalemia[174], by hypophosphatemia (during refeeding phase) [175], or by excessive exercise [176].

2.6. Outcome of ED Males

A delay in diagnosis and referral may contribute to determine a more severe clinical picture in males than in females [6] therefore an early diagnosis and treatment are the most important determinants of a good prognosis both in men and in women.

An important research by Striegel Moore, focused on rates and types of treatment in ED males and females, showed that men received less treatment and once treated received less care in comparison with women, spending fewer days in treatment [177]. Nevertheless, well done studies about outcome in males by Woodside [178] and Burns [179] found a similar rate of response to treatment and a similar long-term prognosis in both sexes.

Andersen, one of the major experts of ED in males stated that "male gender is not an adverse factor in short-term or long-term treatment outcome" [180].

Conclusion

This review has explored the main medical aspects in ED patients with a particular focus on gender differences. According to several authors we cannot define the clinical picture in males as substantially different from females' but some peculiarities in males require the physician to pay specific attention:

- A healthy weight is more difficult to define in males than in females.
- In men the diagnostic value of BMI is more limited than in women. Actually minimal healthy weight and BMI are defined in AN females by the resumption of menses: obviously in males a similar event is not present so that their healthy weight is less definable.This may represent one of the reasons why diagnosis and outcome in males may be more difficult to define if we apply criteria prevalently thought for females.
- Muscular shape may hide, in males, an important loss of fat mass leading to severe medical complications: in these cases the analysis of body composition during the global assessment may be more useful than the BMI in order to better define the risk of physical complications.
- The nutritional intervention in men generally requires a higher caloric intake in comparison with females
- Adolescent males may have a higher risk for short stature and osteoporosis, therefore an early and intense treatment should be provided to these young patients

REFERENCES

[1] American Psychiatric Association Practice guideline to the treatment of patients with an eating disorders. *Am J Psychiatry*, vol. 163, 7, 2006.

[2] National Collaborating centre for Mental health. Eating Disorders. Core interventions in the treatment and management of anorexia nervosa, bulimia nervosa and related eating. National Clinical Practice Guideline. N.9. Leicester and London: British Psychological Society and Gaskell. 2004.

[3] Braun, DL; Sunday, SR; Huang, A; Halmi, KA. More males seek treatment for eating disorders. *Int J Eat Disord*,1999 25, 415-424.

[4] Button, E; Aldridge, S; Palmer, R. Males assessed by a specialized adult Eating Disorders service: patterns over time and comparisons with females. *Int J Eat Disord,,* 2008 41, 758-761.

[5] Harvey, AJ; Robinson, DJ. Eating Disorders in men: Current considerations. *J Clin Psychol Med Settings,* 2003 10, 297-306.

[6] Siegel, HJ; Hardoff, D; Golden, NH; Shenker, R. Medical complications in male adolescent with anorexia nervosa. *J Adolesc Health*, 1993 16, 448-453.

[7] Mosley, PE. Bigorexia: bodybuilding and muscle dismorphia. *Eur Eat Disord Rev*, 2009 17 (3), 191-8.

[8] Strober, M; Freeman, R; Lampert ,C. Controlled family study of anorexia nervosa and bulimia nervosa : evidence of shared liability and transmission of partial syndromes. *Am J Psychiatry*, 2000 157, 393-401.

[9] Bulik, CM; Sullivan, PF; Wade, TD; Kendler, KS. Twin studies of Eating Disorders: A review. *Int J Eat Disord,* 2000 27, 1-20.

[10] Strober, M.; Bulik, CM. Genetic epidemiology Eating Disorders. In Fairburn CG, Brownell KD, eds. *Eating disorder and obesity* second ed., NY, 2002, 238-242.

[11] Woodside, DB; Field, LL; Garfinkel, PE; Heinmaa, M. Specificity of EATING DISORDERS diagnoses in families of probands with anorexia nervosa and bulimia nervosa. *Compr Psychiatry,* 1998 39, 261-4.

[12] Strober, M; Lampert, C; Morrell,W; Burroughs, J; Jacobs C. A controlled family study of anorexia nervosa: Evidence of familial aggregation and lack of sharEating Disorders transmission with affective disorders. *Int J Eat Disord,*1990 9 (3), 239-253.

[13] Grice, DE; Halmi, KA; Fichter, MM; Strober, M; Woodside, DB; Treasure, JT; Kaplan, AS; Magistretti, PJ; Goldman, D; Bulik, CM; Kaye, WH; Berrettini WH. Evidence for a susceptibility gene for anorexia nervosa on chromosome 1. *Am J Hum Genet,* 2002 70 (3), 787-92.

[14] Yanez, AM; Peix, MA; Atserias, N; Arnau, A; Brug J. Association of eating attitudes between teenage girls and their parents. *Int J Soc Psychiatry,* 2007 53 (6), 507-13.

[15] Strober, M; Freeman, R; Lampert, C; Diamond, J; Kaye, WH. Males with anorexia nervosa: a controlled study of EATING DISORDERS in first- degree relatives. *Int J Eat Disord,* 2001 29, 263-269.

[16] Raevuori, A; Keski-Rahkonen, A; Hoek, HW; Sihvola, E; Rissanen, A; Kaprio, J. Lifetime anorexia nervosa in young men in the community: five cases and their co-twins. *Int J Eat Disord,* 2008 41(5), 458-463.

[17] Raevuori, A; Hoek, WH; Susser, E; Kaprio, J; Rissanen, A and Keski- Rahkonen, A.Epidemiology of anorexia nervosa in Men : A nationwide study of finnish twins. PLoS ONE. 2009 4 (2), e 4402.

[18] Patel, P; Wheatcroft, R; Park, RJ; Stein, A. The children of mothers with ED. *Clin Child Fam Psychol Rev,* 2002 5 (1), 1-19.

[19] Carlat, DJ; Camargo, CA; Herzog, DB. Eating disorders in Males: A report on 135 patients. *Am J Psychiatry,* 1997 154,1127-1132.

[20] Sreenivasan, U. Anorexia nervosa in boys. *Can Psychiatr Assoc J,* 1978 23 (3),159-62.

[21] Crisp,AH; Burns,T; Bhat, AV. Primary anorexia nervosa in the male and female: a comparison of clinical features and prognosis. *Br J Med Psychol,*1986 59, 123-32.

[22] Crisp, A. Anorexia Nervosa in Males: Similarities and Differences to anorexia nervosa in females. *Eur Eat Disord Rev*, 2006 4, 163-167.

[23] Cnattingius, S; Hultman, CM; Dahl, M; Sparen, P. Very preterm birth ,birth trauma,and the risk of anorexia among girls. *Arch Gen Psychiatry,* 1999 56, 634-638.

[24] Favaro, A; Tenconi, E; Santonastaso, P. Perinatal factors and the risk of developing anorexia nervosa and bulimia nervosa. *Arch Gen Psychiatry*, 2006 63 (1), 82-8.

[25] National Health and Nutrition Examination Survey, CDC Growth Charts, UnitEating Disorders States 2000

[26] Crisp, AH. Premorbid factors in adult disorders of weight, with particular reference to primary anorexia nervosa (weight phobia). A literature review. *J Psychosom Res*, 1970 14 (1), 1-22.

[27] Sharp, C; Clark, S; Dunan, J et al. Clinical presentation of anorexia nervosa in males: 24 new cases. *Int J Eat Disord,* 1994 15, 25-134.

[28] Carlat D, Camargo C: Review of bulimia nervosa in males. *Am J Psychiatry* 1991 148, 831- 843.

[29] Sancho, C; Arija, MV; Asorey, O; Canals, J. Epidemiology of Eating Disorders: a two year follow up in an early adolescent school population. *Eur Child Adolesc Psychiatry,* 2007 16 (8) 495-504.

[30] Bulik, CM; Klump, KL; Thornton, L; Kaplan, AS; Devlin, B; Fichter, MM; Halmi, KA; Strober, M; Woodside, DB; Crow, S; Mitchell, JE; Rotondo, A; Mauri, M; Cassano, GB; Keel, PK; Berrettini, WH; Kaye, WH. Alcohol use disorder comorbidity in EATING DISORDERS: a multicenter study. *J Clin Psychiatry*, 2004 65 (7),1000-6.

[31] Penas Lledo, E; Rancho, L; Walzer, G. Eating attitudes and the use of alcohol, tobacco and exercise among male and female adolescents. *Eat Behav*, 2002 3 ,101-111.

[32] Holderness, CC; Gunn-Brooks, J; Waren, PM; Marx, L and Marx, V. Co-morbidity of eating disorders and substance abuse: Review of the literature. *Int J Eat Disord* ,1994 16 (1) 1-34.

[33] Herzog, DB et al. Sexual conflict and EATING DISORDERS in 27 males. *Am J Psychiatry,* 1984 141, 989-990.

[34] Herzog, DB et al. (1990). Sexuality in Males with ED. In A. Andersen (Eating Disorders.), *Males with ED* (p. 47). New York: Brunner/Mazel.

[35] Fitcher, MM; Daser, C. Anorexic Syndromes in the male. *J Psychiatr Res*, 1985 9, 305-313.

[36] Fichter, MM; Daser, C. Symptomatology, psychosexual development and gender identity in 42 anorexic males. *Psychol Med*, 1987 17, 409-418.

[37] Pope, HG Jr; Hudson,JI; Jonas, JM. Brief Communication: Bulimia in Men: A Series of Fifteen Cases. *J Nerv Ment Dis* 1986 174 (2), 117-9.

[38] Robertson, P; Rosenvinge, J. Insulin dependent diabetes mellitus: a risk factor in anorexia nervosa or bulimia nervosa ? An empirical study of 116 women. *J Psychosom Res,* 1990 34, 535-541.

[39] Fairburn, CG; Peveler, RC; Davies, B; Mann, JI; Mayou, RA. ED in young adults and insulin-dependent diabetes mellitus: a controlled study. *Br Med J,* 1991 303, 17-20.

[40] Steel, JM; Young, RJ; Lloyd, GG; Clarke, BF. Clinically apparent ED in young diabetic women: association with painful neuropathy and other complications. *Br Med J* 1987 294, 859-862.

[41] Jones, JM; Lawson, ML; Danemann, D; Olmsted, MP; Rodin, G. Eating disorders in adolescent female with and without type 1 diabetes: Cross sectional study. *Br Med J,* 2000 320,1563-1566.

[42] Mannucci, E; Rotella, F; Ricca, V; Moretti, S; Placidi, GF; Rotella, CM. ED in patients with type 1 diabetes: a meta- analysis. *J Endocrinol Invest,* 2005 28(5), 417-9.

[43] Nissim, R; Rodin, G; Daneman, D; Rydall, A; Colton, P; Maharaj, S; Jones, J. Eating disturbances in adolescent girls with type 1 diabetes mellitus. *Harefuah,* 2002 141(10), 902-7, 929.

[44] Rodin, G. ED in young women with type 1 diabetes mellitus. *J Psychosom Res J,* 2002, 53 (4), 943-949.

[45] Takii, M; Uchigata, Y; Tokunaga, S; Amemiya, N; Kinukawa, N; Nozaki, T; Iwamoto, Y; Kubo, C. The duration of severe insulin omission is the factor most closely associated with the microvascular complications of type 1 diabetic females with clinical ED. *Int J Eat Disord* , 2008 41(3), 259-264.

[46] Herpertz, S; Albus, C; Wagener, R; Kocnar, M; Wagner, R; Henning, A; Best, F; Foerster, H; Schulze Schleppinghoff, B; Thomas, W; Köhle, K; Mann, K; Senf, W. Comorbidity of diabetes and ED. Does diabetes control reflect disturbed eating behaviour? *Diabetes Care,* 1998 21(7), 1110-6.

[47] Colton, P; Olmsted, M; Daneman, D; Rydall, AC and Rodin, MG. Five years prevalence and persistence of disturbed eating behaviour and ED in girls with type one diabetes. *Diabetes care,* 2007 30, 2861-2862.

[48] Peveler, RC; Fairburn, CG. The treatment of bulimia nervosa in patients with diabetes mellitus. *Int J Eat Disord,* 2002 32, 230-239.

[49] Nielsen, S; Emborg, C and Mølbak, A-G. Mortality in Concurrent Type 1 Diabetes and Anorexia Nervosa. *Diabetes Care,* 2002 25 (2), 309-312.

[50] Friedman, S; Vila, G; Timsit, Boitard, C; Mouren-Simeoni, MC. Eating Disorders and insulin-dependent diabetes mellitus (IDDM): relationship with glycaemic control and somatic complications. *Acta Psychiatr Scand,* 1998 97(3), 206-212.

[51] Neumark- Sztainer, D; Patterson, J; Mellin, A; Ackard, MD. Weight control practices and disordered eating behaviours among adolescent females and males with type 1 diabetes. *Diabetes care,* 2002 25 (8), 1289-1296 .

[52] Leffler, DA; Dennis, M; Edwards George, JB; Kelly, CP. The interaction between eating disorders and celiac disease: an exploration of 10 cases. *Eur J Gastroenterol Hepatol,* 2007 19(3), 251-5.

[53] Yucel, B; Ozbey, N; Demir, K; Polat, A; Yager, J. Eating Disorders and celiac disease: A case report. *Int J Eat Disord,* 2006 39 (6), 530 – 532.

[54] Karwautz, A; Wagner, G; Berger, G; Sinnreich. U; Grylli, V; Huber, WD.Eating pathology in adolescent with celiac disease. *Psychosomatics*, 2008 49(5), 399-406.
[55] Woodside D. Blake, FRCPC. Eating Disorders in Men: An Overview. *Healthy Weight Journal*, 2002 16 (4), 6-9.
[56] Center for Disease Control and Prevention, United States 2000 Growth Charts.
[57] Sullivan, PF. Mortality in anorexia nervosa. *Am J Psychiatry*, 1995 152(7), 1073-4.
[58] Fitcher, MM; Quadflieg, N; Hedlund, S. Twelve-year course and outcome presictors of anorexia nervosa. *Int J Eat Disord* 2006 39 (2), 87-100.
[59] Steinhausen, HC. The outcome of anorexia nervosa in the 20th century. *Am J Psychiatry*, 2002 159(8), 1284-93.
[60] Papadopoulos, FC. Excess mortality, causes of death and prognostic factors in anorexia nervosa. *Br J Psychiatry*, 2009 194 (1),10-7.
[61] Pike,MK. Long term course of anorexia nervosa: response, relapse, remission and recovery. *Clin Psychol Rev,* 1998 18 (4), 447-475.
[62] Fairburn, CG; Cooper, Z; Bohn, K; O'Connor, ME; Doll, HA ;Palmer, RL. The severity and status of eating disorder NOS :implications for DSMV. *Behav Res Ther,* 2007 45(8), 1705-15.
[63] Konrad, KK; Carels, RA and Garner, DM. Metabolic and psychological changes during refeeding in anorexia nervosa. *Eat Weight Disord,* 2007 12 (1),20-26.
[64] Onur, S; Haas,V; Bosy-Westphal, A; Hauer, M; Paul,T; Nutzinger, D; Klein, H and Müller, MJ. L-Tri-iodothyronine is a major determinant of resting energy expenditure in underweight patients with anorexia nervosa and during weight gain. *Eur J Endocrinol*, 2005 152 (2), 179-184.
[65] Kollai, M; Bonyhay ,I; Jokkel,G; Szonyl, L. Cardiac vagal hyperactivity in adolescent anorexia nervosa. *Eur Heart* J, 1994 15, 113-18.
[66] Misra, M; Aggarwal, A; Miller, KK; Almazan, C; Worley, M; Soyka, A; Herzog, B.D and Klibanski, A. Effects of anorexia nervosa on clinical, hematologic ,biochemical and bone density parameters in community- dwelling adolescent girls. *Pediatrics,* 2004 114 (6), 1574- 1583.
[67] Miller, KK; Grinspoon, SK; Champa, J; Hier, J; Herzog, D; Klibanski, A. Medical findings in outpatients with anorexia nervosa. *Arch Intern Med,* 2005 165, 561-66.
[68] Dhoble, A; Puttarajappa, C; Patel, MB; Thakur, RK. Heart rate variability in a man with anorexia. *Am J Med,* 2008 121 (12), e 5-6.
[69] Murialdo, G; Casu, M; Falchero, M; Brugnolo, A; Patrone, V; Cerro, PF; Ameri, P; Andraghetti, G; Briatore, L; Copello, F; Cordera, R; Rodriguez, G; Ferro, AM. Alterations in the autonomic control of heart rate variability in patients with anorexia or bulimia nervosa: correlations between sympathovagal activity, clinical features, and leptin levels. *J Endocrinol Invest*, 2007 30 (5), 356-62.
[70] Algra, A; Tijssen, JG; Roelandt JR; Pool, J; Lubsen, J. QTc prolongation measured by Standard 12-lead electrocardiography is an independent risk factor for sudden death due to cardiac arrest. *Circulation*, 1991 83 (6), 1888-94.
[71] Isner, JM; Roberts, WC; ,Heymsfield, SB; Yager, J. Anorexia Nervosa and sudden death. *Ann Intern Med,* 1985 102, 49-52.
[72] Cooke, RA; Chambers, JB; Singh, R;Todd, GJ; Smeeton, NC; Treasure, J et al.QT interval in anorexia nervosa. *Br Heart J,* 1994 72, 69-73.

[73] Lesinskiene, S; Barkus, A; Ranceva, N; Dembinskas, A. A meta-analysis of heart rate and QT interval alteration in anorexia nervosa. *World J Biol Psychiatr,* 2008 9 (2), 86-91.

[74] Okin, PM; Devereux, RB; Howard, BV; Fabsitz, RR; Lee, ET; Welty, TK. Assessment of QT Interval and QT Dispersion for Prediction of All-Cause and Cardiovascular Mortality in American Indians: The Strong Heart Study. Clinical Investigation and Reports. *Circulation*, 2000 101 (1), 61.

[75] Vázquez, M; Olivares, JL; Fleta, J; Lacambra, I; González, M. Cardiac disorders in young women with anorexia nervosa. *Rev Esp Cardiol,* 2003 56 (7), 669-73.

[76] Krantz, MJ; Donahoo, WT; Melanson, EL; Mehler, PS. QT interval dispersion and resting metabolic rate in chronic anorexia nervosa. *Int J Eat Disord*, 2005 37 (2),166-70.

[77] Galetta, F; Franzoni, F; Cupisti, A; Belliti, D; Prattichizzo, F; Rolla, M. QT interval dispersion in young women with anorexia nervosa. *J Pediatr*, 2002 140 (4), 456-60.

[78] Takimoto, Y; Yoshiuchi, K; Kumano, H; Yamanaka, G; Sasaki, T; Suematsu, H; Nagakawa, Y; Kuboki, T. QT Interval and QT Dispersion in ED. *Psychother Psychosom,* 2004 73, 324-328.

[79] Swenne,I; Larsson, PT. Heart risk associated with weight loss in anorexia nervosa and ED: risk factors for QTc interval prolongation and dispersion. *Acta Paediat,* 1999 88 (3), 304-9.

[80] Wolbrette, D; Naccarelli, G; Curtis, A; Lehmann, M; Kadish, A. Gender differences inarrhythmias. *Clin Cardiol,* 2002 25 (2), 49-56.

[81] De Simone, G; Scalfi, L; Galderisi, M et al.. Cardiac abnormalities in young women with anorexia nervosa. *Br Heart J* 1994 71, 287-292.

[82] Oka, Y; Ito, T; Matsumoto, S; Suematsu, H; Ogata, E. Mitral valve prolapse in patients with anorexia nervosa. Two-dimensional echocardiographic study. *Jpn Heart J ,* 1987 28 (6)873-82.

[83] Johnson, GL; Humphries, LL; Shirley, PB; Mazzoleni A; Noonan JA. Mitral Valve Prolapse in Patients With Anorexia nervosa and Bulimia. *Arch Intern Med,* 1986 146 (8), 1525-1529.

[84] Ramacciotti, C.E; Coli, E; Bladi, O and Dell'Osso, L. Silent pericardial effusion in a sample of anorexic patients. *Eat Weight Disord* 2003 8 (1), 68-71.

[85] Frölich, J; von Gontard, A; Lehmkuhl, G; Pfeiffer, E; Lehmkuhl, U. Pericardial effusions in anorexia nervosa. *Eur Child Adolesc Psychiatry*. 2001 10 (1), 54-7.

[86] Polli, N; Blengino, S; Moro, M; Zappulli, D; Scacchi, M; Cavagnini, F. Pericardial effusion requiring pericardiocentesis in a girl with anorexia nervosa. *Int J Eat Disord*, 2006 39 (7), 609-11.

[87] Solvetti, SM; Magnani, M; Santilli, A; Di Liso, G; Diamanti, A; Pompei, E; Gambarara, M; Montecchi, F; Ragonese, P.The Heart in anorexic teenage girls. *G.Ital Cardiol* 1998 28, 131-139.

[88] Inagaki, T; Yamamoto, M; Tsubouchi, K; Miyaoka, T; Uegaki, J; Maeda, T; Horiguchi, J; Yamane,Y; Kato, Y. Echocardiographic investigation of pericardial effusion in a case of anorexia nervosa. *Int J Eat Disord*, 2003 33 (3), 364-6.

[89] Olivares, JL; Vazquez, M; Fieta, J; Moreno, LA; Perez-Gonzalez, JM;Bueno, M. Cardiac findings in adolescents with anorexia nervosa at diagnosis and after weight restoration. *Eur J Pediatr,* 2005 164 (6), 383-6.

[90] Birmingham, CL and Gritzner, S. Heart failure in anorexia nervosa :case report and review of the literature *Eat Weight Disord,* 2007 12, 7-10.

[91] Mont, L; Castro, J; Herreros, B; Pare', C; Azqueta, M;,Magrina, J; Puig, J; Toro, J; Brugada, J. Reversibility of cardiac abnormalities in adolescents with anorexia nervosa after weight recovery *J Am Acad Adolesc Psychiatry,* 2003 42 (7), 808-813.

[92] .Hutter, G; Ganepola, S; Hofmann, W-K. The Hematology of Anorexia Nervosa. *Int J Eat Disord,* 2009 42 (4), 293-300.

[93] Böhm, J; Gelatinous transformation of the bone marrow: the spectrum of underlying diseases. *Am J Surg Pathol,.* 2000 24 (1) 56-65.

[94] Sen R, Singh S, Singh H, Gupta A, Sen Clinical profile in gelatinous bone marrow Transformation. *J Assoc Physicians India,* 2003 51, 585-8.

[95] Tavassoli, M; Eastlund, DT; Yam, LT; Neiman, RS; Finkel, H. Gelatinous transformation of bone marrow in prolonged self-induced starvation. *Scand J Haematol,.* 1976 16 (4), 311-9.

[96] Boullu-Ciocca, S; Darmon, P; Sébahoun, G; Silaghi, A; Dutour-Meyer. A Gelatinous bone marrow transformation in anorexia nervosa. *Ann Endocrinol* (Paris), 2005 66 (1), 7-11.

[97] Pearson, HA. Marrow hypoplasia in anorexia nervosa. *J Pediatr,* 1967 71, 211-215.

[98] Mant, MJ; Faragher, BS. The Haematology of anorexia nervosa. *Br J Haematol,* 1972 23 737- 749.

[99] Warren, MP; Vande Wiele, RL. Clinical and metabolic features of anorexia nervosa. *Am J Obstet Gynecol,* 1973 117, 435-449.

[100] Abella, E; Feliu, E; Granada, I; Millá, F; Oriol, A; Ribera, JM; Sánchez-Planell, L; Berga, LI; Reverter, JC; Rozman, C. Bone marrow changes in anorexia nervosa are correlated with the amount of weight loss and not with other clinical findings. *Am J Clin Pathol,* 2002 118 (4) 582-8.

[101] Dexter, TM; Allen, TDand Lajtha, LG.Conditions controlling the proliferation of haemopoietic stem cell in vitro. *J Cell Physiol,* 1976 91, 335-344.

[102] Vande Berg, BC; Malghem, J; Devuyst, O; Maldague, BE; Lambert, MJ. Anorexia nervosa: correlation between MR appearance of bone marrow and severity of disease. *Radiology,* 1994 193 (3), 859-64.

[103] Geiser, F; Mürtz, P; Lutterbey, G; Träber, F; Block, W; Imbierowicz, K; Schilling, G; Schild, H; Liedtke, R. Magnetic resonance spectroscopic and relaxometric determination of bone marrow changes in anorexia nervosa. *Psychosom Med,* 2001 63 (4), 631-7.

[104] Lambert, M; Hubert, C; Depresseux, G; Vande Berg, B; Thissen, JP; Nagant de Deuxchaisnes, C; Devogelaer, JP. Hematological changes in anorexia nervosa are correlated with total body fat mass depletion. *Int J Eat Disord,* 1997 21 (4), 329-34.

[105] Polli, N; Scacchi, M; Pecori Giraldi, F; Sormani, M; Zappulli, D; Cavagnini, F. Low insulin-like growth factor I and leukopenia in anorexia nervosa. *Int J Eat Disord,* 2008 41 (4), 355-9.

[106] Van de Zande, VL; Mazza, JJ; Yale, SH. Hematologic and metabolic abnormalities in a patient with anorexia nervosa. *WMJ,* 2004 103 (2), 38-40.

[107] Maréchaud, R; Abadie, JC; Babin, P; Lessart, M; Sudre, Y. Reversible bone marrow hypoplasia in a case of male anorexia nervosa. *Ann Med Interne* (Paris), 1985 136(1), 36-40.

[108] Hartgens, F; Kuipers, H. Effects of androgenic-anabolic steroids in athletes. *Sports Med*, 2004 34 (8), 513-54.

[109] Golla, JA; Larson, LA; Anderson, CF; Lucas, AR; Wilson, WR; Tomasi, TB Jr. An immunological assessment of patients with anorexia nervosa. *Am J Clin Nutr*, 1981 34 (12), 2756-62.

[110] Devuyst, O; Lambert, M; Rodhain, J; Lefebvre, C; Coche, E. Haematological changes and infectious complications in anorexia nervosa: a case-control study. *Q J Med* ,1993 86 (12), 791-9.

[111] Hotta, M; Nagashima, E; Takagi, S; Itoda, I; Numata ,T; Kobayashi, N; Takano, K. Two young female patients with anorexia nervosa complicated by Mycobacterium tuberculosis infection. *Intern Med,* 2004 43 (5), 440-4.

[112] Cason, J; Ainley, CC; Wolstencroft ,RA; Norton, KR; Thompson, RP. Cell-mediated immunity in anorexia nervosa. *Clin Exp Immunol.* 1986 64 (2), 370-5.

[113] Nova, F; Samartin, S; Gomez, S; Morandè, G; Marcos, A. The adaptive response of the immune system to the particular malnutrition of Eating Disorders. *Eur J Clin Nutr,* 2002 56 (Suppl. 3), S34-7.

[114] Danziger, Y; Mukamel, M; Zeharia, A; Dinari, G; Mimouni, M. Stunting of growth in anorexia nervosa during the prepubertal and pubertal period. *Isr J Med Sci,* 1994 30 (8), 581-4.

[115] Misra, M. Long-term skeletal effects of ED with onset in adolescence. *Ann N Y Acad Sci,* 2008 1135, 212-8.

[116] Modan-Moses, D; Yaroslavsky, A; Novikov, I; Segev, S; Toledano, A; Miterany, E; Stein, D. Stunting of growth as a major feature of anorexia nervosa in male adolescents. *Pediatrics.* 2003 111(2), 270-6.

[117] Pfeiffer, RJ; Lucas, AR; Ilstrup, DM. Effect of anorexia nervosa on linear growth. *Arch Pediatr,* 2003 10 (9), 836-40.

[118] Root, AW; Powers, PS. Anorexia nervosa presenting as growth retardation in adolescents *J Adolesc Health Care,* 1983 4, 25-30.

[119] WHO Scientific Group on the Prevention and Management of Osteoporosis (2000) : Geneva, Switzerland) (2003). "Prevention and management of osteoporosis: report of a WHO scientific group."

[120] Lennkh, C; de Zwaan, M; Bailer, U; Strnad, A; Nagy, C; El -Giamal, N; Wiesnagrotzki, S;Vytiska, E; Huber, J; Kasper, S. Osteopenia in anorexia nervosa: specific mechanisms of bone Loss. *J-Psychiatr-Res,* 1999 33, 349-56.

[121] Rigotti, NA; Nussbaum, SR; Herzog, DB; Neer, RM. Osteoporosis in women with anorexia Nervosa. *N Engl J Med,* 1984 311, 1601-06.

[122] Grinspoon, S; Thomas, E; Pitts, S; Gross, E; Mickley, D; Miller, K; Herzog, D and Klibanski, A. Prevalence and Predictive Factors for Regional Osteopenia in Women with Anorexia Nervosa. *Ann Intern Med* 2000 133, 790-794.

[123] Bachrach, L; Guido, D; Katzman, D; Litt, I; Marcus, R. Decreased bone density in adolescent girls with anorexia nervosa. *Pediatrics,* 1990 86, 440-447.

[124] Biller, BM; Saxe, V; Herzog, DB; Rosenthal, DI; Holzman, S; Klibanski, A. Mechanisms of osteoporosis in adult and adolescent women with anorexia nervosa. *J Clin Endocrinol Metab,* 1989 68, 548–554.

[125] Rigotti, NA; Neer, RM; Skates, SJ; Herzog, DB; Nussbaum, SR. The clinical corse of osteoporosis in anorexia nervosa. *Jama* 1991 265, 1133-1138.

[126] Lucas, AR; Melton, LJ; Crowson, CS; O'Fallon, WM. Long-term fracture risk among women with anorexia nervosa: a population-based cohort study. *Mayo Clin Proc,* 1999 74 (10), 972-7.

[127] Grinspoon, S; Miller, K; Coyle, C; Krempin, J; Armstrong, C; Pitts, S; Herzog, D; Klibanski, A. Severity of Osteopenia in Estrogen-Deficient Women with Anorexia Nervosa and Hypothalamic Amenorrhea. *J Clin. Endocrinol Metab,* 1999 84, 2049-55.

[128] Baker, D; Roberts, R; Towell, T. Factors predictive of bone mineral density in eating-disorderded women: a longitudinal study. *Int J Eat Disord,* 2000 27, 29-35.

[129] Maugars, YM; Berthelot, JM; Forestier, R; Mammar, N; Lalande, S; Venisse, JL; Prost, AM.Follow-up of bone mineral density in 27 cases of anorexia nervosa. *Eur J Endocrinol,* 1996 135 (5), 591-7.

[130] Hotta, M; Fukuda, I; Sato, K; Hizuka, N;. Shibasaki, T and Takano, K. The Relationship between Bone Turnover and Body Weight, Serum Insulin-Like Growth Factor (IGF) I, and Serum IGF-Binding Protein Levels in Patients with Anorexia Nervosa. *J Clin Endocrinol. Metab,* 2000 85(1), 200 - 206.

[131] Misra, M; Klibanski A. Anorexia nervosa and osteoporosis. *Rev Endocr Metab Disord,* 2006 7 (1-2), 91-9.

[132] Herzog, W; Minne, H; Deter, C et al. Outcome of bone mineral density in anorexia nervosa patients 11.7 years after first admission. *J Bone Miner Res,* 1993 8, 597–605.

[133] Katzman, DK. Medical Complications in Adolescents with Anorexia Nervosa: A Review of the Literature. *Int J Eat Disord,* 2005 37, 552-559.

[134] Klibanski, A; Biller, BM; Schoenfeld, DA; Herzog, DB; Saxe, VC. The effects of estrogen administration on trabecular bone loss in young women with anorexia nervosa. *J Clin Endocrinol Metab,* 1995 80 (3), 898-904.

[135] Sim, LA; McGovern, L; Elamin, MB; Swiglo, BA; Erwin, PJ; Montori, VM. Effect on bone health of estrogen preparations in premenopausal women with anorexia nervosa: A systematic review and meta-analyses. *Int J Eat Disord* , Published Online: 6 Apr 2009.

[136] Miller, KK; Lee, EE; Lawson, EA; Misra M, Minihan, J; Grinspoon, SK; Gleysteen, S; Mickley, D; Herzog D, Klibanski A. Determinants of skeletal loss and recovery in anorexia Nervosa.. *J Clin Endocrinol Metab,* 2006 91 (8), 2931-7, Epub 2006 May 30.

[137] Mehler, PS; MacKenzie, TD. Treatment of Osteopenia and Osteoporosis in Anorexia Nervosa A Systematic Review of the Literature. *Int J Eat Disord,* 2009 42 195-201.

[138] Grinspoon, S; Thomas, L; Miller, K; Herzog, D and Anne Klibanski. Effects of Recombinant Human IGF-I and Oral Contraceptive Administration on Bone Density in Anorexia Nervosa. *J Clin Endocrinol Metab,* 2002 87 (6), 2883-2891.

[139] Patlas, N; Golomb, G; Yaffe, P; Pinto, T; Breuer, E; Omoy, A. Transplacental effects of bisphosphonates on fetal skeletal ossification and mineralization in rats. *Teratology,* 1999 60 (2), 68-73.

[140] Zipfel,S; Seibel, MJ; Lowe, B; Beumont, JP; Kasperk, C and Herzog, W. Osteoporosis in ED: A Follow-Up Study of Patients with Anorexia and Bulimia Nervosa. *J Clin Endocrinol. Metab*, 2001 86 (11), 5227 - 5233.

[141] Andersen, AE; Woodward, PJ; LaFrance, N. Bone mineral density of eating disorder subgroups. *Int J Eat Disord.* 1995 18 (4), 335-42.

[142] Nguyen, TV; Maynard, LM; Towne, B; Roche, AF; Wisemandle, W; Li, J; Guo, SS; Chumlea, WC; Siervogel, RM. Sex differences in bone mass acquisition during growth: the Fels Longitudinal Study. *J Clin Densitom*, 2001 4 (2), 147-57.

[143] Mehler, PS; Sabel, AL; Watson, T; Andersen, AE. High risk of Osteoporosis in male patients with ED. *Int J Eat Disord* , 2008 41, 666-672.

[144] Misra, M; Katzman, DK; Cord, J; Manning, SJ; Mendes, N; Herzog, DB; Miller, KK; Klibanski A. Bone metabolism in adolescent boys with anorexia nervosa. *J Clin Endocrinol Metab*. 2008 93(8), 3029-36. Epub 2008 Jun 10.

[145] Andersen, EA; Watson T; Schlechte, J. Osteoporosis and osteopenia in men with eating Disorders. *Lancet,* 2000 355, 1967-68.

[146] Lane, JM; Serota, AC; Raphael, B. Osteoporosis: differences and similarities in male and female patients. *Orthop Clin North Am*, 2006 37 (4), 601-9.

[147] Ringe, JD.Treatment of osteoporosis in men. *JMHG,* 2007 4 (3), 326-333.

[148] Tomova, A; Kumanov, P. Sex differences and similarities of hormonal alterations in patients with anorexia nervosa. *Andrologia,* 1999 31, 143-147.

[149] Munoz, M and Argente, J. Anorexia nervosa in female adolescents: endocrine and bone mineral density disturbances. *Eur J Endocrinol,* 2002 147, 275–286.

[150] Kohmura, H; Miyake, A; Aono ,T;Tanizawa, O.Recovery of reproductive function in patients with anorexia nervosa :a 10 year follow up study. *Eur J Obstet Gynecol Reprod Biol*, 1986 22 (5-6), 293-6.

[151] Golden, NH; Jacobson, MS; Schebendach, J; Solanto, MV; Hertz, SM; Shenker, IR.Resumption of menses in anorexia nervosa. *Arch Pediatr Adolesc Med,* 1997 151 (1), 16-21.

[152] Shomento, SH; Kreipe, RE. Menstruation and fertility following anorexia nervosa. *Adolesc Pediatr Gynecol ,* 1994 7, 142-146.

[153] Fichter, MM; Daser, C. Symptomatology, psychosexual development and gender identity in 42 anorexic males. *Psychol Med,* 1987 17, 409-418.

[154] Ayers, JW; Komesu, Y; Romani, T. Anthropomorphic,hormonal, and psychologic correlates of semen quality in endurance-trained male athletes. *Fertil Steril,* 1985 43, 917-921.

[155] Gold, PW; Gwritsman, H; Augerinos, PC; Nieman, LK; Galluci, WT; Kaye, W. Abnormal hypothalamic pituitary–adrenal function in anorexia nervosa. Pathophysiology mechanisms in underweight and weight-corrected patients. *N Engl J Med* 1986 314, 1339–1342.

[156] Golden, NH; Kreitzer, P; Jacobson, MS et al. Disturbances in growth hormone secretion and action in adolescents with anorexia nervosa.. *J Pediatr*, 1994 125, 655–660.

[157] Misra, M; Miller, KK; Bjornson, J. Alterations in growth hormone secretory dynamics in adolescent girls with anorexia nervosa and effects on bone metabolism. *J Clin Endocrinol Metab,* 2003 88, 5615.

[158] Støving, RK; Veldhuis, JD; Flyvbjerg, A;, Vinten, J; Hangaard, J; Koldkjaer, OG et al. Jointly amplified basal and pulsatile growth hormone (GH) secretion and increased process irregularity in women with anorexia nervosa: indirect evidence for disruption of feedback regulation within the GH-insulin-like growth factor I axis. . *J Clin Endocrinol Metab,* 1999 84, 2056–2063.

[159] Argente, J; Caballo, N; Barrios, V; Munoz, MT; Pozo, J; Chowen, JA. Multiple endocrine abnormalities of the growth hormone and insulin-like growth factor in patients with anorexia nervosa :effects of short and long.term weight recuperation. *J Clin Endocrinol Metab,* 1997 82, 2084-2092.
[160] Greenfeld, D; Mickey, D; Quinlan, D; Roloff, P. Hypokaliemia in outpatients with eating Disorders. *Am J Psichiatry,* 1995 152, 60-83.
[161] Mehler, PS; Crews, C and Weiner K. Bulimia: Medical Complications. *J Womens Health,* 2004 13 (6), 668-675.
[162] Crook, MA; Hally, V; Panteli, JV. The importance of the refeeding syndrome. *Nutrition,* 2001 17, 632-637.
[163] Birmingham, CL; Puddicombe, D; Hlynsky, J. Hypomagnesemia during refeeding in anorexia nervosa. *Eat Weight Disord,* 2004 9, 236-237.
[164] Rich, LM; Caine, MR;Findling, W; Shaker, JL. Hypoglycemic coma in anorexia nervosa .Case report and review of the literature. *Arch Intern Med,* 1990 150, 894-895.
[165] Yanai, H; Yoshida, H; Tomono, Y; Tada, N. Severe hypoglicemia in a patient with anorexia nervosa. *Eat Weight Disord,* 2009 13; e1-e3.
[166] Thissen, JP; Ketelslegers, JM. Endocrine response to undernutrition from the experimental model to human physiology. *Clinical Issues in Growth Disorders : Evolution, Diagnosis and Therapy.* 1994 Eds A. Prader and R. Rappaport, London Freund Publishing house Ltd :131-150
[167] Weltzin,TE; Weisensel, N; Franczyk D; Burnett, K; Klitz, C; Bean P. Eating Disorders in men: Update. *JMHG,* 2005 2 (2), 186-193.
[168] Schneider, JA; Agras, SW. Bulimia in males :a matched comparison with females. *Int J Eat Disord,* 1987 6 (2), 171 – 330.
[169] Carlat, DJ; Camargo, CA Jr. Review of bulimia nervosa in males. *Am J Psychiatry,* 1991148, 831-843.
[170] Mitchell, JE; Boutacoff, LI. Laxative abuse complicating bulimia: Medical and treatment Implications. *Int J Eat Disord,,* 2006 5 (2), 325 – 334.
[171] Rome, SE; Ammerman, S. Medical complications of Eating Disorders: an update. *J Adolesc Health,* 2003 33, 418-426.
[172] Yasuhara, D; Naruo, T; Taguchi, S; Umekita, Y; Yoshida, H; Nozoe, S. End-stage kidney" in longstanding bulimia nervosa. *Int J Eat Disord,* 2005 38 (4), 383-5.
[173] Abdel-Rahman, EM; Moorthy, AV. End stage renal disease (ESRD) in patients with eating disorders . *Clin.Nephrol* , 1997 47, 106-111.
[174] Dive, A; Donckier, J; Lejeune, D; Buysschaert, M. Hypokalemic rhabdomyolysis in anorexia nervosa. *Acta Neurol Scand,* 1991 83 (6), 419.
[175] Wada, S; Nagase, T; Koike,Y; Kugai N; Nagata, ,N. A Case of Anorexia Nervosa with Acute Renal Failure Induced by Rhabdomyolysis: Possible Involvement of Hypophosphatemia or Phosphate Depletion. *Internal Medicin* ,1992 31 (4), 478-482.
[176] Walder,A; Baumann,P. Increased creatinine kinase and rhabdomyolysis in anorexia nervosa. *Int J Eat Disord,* 2008 41 (8), 766 – 767.
[177] Striegel-Moore, RH; Leslie, D; Petrill, SA; Garvin, V; Rosenheck, RA. One-year use and cost of inpatient and outpatient services among female and male patients with an eating disorder: evidence from a national database of health insurance claims. *Int J Eat Disord,* 2000 27 (4), 381-9.

[178] Woodside, DB; Kaplan, AS. Day hospital treatment in males with Eating Disorders: response and comparison to females. *J Psychosom Res,* 1994 38, 471–475.

[179] Burns,T and Crisp, AH. Outcome of anorexia nervosa in males. *Br J Psychiatry*, 1984 145, 319-325 .

[180] Andersen, AE; Holman, JE. Males with Eating Disorders: challenges for treatment and research. *Psychopharmacol Bull.* 1997 33 (3), 391-7.

Chapter 3

SKIN SIGNS IN EATING DISORDERS

R. Strumia

ABSTRACT

Dermatologists are interested in EDs because there are at least 40 skin signs in patients with these disorders and some of them are considered guiding signs because they allow physicians to suspect the presence of a still hidden ED.

Skin signs are due to starvation, self-induced vomiting, drug consumption and concomitant psychiatric illness.

A body mass index of < or = 16 can be considered a critical value at which skin changes are more frequent. Frequent skin signs include xerosis and dry skin, carotenoderma, hypertrychosis (lanugo- like body hair), escoriated acne, acral coldness and acrocyanosis, cheilitis, alopecia, nail changes, calluses on dorsum of hands (Russell's sign) due to self-induced vomiting, and self-induced trauma. Guiding signs include: hypertrichosis, Russell's sign, self-induced dermatitis. The role of the dermatologist in eating disorders is to suspect the presence of hidden EDs: guiding signs are very important for this and also to improve the knowledge of skin signs in EDs through a collaboration with the specialists who work in an Eating Disorder Centre.

INTRODUCTION

In EDs, many skin signs have been reported, and skin signs may help in leading to the diagnosis of a not yet recognized ED. Reviewing the literature, Tyler et al [1] found 40 dermatological signs in ED patients. In the last few years new complete reviews of skin signs of EDs have been published [2-8]. Skin signs are the expression of underlying disorders, of vomiting, of abuse of drugs such as laxatives and diuretics, and of psychiatric morbidity. Gupta et al [8] classified the skin signs of EDs into four groups: those caused by starvation and/or malnutrition, those due to self-induced vomiting, findings caused by drug consumption and those caused by concomitant psychiatric illness. Based upon his data, Glorio [6] in 200 patients with EDs identified two groups of signs: frequent signs (xerosis, alopecia, caries, opaque and fragile hair, nail fragility) and guiding signs (hypertrichosis, Russell's sign, perimylolysis, self-induced dermatitis).

Hediger et al [7] documented that a BMI < or = 16 can be considered a critical value at which skin changes are more frequent.

Skin Signs Due to Starvation

Symptoms due to dietary change or starvation include, xerosis, lanugo-like body hair, telogen effluvium, carotenoderma, acne, hyperpigmentation, seborrheic dermatitis, acrocyanosis, perniosis, petechiae, livedo reticularis, interdigital intertrigo, paronychia, generalized pruritus, acquired striae distensae, slower wound healing, prurigo pigmentosa, edema, linear erythema craquelé, acral coldness, pellagra and scurvy, acrodermatitis entheropathica and miscellanea.

Xerosis may be observed in almost all of the patients. Prolonged total caloric deprivation gives rise to reduced sebaceous gland secretion. A definite correlation with compensatory hypothyroidism has not yet been demonstrated. Xerosis is often associated with hyperpigmentation (so called "dirty skin").

Lanugo-like body hair is a frequent sign in AN, especially in younger patients. It does not appear when starvation is due to other causes. It presents as fine, downy, pigmented hairs on the back, abdomen and forearms. It is not a sign of virilization and has been associated with decreased activity of the 5-alpha-reductase enzyme system, probably due to hypothyroidism. Telogen effluvium shows a diffuse pattern, sometimes with frontal predominance. Opaque hair often occurs.

Acne may be referred to endocrine changes occurring in starvation but acne itself may lead to a change eating patterns. In psychologically vulnerable girls a new dieting behaviour, adopted to control their acne, may lead to weight loss and in some cases to develop AN.

Carotenoderma is due to marked ingestion of carotenoid-rich vegetables low in calories. It results from carotene deposition in the tissue causing yellowing of the skin.

Acrocyanosis is more prevalent among the more severely ill patients. It is associated with pallor of the face and trunk, slower pulse rates and higher fasting plasma glucose levels. It could represent a more extreme form of heat conserving mechanism not uncommon in anorectics.

Purpura is the result of bone marrow depression from starvation and subsequent thrombocytopenia. Life-threatening episodes of thrombocytopenia are reported in the typical restricting-type of AN with purpura, gingival, nasal gastrointestinal bleeding and apparent bone marrow hypoplasia [10].

In our experience we have found this sign in 11.7% with a preponderance in males with AN. The morphologic aspect is indistinguishable from those of individuals without AN.

Mucosal signs due to starvation include cheilitis and gingivitis. Nail fragility, longitudinal ungueal striae, onychocryptosis, and periungueal erythema have been reported. Pili torti in AN may be due to malnutrition combined with ingestion of exaggerated amounts of yellow vegetables and vitamin supplements, causing a significant increase in levels of serum carotens (possible link between excess vitamin A and pili torti) [11].

Skin Signs Due to Vomiting

One of the most characteristic skin signs in purging type AN and in BN is the Russell's sign (knuckle calluses). The lesions involve calluses on the dorsal aspects of the dominant hand induced by the patients'repeated introduction of the hand into the mouth. It is a guiding sign in the diagnosis of EDs.

Skin Signs Due to Abuse of Drugs

In purging type AN patients may undergo the adverse reactions of drugs, such as laxatives, diuretics and appetite suppressants, which they use. Finger clubbing may be due to abuse of laxatives containing senna.

Skin Signs Due to Psychiatric Morbidity

Self-induced trauma often coexists with AN. The disorder varies from unconscious picking at the skin to severe self-destructive actions. Artifact scars as a visible result of this behaviour is reported in 13% of adult anorectics and in 30% of children and adolescents [5-8].

Skin signs are generally similar in both AN and BN even if some differences can be found. The prevalence of xerosis in BN is slightly lower than in AN. Telogen effluvium and acne are perhaps more frequent in BN; Russell's sign, dental enamel erosion and salivary gland enlargement are pathognomonic of purging behaviour and are also common in BN.

Skin Signs in Males with EDs

Owing to the prevalence of the restrictive type of AN in males, with less vomiting and laxative abuse, skin signs due to vomiting such as scraped or raw areas on the patient's knuckles (Russell's sign) and perimylosis, are less frequently observed. Lanugo-like body hair as well, a soft, downy body hair that often develops on the chest and arms of anorexic women, is difficult to evaluate in men or is absent. Moreover, skin signs that are frequent in women such as opaque and fragile hair, nail fragility and self-induced dermatitis were absent in our patients. Therefore, the dermatologic diagnosis of male AN must be based on different parameters.

In our patients, haematic crasis and the endocrine system were mostly compromised and skin changes were the expression of that pathology [15].

Further investigations on larger series are requested to better understand the dermatologic complications of AN in males but, based on our data, we can conclude that the classification of skin signs of EDs into four groups is not completely adequate for male AN. We have not identified any dermatologic guiding sign to help suspect an early diagnosis of AN in males. Nevertheless, the existence of AN in males and the preponderance of haematic alterations in these patients [16] must be kept in mind because some skin symptoms such as purpura, and laboratory tests simulate leukemia and other severe diseases.

REFERENCES

[1] Tyler, I; Wiseman, C; Crawford, RI; et al. Cutaneous manifestations of ED. *J Cutan Med Surg.* 2002 6, 345-53.

[2] Siddiqui, A; Ramsay, B; Leonard, J. The cutaneous signs of ED. *Acta Derm Venereol* (Stockh) 1994 74, 68-69.

[3] Marshman, GM; Hanna, MJ; Ben-Tovim DI; et al. Cutaneous abnormalities in anorexia nervosa. *Australas J Dermatol* 1990 31(1),9-12.

[4] Strumia, R; Varotti, E; Manzato, E; et al. Skin signs in anorexia nervosa. *Dermatology* 2001 203,314-7

[5] Strumia, R; Manzato, E; Gualandi M. Cutaneous manifestations in anorexia nervosa in males. *JEADV* 2002 16 Suppl.1,303.

[6] Glorio, R; Allevato, M; De Pablo, A; et al. Prevalence of cutaneous manifestations in 200 patients with ED. *Int J Dermatol* 2000 39,348-53.

[7] Hediger, C; Rost, B; Itin, P. Cutaneous manifestations in anorexia nervosa. *Schweiz Med Wochenschr* 2000 130(16),565-75.

[8] Gupta, MA; Gupta, AK; Haberman, HF. Dermatologic signs in anorexia nervosa and bulimia nervosa. *Arch Dermatol* 1987 123,1386-90.

[9] Gupta, MA; Gupta, AK; Voorhees, JJ. Starvation-associated pruritus: a clinical feature of ED. *J Am Acad Dermatol* 1992 27(1),118-20.

[10] Abella, E; Feliu, E; Granata, I; et al. Bone marrow changes in anorexia nervosa are correlated with the amount of weight loss and not with other clinical findings. *Am J Clin Pathol* 2002 118(4),582-8.

[11] Lurie, R ; Danziger, Y ; Kaplan, Y ; et al. Acquired pili torti: a structural hair shaft defect in anorexia nervosa. *Cutis* 1996 57,151-6.

[12] Ishiguro, N; Hirohara, D; Hotta, M; et al. Linear erythema craquelé due to acute oedema in anorexia nervosa. *Br J Derm* 2001 145,357.

[13] Schulze, UM; Pettke-Rank, CV; Kreienkamp, M; et al. Dermatologic findings in anorexia and bulimia nervosa of childhood and adolescence. *Pediatr Dermatol* 1999;16(2):90-4.

[14] Garcia Hidalgo, L; Dermatological Complications of Obesity. *Am J Clin Derm* 2002 3,497-506.

[15] Strumia, R; Manzato, E; Gualandi, M. Cutaneous manifestations in anorexia nervosa in males. *JEADV* 2002 16 Suppl.1,303.

[16] Abella E, Feliu E, Granada I, Milla F, Oriol A, Ribera JM, Sanchez-Planell L, Berga LI, Reverter, JC; Rozman, C. Bone marrow changes in anorexia nervosa are correlated with the amount of weight loss and not with other clinical findings. *Am J Clin Pathol* 2002 118,582-8

PART III. THE EXPERIENCE OF THE EATING DISORDER UNIT IN FERRARA (I)

PREFACE PART THREE

THE EXPERIENCE OF EATING DISORDER UNIT IN FERRARA, ITALY

We conclude this book with the presentation of our experience in the ED Unit in Ferrara (Italy).

Initially we describe our multiprofessional team and the different types of our intervention in the Diagnostic and Treatment phases.

The clinical activity of last decade will be reported, the different diagnostic groups and the multiple types of treatment settings in our Unit will be shown.

Finally we will present some clinical cases of ED males, followed in our Centre.

We have chosen some cases of medical and psychiatric interest, which may address specific clinical aspects, already treated in the theoretical part.

The aim of these clinical vignettes is to help PCPs to early recognize ED subjects and diagnose them as soon as possible also taking into account the medical complications.

In each clinical case we have given an overview of psychiatric, medical and nutritional assessment and, at the end, we have summarized the points of greatest complexity (the delay of diagnosis is one of these points).

PCPs, if aware of all the possible clinical manifestations, have a vital role in early diagnosis and play a crucial role for a right approach to the likely ED subject: this is particularly true in case of an uncooperative subject.

Actually, improving secondary prevention remains a priority in the care of ED.

We have not dwelt upon the course of the treatments made by different patients at our Centre (only for some of them we gave outcome scores) because the exposition of the wide variety of treatments of EDs overcomes the scope of our work.

Chapter 1

THE EATING DISORDER UNIT IN FERRARA, ITALY

E. Manzato

The Eating Disorder Unit works inside S.Anna Hospital in Ferrara, a North Italian town, since 1997.

This Unit is a public structure depending on the National Health Service and it is organized as a multidisciplinary centre.

Admission to the unit is charged by a ticket; when a diagnosis of ED is defined (according to the DSM-IV criteria) the subject is free of charge as provided for ED patients, in Italy.

Access to the centre may be requested by primary care physicians, paediatricians and all those specialists who suspect an ED.

Sometimes relatives or patients themselves may directly ask for an evaluation.

The unit is addressed to patients over 14 years old.

The Centre is organized as a multidisciplinary structure as indicated by the most accepted international guidelines (APA 2000 and 2006, NICE 2006, New Zealand 2006) and by the national and regional guidances.

The team consists of a psychiatrist, an expert of internal medicine, a dietician and some psychotherapists and psychologists.

The common approach to the patient is organized in three phases: the diagnostic phase, the treatment phase and the monitoring phase.

THE DIAGNOSTIC PHASE

The first evaluation is always made by the psychiatrist, who is the Unit Organizer as well. If the suspicion of ED is validated and if the patient accepts to undergo a diagnostic path, the following steps will be planned:

- individual sessions aimed to assess the psychological status
- a set of self reported inventories in the area of ED and comorbidity (Eating Disorder Inventory, Eating Attitudes Test, Body Attitude Test, Beck's Depression Inventory, Binge Eating Scale)

- family counselling for adolescents
- medical evaluation in order to define clinical general conditions and to choose the more adequate medical intervention and care setting (outpatient, day hospital, hospital).
- nutritional evaluation aimed to define the alimentary patterns and the severity of the most used unhealthy behaviours (dieting, skipping meals, binging-purging practices).

THE THERAPEUTIC PHASE

Type and setting of treatment depend on the severity of general conditions and the compliance of the subject: for the most part, interventions are performed in an outpatient setting where the subjects are followed according to a multidisciplinary approach.

The majority of these outpatients are responsive to treatment, nevertheless some patients do not respond to a lenient approach as they present a higher degree of severity. These patients may require more intensive treatment such as partial hospitalization inside our Day Hospital Unit or even an inpatient treatment.

During partial hospitalization the nutritional rehabilitation process can be helped by having meals with the assistance and encouragement of therapists, or by receiving nutritional infusion therapy.

The most critical patients may need full hospitalization and treatment as inpatients, according to the international guidelines which have defined criteria for admission to inpatient treatment and goals to achieve.

In Ferrara, inside the Medical Department, one bed is always available for eating disordered patients.

In case of severe emaciation or severe medical complications the first goal is to improve the nutritional status and to treat the somatic damage in order to avoid mortality risks and to allow a future psychotherapeutic intervention.

Once good medical stabilization and an adequate weight restoration are acheived the patients will be discharged and the same eating disorder team will continue to take care and follow them in an outpatient setting.

In our team weekly meetings take place, in order to discuss clinical cases with all the staff members. In this context improvements and difficulties of the patients are reassessed to better plan the therapeutic process.

Once the patient is recovered he undergoes a monitoring phase to prevent him from relapses.

The ED Centre has evaluated, in recent years, over a thousand patients (figure with breakdown of diagnosis): we report in Figure 1 the total cases divided by diagnostic class.

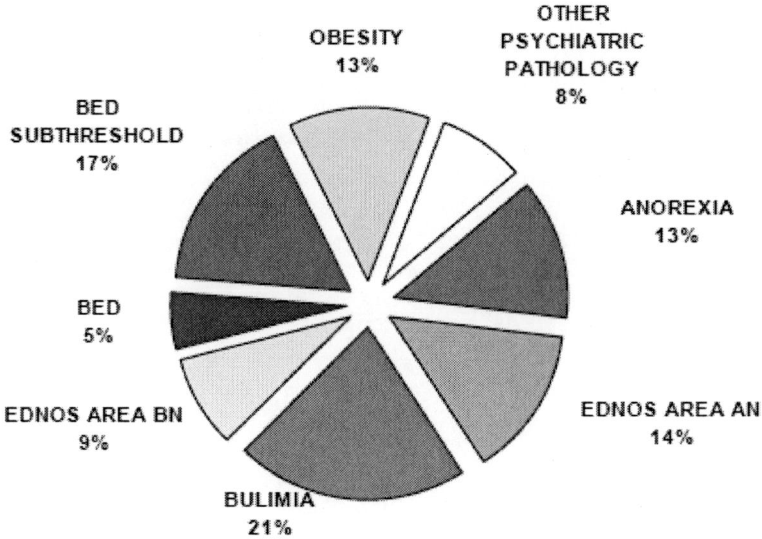

Figure 1. Total of Patients: 1080 BED = Binge Eating Disorder EDNOS = Eating Disorder not Otherwise Specified.

We report now three figures which show the various treatment settings in patients as overall sample (Fig.2) and then subdivided by diagnosis of AN (Fig.3), BN (Fig.4) and EDNOS (Fig.5).

The percentage of males seen in the Unit is definitely low even compared to prevalent data in the literature.

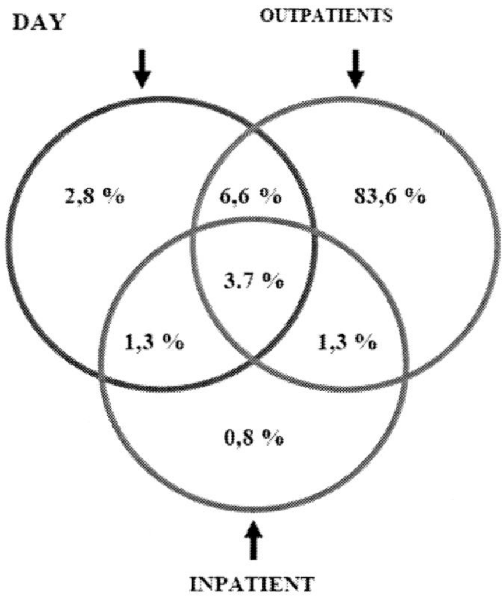

Figure 2. Non-proportional Venn diagram on the method of treatment in 712 patients with ED.

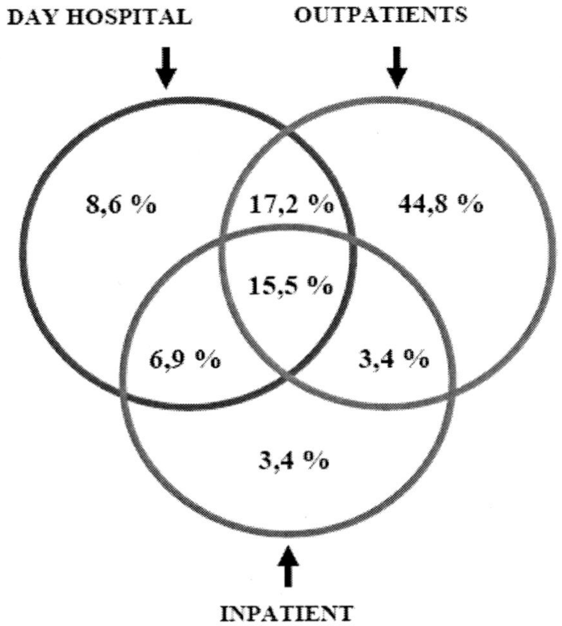

Figure 3. Non-proportional Venn diagram on the method of treatment in 116 patients with Anorexia nervosa.

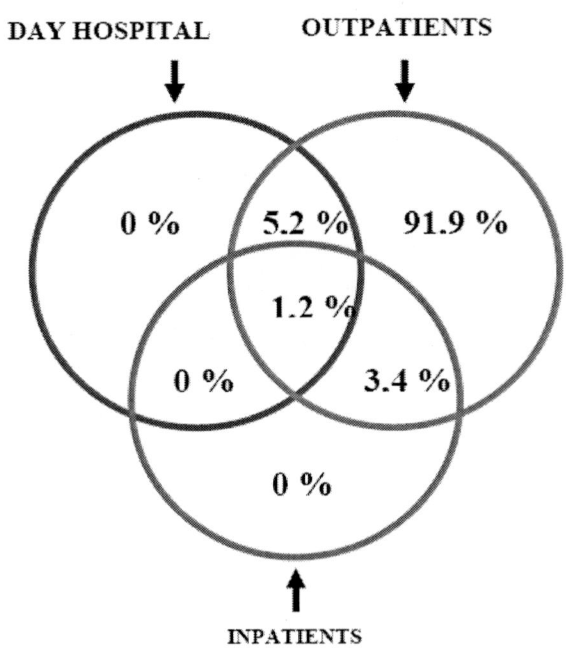

Figure 4. Non-proportional Venn diagram on the method of treatment in 173 patients with Bulimia Nervosa.

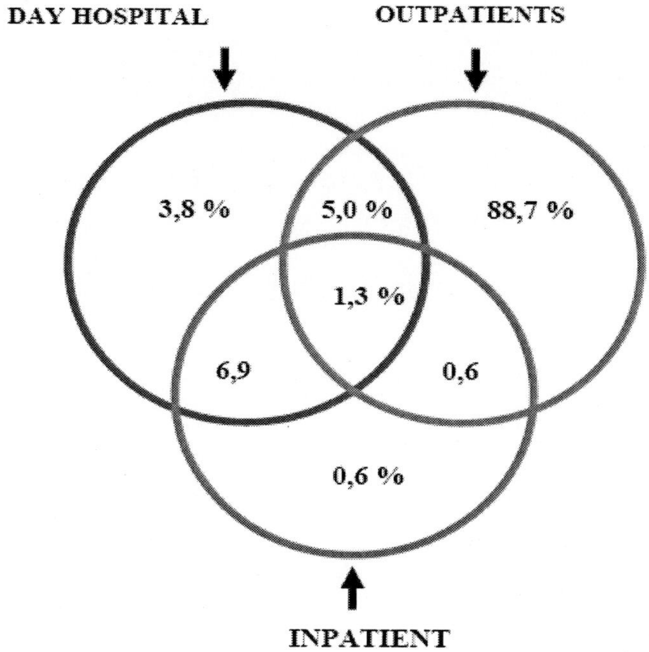

Figure 5. Non-proportional Venn diagram on the method of treatment in 159 patients with EDNOS.

Males treated in the Unit are 79 in total and we report in Table I their diagnostic features.

Table I Males treated in ED Unit of Ferrara

Diagnosis	Frequency	Percent	Valid Percent	Cumulative percent
Other psychiatric pathology	7	8,9	8,9	8,9
Other Pathology	1	1,3	1,3	10,1
An-r	5	6,3	6,3	16,5
BED	8	10,1	10,1	26,6
BN-np	2	2,5	2,5	29,1
BN-p	7	8,9	8,9	38,0
EDNOS anorexic area	10	12,7	12,7	50,6
BED Subthreshold	15	19,0	19,0	69,6
EDNOS bulimic area	1	1,3	1,3	70,9
None	5	6,3	6,3	77,7
Obesity	18	22,8	22,8	100
Total	79	100	100	

The mean positive outcome of the Unit has been around 80% (considering total and partial remissions).

The ED Unit of Ferrara participated in the work of the Regional Group for EDa, established at the Department of Health of the Emilia Romagna region, which in 2003 drafted the document: "Health promotion for eating disorders" Dossier '89 - 04, the official document to address the treatment of EDs in the public health system (a copy of the volume can be downloaded from the website: http://www.regione.emilia-romagna.it/agenziasan/colldoss/index.htm).

In the Ministerial Document of 1998 the reported prevalence values in Italy for subjects between 12 and 25 years were: AN 0.3%, BN 1%, ED-NOS 6%.

According to this data we should expect that in the population of Emilia-Romagna – consisting of more than four million people- somewhere between 4,000 and 8,000 people should be affected by EDs, namely AN/BN. On the contrary, the number of patients under treatment for an ED in specialized public centres of the region Emilia Romagna is significantly below this expected rate.

One of the first problems to be considered is the lack of accessibility to facilities, particularly for adolescents. Another crucial point is the low level of awareness and skills of PCPs and paediatricians in this specific field.

These factors are even more influential on male population where diagnosis is delayed and more difficult also because of limiting cultural and social aspects.

The Regional ED Group developed official guidelines for the treatment of EDs and indicated, as treatment of choice for EDs, the therapeutic integrated protocol in which the management is multi-dimensional and multi-professional. The ED Unit of Ferrara follows these guidelines. The Regional ED Group has been a very important experience in the public structures dealing with EDs, because it has been supporting and enhancing the regional network for EDs.

Case Reports

Case 1

Bob: Long Term Bulimia in a Cyclist

This is the case of a 39 years-old man with a severe diagnosis of purging BN.

This man was a cyclist involved in agonistic performances.

He was referred by his PCP because of chronic fatigue and suspected ED.

When he arrived to our Centre he looked embarrassed and suspicious. He reported he was always tired, was constantly in a bad mood and he felt emotionally flat.

He reported a long list of disadvantages for being ill (both physical and psychological difficulties, both individual and interpersonal); he was seeking help.

He reported he was bingeing and vomiting every day, in average vomiting occurred two to three times a day for the last 25 years.

In fact he started vomiting at the age of 14 because he was slightly overweight (but he felt to be enormously fat). At that time he strongly wanted to lose weight. He began to induce vomiting by putting his fingers down his throat; by inducing himself to vomit after the meals he lost a large amount of weight. It seemed to him that he had found a great tool.

After some years, vomiting after his meals became a regular practice.

Nobody in the original family was aware of this purging behaviour.

He married at the age of 29, he had a baby some years later. His 5 year old son suffered from type-1 diabetes and he had to take insulin after every meal. He and his wife had often discussions about their son's nutrition. Nutrition was really a hard matter for him.

At the age of 28 he started biking, that was one of his father's favourite sporting activities. At the time of assessment he was hyperactive: in fact he ran 100 kilometres a day in spite of the weather: he said "I'm doing very foolish things, I go by bike even when it snows and I do know that it is dangerous, but I can't help doing it."

He was strongly focused on his body and on his body weight. He weighed himself many times a day. At the time of the first visit he had a BMI of 20.8 (63 kilos per 1.74 meters).

He reportedly ate an energetic breakfast with plenty of cornflakes, more than half a litre of milk, dried raisin (roly-poly), coco and other hypercaloric food.

At dinner he always had to eat in restaurants together with his colleagues (he worked in a gas and water delivery company) and for him this was a real "trauma" every day. In these occasions he had big portions of *pasta* and meat and cheese and vegetables, and bread, and fruit and a big slice of cake, everything followed by vomiting. In the evening he tried to eat very little (and his wife was very disappointed about it) otherwise he had another binge episode followed by vomiting.

Eating great amount of food was a problem for him, vomiting was the solution.

The episodes of overeating and vomiting were eventually followed by feelings of guilt and distress.

He completed the self reported questionnaires usually used in our Centre in the assessment phase: the Eating Disorder Inventory evidenced a strong drive for thinness, profound sense of inadequacy and difficulties in interpersonal relationships. He reported to be satisfied with his body weight and shape but the reported score on the body dissatisfaction EDI subscale was low.

At the Beck Depression Inventory he reported moderate levels of depressive symptomatology.

Actually he denied his depression; bulimic symptoms together with the physical tiredness probably let his depressive symptoms remain concealed and therefore he was unaware of them.

The patient did not report medical symptoms, nevertheless a physical assessment was required because of the long duration of his eating disorder characterized by frequent purging behaviour, resistance and compulsive exercise.

At first medical visit his BMI was slightly improved 21,4 (weight 65 kg, height 1,74 meters).

Blood pressure was 130/90, heart rate 48 beats /minute.

The patient had a strong muscularity and his muscular abdominal wall was so contracted that abdominal palpation was almost impossible.

All routine laboratory tests, electrolytes and full blood count were in normal ranges.

Total and free testosterone were lower than inferior limits of normal ranges: respectively 263 ng /dl (normal ranges 270-1070) and 5,03 pg/ml (normal ranges 5,50-40,00) so as FSH and LH respectively 0.4 mUI /ml (normal ranges 2.0-5) and 0.9 mUI/ml (normal ranges 1,5-9); FT4 was at the lower level of normal ranges, TSH was normal.

A flat glucose curve after Oral Glucose Tolerance Test was present and probably due to a delayed gastric emptying and/or to a reduced intestinal absorption, likely enhanced by a latent hypothyroidism. Insulin basal level and insulin levels after glucose load were inside normal ranges.

The patient underwent an oesophago-gastroduodenoscopy (OEGDS), a diagnostic procedure that we usually require even in asymptomatic patients if they have a long duration of vomiting.

The endoscopic and histological picture were consistent with the diagnosis of Barrett's Oesophagus.

Treatment with Pantoprazole (40 mg /die) was initiated and the patient was urged to not discontinue the drug until first follow up- 6 months months.

At discharge a report was sent to his PCP to inform him about the need of regular OEGDS controls due to a higher risk for developing adenocarcinoma.

Besides the necessary medical treatment we decided to cope with his long lasting disorder: the patient began to come twice a week to the Centre both for psychological and nutritional sessions.

During the treatment he aimed first at reducing hyperactivity and he started then to introduce regular and balanced meals. Binge episodes drastically diminished and subsequently he also vomited less. He felt less tired and the relation with his wife started to improve. He had also more time and energy to spend with his child. Difficulties however emerged in his parental role, he thought he was unable to interact with babies: "my wife is able and very good, but I'm not able."

He recalled some episodes from the past related to the relation between him and his father. His father was strict with him and his brother; he always had rules to impose and he did it in a very scary way. He grew up timid. He reported to often be fearful of getting his father angry. In his original family, they seldom spoke to each other. Everything was kept inside and he grew up with the feeling that he couldn't speak about his emotions. During his adolescence he couldn't speak about his troubles or about the difficulties he experienced with his peers and the sense of shame for being overweight. He grew up very uncommunicative. His eating disorder protected him in some way from social life.

In the course of therapy he started to look into himself and to share his thoughts and feelings with the psychologist, and for him it was a stumbling-block! It was really hard work for him!

An important event during treatment occurred, he bought a camper: This was for occasions when he'd go away for trips with his family. He put away the bikes except for short journeys that he made, sometimes alone (but much less than 100 kilometres) or sometimes together with his son.

He reported that he started to feel better, more under control, less tired. His food intake was more adequate. Gradually he diminished and than stopped vomiting.

At a certain point of the treatment depressive symptoms were disclosed. He became more aware of his personal and interpersonal problems: for example he reported that between him and his wife the relation was not very satisfactory and he claimed she was very occupied with their son and worried because of their son's diabetes. He thought that his wife was more engaged with her role of mother than in her role of wife: he felt unconsidered. He felt a decrease in sexual desire and sexual intercourse was rare.

Bulimia nervosa was thought to act like a sort of protection for his interpersonal difficulties. Eating disorders' symptoms seem to have also an antidepressant function.

His symptoms, whose onset was related to the need of controlling his body weight, later became probably a means to cover up his difficulties in his role of husband and father.

He had a worsening in his bulimic symptoms, he started bingeing and vomiting again and was very afflicted and frustrated about this. Besides psychological support he was given SSRI treatment.

After some months he found a new balance: he sometimes had losses of control on food followed by vomit episodes, not daily but sporadically, namely two or three times a month.

He attained and maintained a form of eating disorder not otherwise specified, characterized by a lower frequency and lower intensity of bingeing and vomiting.

He was suggested to begin a more introspective form of psychotherapy that he didn't accept.

He was then referred to his PCP who was invited to make periodically physical examinations and to be alerted on possible relapses.

From the psychological point of view it is worth noting that even in a long term ED patient (with a duration of illness of more than 20 years) a significant improvement is possible.

The patient needed a very long time to find the courage to confide to therapists about his ED.

Symptoms which were considered initially egosynthonic like hyperactivity and vomiting were later abandoned, constructing a more functional and adaptative way of reacting.

After complete remission of ED symptoms a new awareness of interpersonal difficulties emerged and this consequently caused a depressive mood previously concealed by bulimic behaviours. In this phase Bob again started binge and vomiting behaviours but in a less severe way: we can hypothesize that he made a mild an acceptable compromise between the initial severe form of bulimia and the possibility of reaching complete recovery that would have required further psychotherapeutic work.

The patient was in fact not ready and motivated to continue with an introspective form of psychotherapy. He felt generally much better and for him it was enough. He claimed to be satisfied and very proud of himself.

COMMENT

The present case illustrates how purging behaviours (vomiting in this case), starting during adolescence to attain weight loss, can develop into a severe 25 year long form of bulimia.

This case aims at underlining the great importance of the primary care providers: in fact this patient was referred to our Centre by his PCP who suspected an ED: when the patient showed signs of physical tiredness (the only symptom he could initially recognize) he encouraged him to come in contact with our specialized Unit.

As this patient was a cyclist, and he used hyperactivity to keep weight and shape under control, it was difficult to help him discriminate between cycling as sporting activity and compulsive cycling.

PCPs too are asked to early-recognize the difference existing between a healthy sporting activity and an alarming symptom of an ED.

Excessive exercise is, in fact, a symptom that needs to be recognized and faced.

This case gives hope to all patients with a long term ED and to all therapists who work with these eating disordered patients as, even when a long-standing eating disorder is present, a positive outcome can be reached.

From the point of view of the physician this case presents longstanding bulimia, very severe with regard to the presence of purging and non-purging compensatory behaviours, nevertheless not symptomatic for medical complications, excluding asthenia.

Despite this mild clinical picture some relevant physical aspects emerged in the medical assessment.

Oesophagogastroduodenoscopy, performed in absence of specific gastroenteric symptoms, revealed the presence of Barrett's oesophagus, an important risk factor for adenocarcinoma of inferior oesophagus. This finding underscores the importance of endoscopic investigations of upper gastroenteric apparatus in chronic bulimia even though asymptomatic.

Another finding that is worth being stressed is the low level of testosterone and gonadotropins, not so common in bulimic patients but common in athletes of resistance sports. These endocrine changes were consistent with hypogonadotropic hypogonadism of hypothalamic origin similar to those observed in athletes and in AN patients.

Altered glicaemic omeostasis, even if not clinically relevant, was another intriguing speculative aspect, especially if we consider that his son was affected by Type-1 diabetes.

Case 2

Bill: Bulimia Nervosa as a Cathartic Space for a Top Manager

Bill, a 45 year-old man, was referred to our centre by a gastroenterologist in our hospital who evaluated him for gastroenteric symptoms, specifically upper abdominal pain: the specialist, after an accurate history, suspected purging type BN and asked our multidisciplinary team for a complete assessment comprehensive of psychiatric, psychological, medical and nutritional evaluation.

The patient accepted and entered our ED Unit in June 2005.

He was a business man, engaged in a very stressful job and in a complicated relationship with his wife. He had a 10 year-old son, affected by autism

He reported a 28 years long history of ED and depressive moods, which he kept hidden, which begun when he was an adolescent; at that time he lost both parents and remained alone with his sister.

During adolescence he had been an obese boy. At the age of 17 his height was 170 cm and his weight reached a maximum of 103 kg (BMI 35,6). He began a very restrictive diet leading him, in 3 years, to a weight loss of 47.5 kg and to a final weight of 56.5 kg (BMI 19,5).

At the age of 21 he stopped dieting but afterwards, since he was gaining weight again, he decided to practice purging behaviours (vomiting after meals) and later he started to binge. At the age of 31 years, during the florid binge/purge phase, he had a severe and life threatening event related to an extremely severe hypokalemia: a myocardial infarction complicated by cardiac arrest.

The binging/purging cycle was still present at the moment of the first visit at the Centre. From obesity complicated by a binge eating disorder to a restrictive diet and finally to the binging/purging cycle this subject had spent 28 years of his life keeping his problem hidden from his relatives, to his friends and even to his wife.

He showed, initially, many resistances for coming to the Centre: he delayed the appointments, arrived late, left for a long journey between the first and the second psychological session. He claimed he couldn't find the time for coming.

In his role of sales' manager he found it very difficult to accept the different position of being a patient. At the beginning of each session he needed to show self-confidence and assertiveness by smiling in a very open, bright and seductive way. His handshake was excessively vigorous. He acted like a perfect business man, because that was what he was.

He made gallant comments about the therapists. He often tried to get the therapist to speak about herself.

He found it really hard to look at himself like a suffering man and to start thinking and speaking about himself and his difficulties. It was also hard for him to get in touch with his emotional states and his internal feelings. He presented with a profound lack of awareness about his illness. He spent much time and energy denying and under-evaluating his symptoms. It was easier, but not easy, for him to recognize medical complications rather than psychological fractures.

He had a long lasting form of bulimia and his life was characterized by stressful and traumatic events which he tried to avoid facing. His ED, with its repetitive cycles of bingeing, fasting and purging behaviours, could have had an active function in this tentative of denial.

He reported that a precipitant factor for his ED was the death of both parents, which occurred in the same year: his father died of a heart stroke and his mother died a few months later. He and his younger sister remained alone. He precipitated in a depressive state which he tried to contrast by hyperactivity and over-working.

A medical evaluation was required by the physician of ED Centre. From the patient history it emerged that he was a smoker, 20 cigarettes a day, he wasn't an alcohol abuser nor a drug abuser.

A critical hypopotassiemia (1 meq/l) related to purging behaviour was reported at the time of his cardiac arrest in clinical charts.

After the cardiac attack he had always been under treatment with low doses of betablockers (Atenolol 25 mg /die) and with ASA (325 mg/die). During the following years he discontinued clinical cardiologic controls except for an occasional echocardiogram.

At the physical examination the subject appeared to be a well nourished man, slightly overweight; his anthropometric data were : Weight Kg 82, Height cm 170, BMI 28.3.

Spontaneous epigastric pain was the only reported symptom and the only significant finding was an upper abdominal pain enhanced by palpation and prevalent in epigastric area.

Blood pressure was 130/80, heart rate was 64 /minute, both in the normal ranges.

The patient accepted to undergo to a full physical assessment, particularly focused on gastroenteric symptoms; even in absence of specific symptoms, cardiovascular system was re-evaluated.

Laboratory findings : Haematologic parameters were in normal ranges even though white cells, haematocrit and haemoglobin were at the upper limit. All routine biochemistry tests were in normal ranges.

Cardiovascular investigations: ECG showed a sinus rhythm, HR 74 beats /minute and an altered profile of QRS in V1-V4, consistent with previous myocardial infarction.

ECG monitoring 24 H (HOLTER ECG) demonstrated a constant sinus rhythm with a minimum heart rate of 51, a maximum of 120, a median value of 81 and the presence of 21 BEVS, 297 BEV, two BEV couples and two ventricular runs, one of them sustained over six beats.

Transthoracic Ecocardiogram: left ventricle's mass and volumes were into normal ranges, akinesia of left ventricle apex and hypokinesia of interventricular sept in its middle and basal portion were present; ejection fraction (FE) was 45%, an altered diastolic filling pattern was evident in left ventricle, the left atrium and right chambers were not dilated, pericardial effusion was not present: echocardiografic picture was consistent with post-infarction ischaemic cardiopathy.

Maximum exercise ECG with cycle ergometer was negative.

Oesophagogastroduodenoscopy (OEGDS) showed oesophageal ulcer, antral erosive gastritis, duodenitis with flattening of the second duodenal portion.

Histological specimens collected from this area and also from antrum and oesophagus-cardias junction demonstrated respectively a chronic duodenitis of first degree, a superficial and deep chronic quiescent gastritis, a cardiasic mucosa partially lined by squamous epithelium with intestinal metaplasia of foveolar epithelium.

Upper abdomen ultrasonography showed hepatic steatosis of first degree, no other abnormality.

After the assessment the patient accepted both psychological support and pharmacological treatment for medical problems.

In regards to medical complications, cardiac hyperkinetic arrhythmias (runs VPB) were treated at first through a slight increase of betablockers (atenolol from 25 to 50 mg/die), not subsequently tolerated by the patient for increasing asthenia. So, a therapy with propafenone 450 mg bis in die plus the little usual doses of betablockers was initiated.

An ECG monitoring after 4 months showed the disappearance of runs VPB.

Ace inhibitors were prescribed initially, then discontinued for hypotension.

The gastroenteric complications were treated with Proton Pump Inhibitors (PPIs) with good results on symptoms.

From the psychological point of view the patient underwent a cognitive behavioural treatment for BN with individual supportive sessions.

Bill was discharged in October 2005 from Day Hospital with a complete remission of bulimic symptoms and gastroenteric symptoms: a program of clinical follow up was planned.

In February 2006 the patient presented a sudden paresthesia to left emisoma followed by a transient loss of consciousness and vomiting.

A brain TC performed in emergency highlighted two circumscribed ischaemic areas in left para median region of cerebellum and a mild atrophia.

The neurologic examen showed an omonimous lateral emianopsy of upper right quadrant confirmed by campimetric examination.

Routine biochemistry tests were negative, thyroid hormones were in normal ranges, blood parameters ruled out haematologic diseases.

Diagnostic tests exploring the existence of congenital or acquired abnormalities of the coagulative system and/or vasculitis were inconsistent with these diagnoses.

Total cholesterol and LDL calculated cholesterol were respectively 256 and 179 mg/dl. Omocistein was mildly elevated 18.9 micromol/L (normal ranges 5-15).

Echo-doppler of the supra-aortic trunks demonstrated only intimal thickening associated to a little ateromasic lesion in the anterior wall of carotid bifurcation, in absence of significant changes in flow velocity. Brain RM showed two lesions: one, older, in left paramedian cerebellar region, the other one, subacute, in left occipital region.

AngioRNM with investigation of extracranic circulation demonstrated hypoplasia of left vertebral artery.

Transesophageal echocardiogram results were negative for thrombuses in cardiac chambers so that a cardioembolic origin of the ischemic attack resulted less probable.

ECG 24 hours did not put in evidence arrhythmias.

ASA was discontinued by neurologists and the patient began taking ticlopidine 250 mg tablet bis in die.

OUTCOME

During outpatient treatment he started eating according to a more regular pattern, he stopped his bulimic episodes and consequently he stopped vomiting. He could face his preoccupation of weight gain and experimented with a better method of self-caring.

He started thinking that bulimia was a problem itself but also had a role of conceiving other personal and interpersonal difficulties that he couldn't deny. Bulimia was like a cathartic space in his daily life, where everything (his job, his wife and his wife's family and his son) was perceived as excessively demanding.

The patient showed a significant improvement on his ED symptoms during treatment that was confirmed in successive follow-up controls .

Also, regarding medical aspects the neurological picture improved progressively even if the patient was still under control after one year from admission

COMMENT OF THE PSYCHIATRIST

This case report highlights some important points: first of all the great deal of resistance shown by the patient in recognizing his bulimic symptoms. He found it very difficult to think about suffering from an ED and therefore to speak about it with the therapists. This is common in eating disordered patients who feel ashamed of their bulimic symptoms but it can be even more significant in male bulimic patients. After having disclosed his difficulties this patient followed a multidisciplinary treatment that helped him overcome binging and purging.

Another point is the role that bulimic symptoms can play in a very stressful life.

The binging-purging cycle can represent a way of masking, even for a while, the sufferance coming from life stressors. The decision to eat and to vomit can be an illusory space in which one can "find himself," can "decide something" and not be a victim of unmanageable life situations. The problem becomes evident when the bulimic symptoms dominate the will of the patient who finds himself in a passive position.

Last but not least, in this case it is evident how bulimic symptoms can be faced and overcome once the patient engages himself in a specialized, integrated treatment.

COMMENT OF THE PHYSICIAN

From the point of view of the physician this case presents unusual and striking medical features: it cannot represent a typical, common case of bulimia even though cardiovascular arrhythmias and gastroenteric complications are often observed in severe long-standing bulimia.

The patient had passed through two severe ischemic attacks in young age. The first, a cardiac attack, was associated with a florid binging purging phase complicated by a very severe hypokalemia, likely a risk factor for the cardiac event and the consequent arrest.

The second event, an occipital ischemia, occurred in the remission phase of bulimia.

RNM showed also that old cerebellar ischemic areas were present, clinically silent and never diagnosed. We can only hypothesize that multiple discontrol behaviours such as binging/purging and smoking and a highly stressful life were important risk co-factors for severe medical complications in this subject.

Moreover, anatomic factors such as the presence of a congenital left vertebral artery hypoplasia could play a crucial pathogenetic role in posterior circulation stroke. Increase of omocistein and cholesterol could be other possible additional co-factors.

Even if we don't consider the purging bulimic behaviour as the only responsible for all clinical medical complications in this subject we don't exclude that it may have played an important co-pathogenetic role.

Case 3

MARK: ANOREXIA IN A YOUNG ATHLETE

Mark came to our Centre at the age of 21: he had been a sportsman practicing swimming at a very high competitive level until the moment in which he had to stop because of a severe state of malnutrition.

At presentation, he had a BMI of 14.3 as he weighed 44 kg for 175 centimetres of height.

Mark had a familiarity for EDs: his 29 year old sister, who lived out of the family nucleus with her partner, had had an episode of restricting AN at the age of 18. She recovered without any treatment.

Mark started to lose weight at the age of 17 and he linked the onset of his ED to his relationship with a girl who suffered from purging-type AN.

He reported to have been influenced by his girl's behaviours and attitudes: she had excessive concerns about shape, weight and food. He began a restrictive alimentary pattern as she did, also focusing on calculation of caloric intake. Mark began to practice excessive exercise, biking and jogging besides the many hours dedicated to his swimming training.

Despite the fact he had a normal weight his girl often used to take fun of him calling him "fatty" and mock him about his "overeating " (that actually was a normal eating for a sportsman).

He was later abandoned by his girlfriend. In the same year he began his university studies for engineering. He spent his time between hyperactivity on one side and hard working on his studies on the other side, and he strived for the achievement of high results.

Since the ED was worsening and his weight decreasing Mark, began to modify his personality features. He was depressed, he withdrew from peers and friends and became socially isolated, spent many hours closed in his bedroom, working on his personal computer. He had to stop competitive swimming.

He continued to follow a highly restrictive diet by using a rigid daily caloric scheme.

In a short time Mark became severely underweight and for this reason he was initially addressed to a Centre of Mental Disease where he was followed for a short time, but without any result on his anorectic symptoms: in fact he continued to lose weight.

Before coming to our Centre he was referred by his PCP to Gastroenterology for hospitalization indicated by a severe underweight (at that time he reported a BMI of 13) and elevation of liver enzymes.

Mark arrived to our ED Unit, after his teachers strongly suggested him and his family to require an evaluation in an ED Centre.

Two years had passed from the onset of AN to an appropriate referral!

During the first meeting with the psychologist he showed his identity certification with a photo of himself in which he appeared very, very nice-looking, normal-weight, with a well defined muscle mass, and he said: "I was very different. You see, I have lost everything!."

The patient was evaluated in a few days by all the components of our ED Unit: psychiatrist, psychologist, clinician and dietician. His family was also involved in the care.

The patient's personal history and family history were negative for the presence of other psychiatric diseases except for a previous episode of anorexia in his sister.

His parents reported a normal psychophysical development of their son without any difficulty in his nutrition when he was a child.

They underlined "perfectionism" as a core feature of Mark's personality. He had the ambition to be the best, both in studies and in sports; he had been planning for success all his life - they reported that he always said: " I will go to University, I will get a degree with full marks, I will get married at the age of twenty five." Everything had to be planned and organized. They reported he had no difficulty in social relations.

During the first visit Mark appeared very weak, slow reacting, fatigued by the physical status of emaciation.

He seemed to be aware of his severe physical conditions, nevertheless he still had an intense fear of gaining weight, therefore he regularly went on practicing a strict control on his caloric intake. He was extremely focused on his body appearance that he perceived as unsatisfactory.

At the time of our first assessment he presented a severe restriction of caloric intake, phobic avoidance of different types of food and an excessive slowness in consuming food; he was always calculating the number of calories consumed in each meal.

He completed a battery of self reported questionnaires and he scored 46 on the Beck's Depression Inventory (BDI), indicative of a severe level of depressive symptomatology; he scored 62 at the Body Attitudes Questionnaire (BAQ), indicating a level of difficulties in the attitudes towards his body and body dissatisfaction. On the Eating Disorders Inventory (EDI) he reported high levels of drive for thinness, perfectionism, interpersonal distrust, maturity fears and a low level of interoceptive awareness.

At the internal assessment Mark was pale and profoundly emaciated, his BMI was 14,3. He reported severe weakness and loss of concentration.

His maximum post-pubertal weight was 74 kg as the weight maintained for the longest time (BMI 24). He had a very pronounced muscle mass as he was a competitive swimmer.

The minimum post-pubertal weight had been 40 kg, BMI 13 at 20 years.

Physical examination revealed: oedema at lower limbs, petechiae at superior limbs and periclavear region and muscle mass depletion. Blood pressure was 100/70, pulse rate was 46/minute.

Because of the degree of severity he was hospitalized in our Division of Internal Medicine, a few days after the first evaluation.

He was collaborative and accepted to be hospitalized, even though he was more passive than truly compliant.

Laboratory tests at admission: white blood cells were 1400 /μl (normal ranges 4000-11.000), absolute count of neutrophils was 800/μl (normal ranges 1500-5000), red blood cells were 2.100.000/μl (normal ranges 5-6.5 millions), Hb was 7.1 g/dl (normal ranges 13-18), haematocritus was 20%, mean corpuscular volume (MCV) was 92 fl, at upper limit of normal ranges. Platelets were 133.000/μl (normal ranges (150.000-450.000). This condition was defined as pancytopenia even though white and red cells were more impaired in comparison with platelets. Lymphocyte populations were studied in order to identify alterations in cellular mediated immunity: Ratio CD4 /CD8 was very low 0,61, due to a severe decrease of the absolute number of CD4 (helper) lymphocyte subset.

HIV test was negative.

Serum glucose was low 54 mg/dl (normal ranges 70-120).

Iron was 106 μg/dl, in normal ranges, transferrin was low, 142 mg/dl (normal ranges 171-302), ferritin was high, 718 ng /ml (normal ranges in males 21-385).

Electrolytes: Natrium was 148 meq/l (normal ranges136-146), Potassium was very low 2,9 meq/l (3,5-5,3), Calcium was 4 meq/l (normal ranges 4,5-5,5), phosphorus was in normal ranges.

Total proteins were decreased to a very low level of 4,7 g/dl (normal ranges 6-8) with a high albumin percentage so that the absolute value was decreased only to a value of 3.01 g/dl; prealbumin was decreased to 15 mg/dl (normal ranges 18-45), gammaglobulins were also decreased to a value of 0,47 g/dl (normal ranges 0,68-1,58).

Liver enzymes were elevated, Alanintransferase was 86 U/l (superior limit was 40), Gammaglutamiltransferase was 70 U/l (normal ranges 11-50).

Folic acid and B12 vitamin deficiencies were excluded.

Hormonal parameters: ACTH and seric cortisol were in normal range.

Thyroid function was not impaired. FSH was at lower limit of normal ranges and LH was 0,9 mUI/ml, below normal ranges (normal ranges in male 1.5-9.3), total testosterone was at inferior limit of normality while free testosterone was low , 8,1 pg/ml (normal ranges 14,4-31,6).

Upper abdomen ultrasonography showed hepatic steatosis of first degree, gallbladder micro stones and sand.

Chest x ray was normal.

ECG showed a sinusal bradicardia (HR 47/minute).

Bone marrow aspirate and bone marrow biopsy displayed relevant morphologic changes such as atrophy of fat cells and loss of haematopoietic cells with the deposition of an amorphous and gelatinous material: the cytological/histological pattern was consistent with the diagnosis of “gelatinous transformation (GMT)” or “serous atrophy.”

Since admission Mark was compliant to treatment and for this reason caloric intake was given mostly through regular meals. Oral food intake was integrated by a slowly progressive parenteral infusion of nutrients, liquids, potassium chloride, calcium, phosphorus. He did not present any complication during the refeeding phase.

He was advised against doing any physical activity.

His physical condition improved day by day during 40 days of hospitalization: lower limbs oedema, likely due to anaemia and hypoalbuminemia, and petechiae, likely due to vessel fragility and decrease of fat subcutaneous tissue besides a mild thrombocytopenia, disappeared along the recovery of nutritional status.

At discharge from hospitalization he weighed 51.5 kg (BMI was 16.8), and all haematological and biochemical parameters were significantly improving.

Also ferritin had fallen to normal values in relation to recovery of erythropoiesis.

After discharge from inpatient treatment he underwent a comprehensive multidisciplinary outpatient treatment including nutritional rehabilitation and psychotherapy in addition to medical monitoring. He was regularly followed for almost 18 months (Fig 6-7).

At conclusive discharge his BMI was 24.16 and all haematological, biochemical and anthropometric parameters were normal. Two aspects remained in pathological conditions: one concerning the bone mineral density and the other one regarding the presence of hypogonadism of hypothalamic origin.

In this period for the first time Mark underwent DEXA. A scan at the lumbar spine showed a low BMD 0,840 g /cm square, both T score and Z score were -2.5.

Free testosterone and LH remained persistently below normal values even though a normal weight was achieved in that period: consistent with this data, decrease of libido and sexual activity were reported by the patient. Gonadotropin-releasing factor (GNRH) stimulation of pituitary -gonadic axis was performed, resulting in a normal FSH and LH response enhancement, therefore confirming the central pathogenic role of hypothalamic dysfunction.

It took two years from hospitalization to return to normal values of free testosterone and LH. Fat mass percentage was in that period 25% of total weight.

A second DEXA in this period showed a good improvement of bone mineral density with total BMD 0,993 g/cm square,T score -1,5, Z score -1,5.

From a psychiatric point of view Mark became, along the course of his treatment, progressively more aware of his illness: he described his stressing and competitive way of life, focused on the achievement of the best results, as a "barrier against growth."

During a session with his therapist he said: "I had planned my life with the expectation to reach specific goals, I simply had to achieve them. When I realized I couldn't any more get them I did not know what else I could do."

During his therapeutic path, which combined medical, nutritional and psychological therapy, he worked hard and reached an adequate alimentary pattern, limited his physical activity and achieved better perception and acceptance of his body image.

Follow up tests' scores went back to normal ranges.

It was not always easy for him to get in touch with his internal emotional states as he maintained a sort of rigid attitude.

Mood progressively improved without any pharmacological treatment.

He returned to his university activities and his social life also improved.

COMMENT

This case report presents most of the physical complications of a severe unrecognized restrictive AN with impairment of multiple organs and functions such as pancytopenia, osteoporosis, hypothalamic-hypopituitary hypogonadism, hypokalemia, transaminitis.

The long follow up period allowed us to better evaluate the different timing of improvement and reversibility of even severe medical complications such as: the gelatinous marrow transformation, the decrease of bone mineral density and the hypogonadism of hypothalamic origin.

In addition, this case helps to recall and underline some particular aspects, concerning ED risk factors, delay of referral etc.. already treated in the previous chapters.

In fact, several risk factors were present: he was a resistance athlete and during the phase of active illness he used swimming and other sport activities to lose more weight; he had a familiarity for EDs, he had strong traits of perfectionism and was highly competitive.

Mark's referral was made initially by his PCP to a gastroenterologist and not to a specific ED multidisciplinary centre so that the treatment was delayed from the onset of illness.

Despite the severity of this condition and the difficulties in the referral we can conclude that even such severe forms of anorexia can have a positive outcome when treated according to the main ED guidelines.

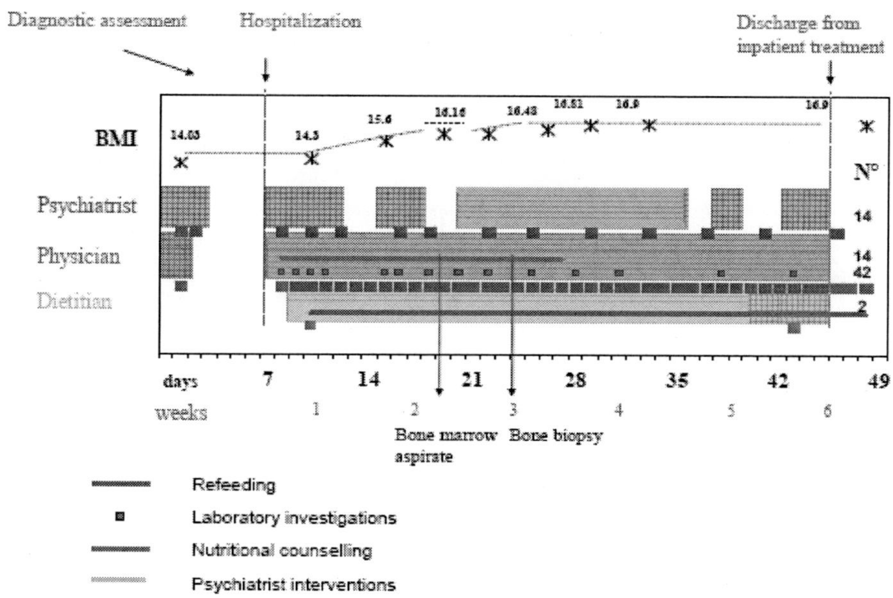

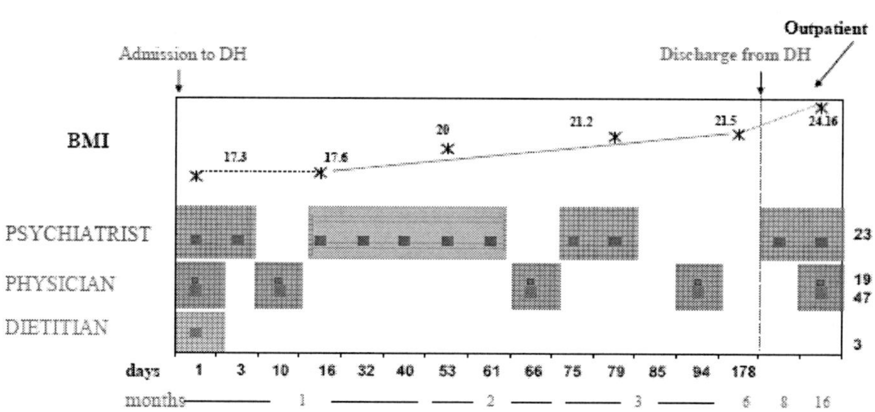

Figures 6 and 7. Timing and frequency of multidisciplinary interventions in the different care settings.

Case 4

ALEX: THE BURDEN OF A COMPLEX FAMILY

Alex, a 23 year-old male patient, arrived to our ED centre because his mother, who was concerned about his weight loss, asked for an evaluation.

Actually, Alex's mother required a "double evaluation": one for his son and one for herself, who was bothered by her weight gain associated with her depressed mood.

Family history: Alex's mother had been previously followed as a patient in our ED Centre four years before, at the age of forty-two. At that time she suffered from ED-NOS of anorectic type: at that time Alex was 19 years old. Here is some data about the mother: since she was an adolescent she was concerned about her body weight and shape; her normal weight was 50 kg for a height of 1,60 (BMI 19,5), the minimum weight was 45 kg which reached at the age of sixteen (BMI 17,6).

She always tried to control her weight both through a restrictive alimentary pattern - a unique meal at dinner, taken while standing up- and through intense exercise: she was a swimmer (as later was her son).

Smoke and coffee helped her to relieve herself from hunger.

Alex's mother, never treated before, was referred to the centre by a physician who followed her for renal problems and suspected the presence of an ED.

She underwent at that time a short pharmacological treatment and psychotherapy with a final outcome of partial remission.

At discharge she was able to maintain her weight in the normal range even she if didn't stop to control her alimentary patterns and to exercise.

Furthermore in Alex's family a cousin (daughter of his mother's sister) had also been treated for a purging bulimia.

As regards to Alex, he is a student of motor science and he is working as a swimming coach and bathing attendant: he is a non-competitive football player as well.

Alex, an only son, was breast-fed, without weaning difficulties, and was mildly overweight during infancy. During adolescence he reached his maximum weight of 94 kg at the height of 176 cm (BMI 30.4) He reported that at that time he was very ashamed of his physical aspects and that his friends used to tease him because he had "too big thighs": thighs are still considered by him an unsatisfactory part of his body.

He never used drugs nor was he an alcohol abuser .

He is living now with his mother (who separated from her husband during the previous year) and with a cousin who lived with them because their house was close to his university.

Since the age of sixteen Alex initiated his control of food intake by calculating calories and trying to eat less than peers and friends did.

At home he observed his mother taking only one meal a day, without sitting down at the table.

His control was not only applied to food intake but it was also exerted on many aspects of his life.

He tended to be extremely tidy, clean, obsessed by checking his homework. His mother described him as exaggerated in tidying and " terrorized by dirt ."

He was often concerned about his school achievements, he wanted to get the best marks and tended to do his homework in a obsessive and perfectionistic manner.

The beginning of ED is reported by Alex to be linked to parents' separation which occurred in the previous year: Alex decided to stay with his mother but he often spent week-ends with the father's new family, perceived as a warm and welcoming family, where he was able to take more regular meals.

The arrival of his male and peer cousin in the house represented a bothersome event for him: Alex began to compare himself with the cousin, to eat less than him and to be jealous of his mother's attitudes toward her nephew.

During the last year food control worsened becoming stronger and stronger: Alex avoided some kind of food and obsessively calculated calories but at beginning his mother did not care.

His body dissatisfaction was enhanced by having a girlfriend who was suffering from purging anorexia. Some months before the arrival to the Centre he had been abandoned by this girlfriend and consequently reported a "depressive mood": he felt sad, he was often crying and became unable to study and to maintain social relations. He felt unsure and inadequate as a male, worried about the possibility of finding another girlfriend.

Weight control associated to compulsive exercise became the focus of Alex's life: Alex was exercising many hours a day. Moreover he began to work as a waiter without discontinuing his university studies.

The anorectic control gave him a feeling of well-being and self esteem.

At admission to the Centre Alex exhibited much concerns about food control and weight gain but he was completely unaware of his disturbance. He reported that, at the beginning, weight loss was caused by psychosomatic food refusal following the breaking off of a sentimental relationship: losing weight had initially caused some positive effects on mood and energy so that he reported to have continued dieting more and more restrictively during their last year together combined with excessive physical exercise.

His mood was not depressive, he reported a pervasive need to control even other aspects of his life, his speech was poor but precise.

His alimentary pattern was too simple, as he had only two meals: lunch was the most critical meal, he used to eat slowly without any binge; he was no longer able to perceive hunger or satiety. A physical evaluation was required.

Medical evaluation: he was a blood donor, never a smoker. Although he was born mildly premature (eight months) his weight at birth was 4.100 kg. During adolescence he reached his maximum weight, he was mildly obese (BMI 30,3 weight 94 height 1,74 cm). The weight maintained for the longest time was 74 kg while the desired weight was 72 kg. In the course of seven years, starting when he was 16, he lost 25 kg, through restrictive dieting and intense physical exercise, reaching the minimum lifetime weight of 69 kg (BMI 22,27) at the age of 23.

Despite of the fact that his BMI at the first visit was within the normal range (23.2), as he weighed 72 Kg, he was complaining for relevant symptoms such as intense weakness, epigastric pain and cold intolerance.

At the physical examination the subject appeared in quite good condition of muscularity and trophism but he presented yellow-orange coloured and cold extremities.

Body temperature was 36.2, blood pressure was 110/80, heart rate was 33 beats /minute. No other pathological sign was evident .

Laboratory findings pointed out the following results: mild haemoglobin decrease 11,9 g/dl (normal ranges 13-18), low iron 47 µg/dl (normal ranges 60-160), hypogammaglobulinemia 0,72 g/dl, total testosterone at the inferior limit 300 ng/dl, free testosterone in normal range, thyroid function in normal ranges.

ECG: Sinus bradicardia with an heart rate of 33 beats /minute was present.

Dxa showed a normal mineral bone density, both T score and Zeta score were -0,1.

Ultrasonography of upper abdomen was negative.

At the end of a full diagnostic phase comprehensive of psychiatric and nutritional evaluation the diagnosis was: ED-NOS (partial syndrome) of anorectic restrictive type, anemia, sinus bradicardia.

The patient accepted psychological, nutritional and medical treatment with the aim to stop excessive exercise and starvation: in the following months he had an improvement of general conditions, an increase of heart rate up to 40 beats /minute and maintained his weight until discharge in January 2004.

Nevertheless he dropped the planned three month follow-up visit. He was expected for that time to check haematologic parameters, total and free testosterone, electrolytes and ECG.

He presented again in February 2005 in worsened general conditions.

He had had a weight loss of 12 kg from October 2004, weighing at this second evaluation 60 kg with a BMI 19,6. He was profoundly weak, he presented a sinus bradicardia with a HR of 49 beats /minute, and hypotension: blood pressure was 80/50.

He reported a minimal caloric intake, only some fruit and vegetables, during the last few weeks.

24 hour ECG monitoring showed a minimal cardiac frequency of 28 beats/minute, maximum 89, median 49 and many events characterized by RR intervals> 2seconds

Echocardiography: pericardial effusion was present and calculated to be nearly 200 ml.

Left ventricle was characterized by: increased dimensions, telediastolic diameter 5,87 cm, decreased global cinesia, globose shape, mass/body surface area of 126 gr/m2 , FE was 60%.

Mitralic valve was prolapsed with a minimum regurgitation jet.

Dxa showed a slight decrease of bone mineral density in comparison with the first analysis even though still in normal ranges. T and Z scores were -0.9 .

Haemodinamic conditions together with progressive worsening of weight indicated the need of hospitalization in a division of general medicine, aimed to improve nutritional status and to control haemodinamic conditions specifically bradicardia and cardiac performance.

The same multidisciplinary team of the centre regularly made consultations during hospitalization and provided, together with the members of the hospital staff, continuity of medical, nutritional and psychiatric care.

At admission laboratory tests showed a decrease of all blood compounds more evident after rehydration, one week from admission: total leucocytes were 2200/μL (normal ranges 4000-11.000), absolute count of neutrophils was 900/ μL (normal ranges 1500-5000), red cells were 3.200.000/ μL (nomal ranges 5-6.5), platelets were 134000/ μL (normal ranges (150.000-450.000).

Iron was 58 μg/dl, Ferritin was 62 ng/ml (normal ranges in males 21-385), Transferrin was 180 mg /dl (normal ranges 202-336).

Total testosterone was decreased to a very low level 108 ng/dl (normal ranges 270-1070) so as free testosterone 2.36 pg/ml (normal ranges 5,50-40).

FSH not dosable, LH 0.4 mUI/ml (normal ranges 1.5-9.3).

Electrolytes were in normal ranges.

BNP (natruretic hormone), ACTH, seric and urinary cortisol and Deidroe-piandrostenedione were in normal ranges.

Thyroid function was depressed: FT3 1,8 pg/ml (normal ranges 2,3-4,2), FT4 0,67 ng/dl (normal ranges 0,80-1,70), TSH 2,73 microUI/ml (0,10-4), Antibodies anti peroxidase and antitireoglobuline not present , Reverse T3 in normal ranges.

Body Impedence Assessment (BIA): the following body composition emerged: Weight 60 kg, lean mass (FFM) 58.8.1 kg with a ratio FFM/weight 98%, FAT mass 1.9 kg with a ratio FAT/weight 2%[1], Basal metabolic rate (BMR) 1646 kcal.

Total body water (TBW) 43,8 Liters with a ratio TBW/weight 73,1 %; TBW was the sum of Intracellular water (ICW) 26,73 Liters, ratio ICW/weight 44,5% and extracellular water (ECW) 17,13 Liters, ratio ECW /weight 28,5 % .

After one week from admission the following investigations were repeated:

ECG 24 hours monitoring: sinusal rhythm, HR min. 33/minute, median 51/min, max 88/min, 8 BEVS ,1 BEV, no pathologic pause.

Echocardiography: pericardial effusion reduced to a little quantity only near the right ventricle wall, improvement of the global contractility, invariate the mitral valve prolapse, left ventricle telediastolic diameter decreased to 5.5 cm.

During his hospitalization the patient received a gradual intravenous alimentation through peripheral catheter along with oral food intake, directed to a slow but progressive supply of nutrients, water and electrolytes. No physical activity was permitted.

Caloric intake reached in ten days 2800 calories (2200 per os+ 600 iv). No refeeding symptom was observed.

Once the vital parameters reached stabilization the patient was discharged and referred again to our Day Hospital Unit where he was followed till September 2005. Then he concluded his treatment.

At that time echocardiography and ECG monitoring were normalized, a persistent leucopenia, specifically neutropenia was still present even though partially restored; haemoglobin and platelets were in normal ranges.

At final discharge the patient, despite the persistence of a partially restrictive alimentary pattern, reached a good clinical and psychological status and a BMI of 21.

---

[1] The values of fat mass in young adult range from 14 (male adolescent) to 26% of total weight, depending on sex, age, exercise, genetic factors, hormonal status and nutritional status.

Comment of the Psychiatrist

In this case we want to highlight some particular aspects that recall aforementioned risk factors and features of male patients.

What is worth noting is the presence of an ED in the mother as risk factor for the development of an ED in the son; the adolescence as a period at risk for the onset of an ED, particularly when life events such as parent's separation occur; the premorbid obesity as a relevant risk factor for the eating disorder, the compulsive exercise as anorectic symptom and, last but not least psychiatric comorbility as a negative prognostic factor.

Comment of the Physician

This case underlines how weight should never be the only criterion to decide hospitalization, particularly in males, for two main reasons: weight loss as percentage of the patient's standard weight may be more important in comparison with current weight, furthermore the predominant lean mass and muscularity may hide the severity of the disease.

In fact in this case even if the patient was in the normal range of BMI he presented important clinical features like severe cardiovascular complications with lifethreatening haemodinamic effects, particularly sinus bradicardia, hyporigenerative pancitopenia related to malnutrition and specifically to a decrease of fat mass/ intramedullar fat cells and hypothalamic hypogonadism.

CONCLUSION

Our hope is that this short guide may have found the readers' interest by stimulating a greater curiosity towards EDs in male gender.

We are aware that much has been written on this peculiar issue and much has still to be explained further. In this perspective we wish to give a little contribution to keep alive the debate on EDs in males, enabling the readers to think of a male ED as a complex phenomenon and to re-think the emblematic figure of the two-faced Janus who faces in two opposite directions. This icon in fact may reflect the swinging between two opposite aspects of male identity, one more linked to the inner *animus,* which is more identified with feminine fragility, the other one more linked to strength and muscularity, which are stereotypic masculine features, as they reflect both protection from external world and the ability to fight and dominate. This could be a possible interpretation of the male dilemma in EDs.

We strongly hope to have conveyed to readers the passion and the devotion that we have always put in our work, that we consider profoundly complex and intriguing. Therefore we thank our patients who have always been a motivating force to go on improving our clinical practice and to keep on studying and training.

Finally we want to thank the publishers who allowed us to share our experience.

AFFILIATIONS

Emilia Manzato, MD
Psychiatrist, chief of ED Unit,
Public University Hospital "Arcispedale S. Anna ", Ferrara, Italy.
e.manzato@ospfe.it

Malvina Gualandi, MD
General Medicine Physician, expert in EDs,
cooperating with ED Unit of Ferrara, Italy
malvinagualandi@virgilio.it

Renata Strumia, MD
Dermatologist, Ferrara, Italy,
cooperating with ED Unit of Ferrara, Italy
restrumi@tin.it

Tatiana Zanetti
Clinical Psychologist, ED Unit of Ferrara, Italy
Department of Neuroscience
University of Padua, Italy
tatiana.zanetti@libero.it

INDEX

A

D

E

F

G

H

I

Q

R

S

T

U

V

W

X

Y